Sensuous Architecture

The Art of Erotic Building

Sensuous Architecture

The Art of Erotic Building

Christian W. Thomsen
With two essays by Angela Krewani

Prestel   Munich · New York

CONTENTS

"Originally Eros is thought of as the systematising principle of the genesis of the world, as a child of strength and beauty…
Eros also addresses the senses, however; physicality and joy, play and pleasure, illusion and dream are the domains of Eros. Those are the wonderful dimensions beyond rationality and functionality which we have largely lost in today's architecture." [1]

Günther Feuerstein

"Architecture, more fully than other art forms, engages the immediacy of our sensory perceptions. The passage of time, light, shadow and transparency; colour phenomena, texture, material and detail all participate in the complete experience of architecture…only architecture can simultaneously awaken all the senses—all the complexities of perception." [2]

Steven Holl

"There is absolutely no doubt that architecture has a sensual, an erotic component—like life itself and the behaviour of people. A sterile conception of architecture, such as has gained ground especially over the last few decades in the Federal Republic of Germany, has had the effect of negating—with its technocratic and materialistic viewpoints—what for us human beings is such an eminently important aspect. And not without consequences for our environment, the sheer desolation of which we experience at first hand every day." [3]

Wolfgang Meisenheimer

If these statements from Günther Feuerstein, Steven Holl and Wolfgang Meisenheimer are true, and there is nothing to confute them, why then has there been so little published on architecture and eroticism? Does it have something to do with deficiencies in the training of our architects? [4] Or with the underestimation of the body and sensuality in industrial and post-industrial societies? [5] With taboos, caused by psychological, cultural and religious repression mechanisms? With the hostile attitude towards sexuality shown by most of our Western churches? With the lack of relevance eroticism has to the drafting and execution of architecture? With the almost exclusively rational and commercial character of most architecture? How can architecture deny the human being's most powerful and creative source of energy, particularly when it claims to be an art form? For there is no doubt that eroticism has something to do with sexuality; it represents to a certain extent the cultural aspect of our sexual instincts, whereas sexuality embodies its natural side. The two are capable

Opposite page:
Georges Rousse, *Rome*, 1987

of overlapping in myriad ways, and are found in a variety of connotational forms depending upon language and culture. But no matter the variety of forms in which they appear, they always involve the sensual attraction between bodies. It is for this reason that the body constitutes the interface between people and architecture. It is not for nothing that since time immemorial we have referred to the 'build' of a body and the 'body' of a building.[6]

It is in this sense that our book is intended as a contribution to the present 'body' discussion, from the perspective of architectural history and theory. The aim is to rescue the word 'erotic' from the shady side of life, where it lingers as a result of the current irresponsible tendency to use superlatives in an inflationary sense, as though in the interest of quick money. Where the word has become clichéd through advertising, where "sex shops" mutate into "eros boutiques" and sex for money is generally equated with eroticism, there is still a vague sense of the cultural nature of eroticism, but such a concept wears thin and is ultimately debased when used to serve unworthy causes. In contrast to this trend, our book introduces arguments supported by carefully chosen examples that are designed to encourage architects to find their way back to a language of the senses, which, as Jacques Derrida has demonstrated in philosophical terms, predates our understanding of the world through language.[7] But it is precisely this sensual, pre-linguistic experience which gives human beings the sense of well-being enabling them intuitively—accompanied by the spirit of discovery and a sense of community—to find their way in the world, to feel at home.

It is through the senses, the long-range senses of seeing and hearing and the close-up senses of smell, touch, and taste, but also skin-sensation, pain and pleasure, that the human body perceives and experiences the world. The brain processes sensual experience and then encodes it intellectually and emotionally. From this point of view, eroticism takes place essentially in the mind. That is where bodies and objects are given an erotic connotation and deemed desirable by

Philippe Starck, *Asahi la Flamme*, interior view, Tokyo, 1989

both body and mind. Eroticism allows us to extend all of our sensual feelers, as it were, and the same is true of the interplay of attraction between bodies of architecture and human bodies. When it comes to eroticism, the intellect and the body, the head and gut, are always one. The differences which do occur, depending, of course, on the historical and social context and the psychology of perception, confirm that what we are dealing with here are cultural constructs.[8]

There is an essential link between man's experience of the world through his own body and creativity,[9] just as there is between the self's experience of the human body and its discovery of identity and a physical sense of space. During the years in which I have been preoccupied with the subject of this book and recording examples of sensual architecture, my experience has paralleled that of Richard Sennett. Sennett was prompted to write his book on cultural history and cultural theory, *Flesh and Stone*, as the story of the city and the relationship between its buildings and streets and the human body. He felt prompted to tackle the subject because of his

Massimo Iosa Ghini, *Bolido Nightclub*, New York, 1988

"…bafflement with a contemporary problem: the sensory deprivation which seems to curse most modern building; the dullness, the monotony, and the tactile sterility which afflicts the urban environment. This sensory deprivation is all the more remarkable because modern times have so privileged the sensations of the body and the freedom of physical life."[10]

Experience gathered from travels and architectural studies has enabled me to gain firsthand impressions that have led me to the conclusion that, where individual buildings are concerned, there are a number which are quite definitely sensual in terms of their interior and exterior architecture,[11] but that in urban settings it is almost impossible to find the same quantity of contemporary architecture that oozes the sensuality typical of historical squares and building complexes.

Since the "rediscovery of the body" in the '80s, discourse on the subject has poured out from a variety of sources. More will be said about this later—in a variety of contexts—in several chapters of this book. The new body cult of the '90s is no doubt related to the apparent demise of the body—or at least its threatened demise—and that in turn is related to modernism's tendency towards abstraction. This trend has fed on the increasing encroachment of science into many contexts of our daily lives,

and the fact that we are raised in a culture based on technology and media, in which through "real time communication" over great distances time cancels out space. Where architecture is concerned, there are two main tendencies to be observed: on the one hand the dominance of purely functional architecture, drafted with Computer Aided Design (CAD) programs, built with prefabricated parts and, to minimize the costs, stripped of all decorative trimmings. On the other hand, there are tendencies towards a reduction in body mass along the lines of a media architecture, in which the walls take the form of a transparent skin or membrane—cubes with playful façades.

The unease about both the "containerization" and the dematerialization of architecture is equally widespread throughout Asia, North America and Western Europe:

"The current over-emphasis on the intellectual and conceptual dimensions of architecture further contributes to a disappearance of the physical, sensual and embodied essence of architecture."[12]

In Western culture it is above all the female body which for centuries has embodied the erotic. That of course has its roots in Christianity, in the myth of original sin—"Eve started it all"—and the heavy Christian restrictions on sexuality. Through the ages the spirit has been

transfigured, the soul went to heaven (or down to hell), and the body has been conquered and put to death. This has been particularly true of Protestantism, whose rigidity is familiar to us through its deliberately functional, sparsely decorated church buildings, structures designed to make a reformist appeal to the human soul. Architecture's tendency to dematerialization and the materialization processes involved in numerous communication and business activities are thus familiar and even agreeable.

In Catholicism—at least in the age of the Baroque and Rococo—and in numerous other creeds there are most certainly examples of highly sensuous sacred architecture. It would, however, be a mistake to presume that erotic

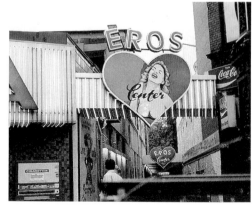

Reeperbahn, red light district, Hamburg

architecture has more than a marginal significance for buildings offering erotic services, even if, as I found out, one sex club proprietor uses architectural features from the inside of a Catholic church for the interior design of his establishment. The backstreet dinginess of our modern "red light districts" is reflected in their dismal architecture. Whereas in the upper middle-class brothel tradition of the 19th century, old "*Gründerzeit*" villas can still work up an erotic ambience, one that does not apply to purposefully built sex barracks where the commodity "woman" is marketed without the least pretence of any architectural packaging that could be described as eroticizing:

> "And yet compared to other cities' modern setups, the brothels which have moved into the old "*Gründerzeit*" houses so typical of Frankfurt are still relatively attractive. The Eros-Centers in Düsseldorf or Hamburg are real sex silos in comparison, soulless and inhuman factories with endless corridors in which you find anything up to thirty women standing in a long line. These buildings are accepted by neither the women nor their clients. The atmosphere there does not have a trace of privacy about it. In contrast, the old brothels live from their charm and the patina that old houses simply possess and—surprisingly enough—retain even when they are not very well maintained."[13]

On leafing back through two hundred years of architectural history, one comes across Claude-Nicolas Ledoux's sketch for the *Oikema*, a house of pleasures and a temple of virtue in which men were supposed to garner sexual prowess in preparation for marriage. Here at least the phallic form of the building was supposed to reflect its function, which does not mean, however, that this amounted to more than just a visual correspondence.

Erotic architecture is all about questions of multisensory spatial perception. Not so much in the sense of those prenatal psychologists, whose studies perpetuate—even in the early '80s, as Erikson's work shows—the stereotypical social roles which have been developing in bourgeois society since the 19th century. In the course of his comprehensive study, Erikson asked ten- to twelve-year-old children to depict scenes with the help of toys:

> "Girls built a room more often than boys by arranging a circle of furniture without walls. This circular structure was broken by something penetrating the circle. Boys had the tendency to build tall structures, like buildings or towers, with streets running between them. Girls tended to lay out the table on which they were playing as the interior of a house, whereby they used building bricks sparingly and simply."[14]

Girls are responsible for interiors, boys for exteriors and tall structures. It is as simple as that for

Michele Saee (Building), *Boutique Ecru*, Los Angeles, 1988

Erikson, and he concludes from his observations that the dominance of gendered modes over the modalities of spatial organization leads to a fundamental difference in the spatial perception and experience of the two sexes.

It is in the light of contemporary social developments and recent research that we want to free ourselves as much as possible from traditional stereotypes and, in keeping with the modern debate on gender, to distinguish among gender roles, activity roles and biological gender. This is not only because androgynous tendencies are on the increase or, as a result of intellectual, emancipatory and more general developments in society, because we want to adopt neither a "typically male" nor a "typically female" view of our thematic spectrum. Rather, we do it because we are convinced that this "typical" view no longer exists, that as part of

the trend towards individualistic lifestyles, activity roles and sexual identities, it has disintegrated or is in the process of disintegrating into a complex system of individually variable structures.

We see our view confirmed by the research of Aaron Betsky, who not only detects strong tendencies towards nomadic lifestyles in industrial and postindustrial societies in his book *Building Sex*,[15] but also revives the centuries-old architectural discussion concerning Laugier's "rustic cabin" and propagates the idea of the tent, being both male and female, as the architectural archetype. For Betsky, too, gender is a social construct. Recognizing it as such[16] has far-reaching consequences not only for the building but also for the analysis of architecture:

> "We *should*, I shall argue, dream of weaving together a realm of men and women. We can

Issey Miyake,
Paris spring collection
1995

Street in Menton,
Côte d'Azur,
Southern France

San Gimignano,
Tuscany,
Clan towers

appeared in the weekly glossies and news magazines in March 1995, a good-looking and well-dressed woman, who looks very natural and not at all like a model, is unabashedly throwing seductive looks at a half naked man who is in the process of taking off his jeans. The man's eyes are covered and the background is that of a bar with ambience generated by elements of stylized Egyptian architecture. The advertisement radiates freshness, fun and casual eroticism, and it becomes obvious that our star models, who have been reduced to just a few standard types, are in fact no more than aesthetically beautiful mobile surfaces, living advertising 'media' in fact, which no longer have anything in common with the variety of individual life patterns of today's men and women because the architecture of their bodies has been mutated into a standardized ideal. Issey Miyake has recognized this fact and often eschews employing models altogether; instead, his customers present his creations, among them many architects, artists, philosophers, writers and academics. He thus proves that even ageing bodies can radiate eroticism, because their life comes from within, they have charisma. Dressed in

imagine a world in which interior and exterior flow together, structure dissolves into surface, comfort and abstractions are intertwined. It is… a world where we fold ourselves into a texture of culture, a landscape that gives birth to many different sexes and forms."[17]

This can be observed, for example, in advertising strategies of the mid-'90s in which a reversal of roles based on traditional behavioural patterns is celebrated. In an advertisement for the fashion company Joseph Janard, which

Antonio Gaudí, *Casa Milà*, Barcelona, 1906–10

Miyake's creations, even an eccentric ninety-year-old female member of the Parisian nobility can exude eroticism.

The same is the case with architectural styles and our perception of the built environment. Although architecture may be sensual by the very means of its construction, the choice of materials, colours and textures, it is only specific spatial relationships, and symbols and what we associate with them[18] that give it an erotic aura. Why do towns in Tuscany or Provence often appear so sensous and erotic? It is because they show such clear signs of life—layers, cracks, peeling paint, textures—because in their dimensions the houses still relate to the scale of the human body; because to protect themselves from the sun they veil and unveil themselves, they know how to use light in a variety of ways as a material and a dimension of building; because they are like skins, equipped with tactile sensors, and because from out of their darkened interiors they issue vague promises, full of secrets. And also because they are emphatically physical and have a playful way of showing it off. Houses are like the facial landscapes of people who have gathered a wealth of maturity and experience. It is ambiguity, ambivalence, transience, and the rust of life and materials which make them erotic, and often it is only certain aspects of a building and not the whole which can be counted as erotic architecture: its entrances, stairways, hallways, courtyards and swatches of façade.

This is often especially true of old buildings which have been revitalized, like the old warehouses on Hamburg's docks or Butler's Wharf and the street Shad Thames in the Bermondsey docklands of London's East End. The combination of architecture, photography and painting is capable of capturing such effects particularly well, and of intensifying their symbolism, as is brilliantly demonstrated in the work of the French painter and photographer Georges Rousse. With the use of very economical means, Rousse achieves a dimension of art which for the most part eludes the spoken or written word, to which one reacts—for example when confronted with his series of "Embrasures" (1987)—with a surge of adrenalin, as though struck by lightning, because of the realization that here essential aspects of the relationship between architecture and eroticism have been captured in a still shot:

"The rooms (on the other hand) playfully recall the mysticism of an extinct culture. They are brought to life by the dramatic lighting. We are looking at buildings which were forgotten somewhere and are slowly falling into decay. (…) It is the invisible elements in Rousse's pictures which lend them their

Michael Ludwig Rohrer, *Favorite Castle* near Rastatt, Germany, cabinet of mirrors, 1710–15

urgency. (…) Rousse creates moments of a collective remembrance which faded into oblivion."[19]

A lot of good film directors make use of the ambiguities of ageing architectural settings when they shoot erotic scenes in slightly dingy rather than sterile, high-gloss surroundings. The same is true of fashion photographers, the stars of their profession. Whenever they want to give a new collection a distinctly erotic feel, they photograph their models against a backdrop of old

run-down buildings or the multicultural bustle of ancient Parisian alleys. Feuerstein has referred to this as "perambulatory" art:

"Drifting from place to place, always on the move, an art of experience, coeval with a process-orientated art form—only by means of movement is it possible to exhaust the whole palette of experiences and appreciate architecture with all the senses. Architecture and Eros both can be experiences which via the senses can reach down into man's deepest substance."[20]

Arata Isozaki, *Disney Building,* Orlando, Florida, 1990

Using this combination of architecture and eroticism, photographers and film directors manage to psychologically deepen our understanding of architecture and its effects on people and products, while at the same time symbolically sophisticating character and plot.

For this purpose the element of play is particularly important, an aspect perhaps most impressively demonstrated by the architects of the famous Loire valley summer residences, the various small German Baroque and Rococo castles or those even more intimate specimens of garden architecture in which the moneyed and noble classes in 18th-century England took such delight. Peter Greenaway, a talented painter and film director, a man gifted with an impressive knowledge of the history of art as well as a truly perfidious erotic imagination, playfully spins a subtle and complex web of erotic symbols and signals from architecture and landscape gardening in his films.

There are, of course, examples of modern architecture which demonstrate how to play, if only ambiguously, with erotic symbols. One thinks, for example, of Hans Hollein's design for a dockhead building on the Rhine at Düsseldorf (1994), the lucid, ingenious, ostentatious symbolism of Arata Isozaki's Disney World building in Orlando, Florida (1990), the eroticizing effect of Philippe Starck's colour combinations in a world of billowing, sensual shapes for both interior and exterior architecture.

Eroticism is more than mere sensuality, even if there is no clear-cut line dividing the two. One is reminded of the tremendously powerful, sensual sculptures of Louis Barrigan's coloured walls, and of the vibrant blends of multicultural influences in Mark Mack's Californian villas. Those are houses built for the senses, structures that derive their erotic charge from architectural detail, as indeed it is often details which transmit erotic signals. Here again George Rousse has composed some superb examples.

But there is also the eroticism of leather and rubber fetishists to consider, of sadomasochists, of piercers and various others who regularly keep the mainstream supplied with provocatively creative stimuli. This sort of eroticism is associated with the specific aesthetics of smooth, cold, glistening, soft or supple surfaces, with strength and power, and it is correspondingly also found in architecture. If one takes a fresh look at some forms of high-tech architecture, as Angela Krewani does, one sees how they suddenly reveal themselves to be male fantasies of flaying and dismemberment, the apostles of sadistic manipulation to a piece of architecture that acts as a body surrogate. As a reversal of this phenomenon, Veruschka von Lehndorff has shown how architecture and technology deprived of their original function can merge with the human body to produce an eroticism of "deadness".[21]

All these examples support Wolfgang Meisenheimer's theory:

"But for thousands of years architecture has been giving man a second form of help: it alleviates the search for his own self! Again and again, amidst the restlessness of life, an age-old yearning drives mankind to ask about its identity. And rooms built during the processes of self-projection or self-inquiry play an essential role."[22]

As an architect and an artist, Meisenheimer stands for a holistic approach, for integrating the draft stage and the final product. He lives his life according to that approach, too, and that makes him into the rounded and equable person he is.

But not all subscribe to the idea of holism, especially not in such times of conflict and precarious balance as today's. Coop Himmelblau's Deconstructivism bears witness to this with architectural eloquence and aggressive eroticism. And Bernard Tschumi, one of the leading theorists in architecture today and the self-styled high priest of disjunction, sings the praises of Deconstructivism[23] in theoretical tones, according to which everything today is disjunctive, dissociative and discontinuous; life is erratic, as are the various realities, there is neither totality nor meaningful value judgements, nothing finite, history no longer has any monitoring function, everything is in fragments and layers, and that is the foundation upon which architecture has to model itself. But eroticism still exists, and for Tschumi its architectural manifestation is in inventiveness, mobility and dynamics, in colour, in a spirit of adventure and open-mindedness to cross-connect, to establish new links and to break off old ones. For him eroticism grows out of the union between theoretical concept and spatial structure.[24] This is a conceptual form of eroticism as blueprint, but it is an eroticism that can be experienced directly in the architecture Tschumi has built to address a variety of senses, if only it is allowed to soak in.

We are living in an era of pluralism, and it would be a considerable waste of time and effort to even attempt to reduce such a complex and personal topic as eroticism to one common

Vera v. Lehndorff / Holger Trülzsch,
Living Matter in a Space,
1978

Mark Mack, *House Baum*, view to the courtyard, San Francisco, 1987–88

Bernard Tschumi,
Folly, Parc de la Villette,
Paris, 1987–91

denominator. But the few examples briefly discussed here, chosen from the many which appear in this book, serve to demonstrate something more: our wish is to go beyond the architectural "body" theory already mentioned and present our contribution to the cultural history of eroticism, of erotic architecture and its rami-

fications, together with the interaction of architecture with various spheres of life, using examples from art, the media and also from the erotic world of consumer goods. Because this entails breaking new ground in the process, we ask to be conceded the leeway to make mistakes.

When, for political or economic reasons, architects in this century were not able or allowed to build, they resorted to the literary-theoretical manifesto to articulate and publicize their largely forward-looking ideas on architecture. Although we are not architects, but instead academic researchers and architecture aficionados, we wish to uphold this tradition and therefore present as our creed and theoretical basis for reference a

Manifesto of Erotic Architecture

Erotic architecture is the expression of a building tradition with a positive outlook on life.

Erotic architecture conceives of all architecture as the multisensory interplay of shapes, colours, bodies, and light integrated into the network of cultural communication and tradition.

Erotic architecture professes its belief in the physical nature of all architecture and in the physical and emotional sensations which it triggers in the process of communication, in so far as they possess a hedonistic element and orientation. It is aware of the fact that immaterial forms of architecture will play an increasingly important part in the future and that body-simulations will take over from real bodies, possibly leading to new forms of sensuality and ways of experiencing architecture.

Erotic architecture plays with surfaces, layers, materials, with visual stimuli, symbols and the functions of sexual attraction between bodies, skin, surfaces and interiors. Its playfulness is expressed in a contradictory interplay of veiling and unveiling, of covering up and opening out, of luring in and fending off, of exterior and interior.

The game played by erotic architecture is at once narrative and signal. It rouses cravings and satisfies desires. It prefers states of suspense and protraction to the direct fulfilment of a function. This game is capable of creating all sorts of associations in the mind, but its aim is to unite the head and the belly, fantasy and urge. The game played by erotic architecture stimulates the imagination and offers the prospect of pleasure, thus giving rise to a variety of discourse. Erotic architecture is the ars amatoria in the story of building.

In addition to fostering aesthetic well-being, erotic architecture serves to promote the holistic well-being of bodies, both private and communal; the well-being of the individual and society.

"Architects must stop thinking only in terms of materials. In this respect present-day architecture is in the process of both reforming itself as a medium and expanding its repertoire of techniques. There are many fields outside building which influence architecture, just as architecture and 'architects' cover a wide variety of fields. Everyone is an architect. Everything is architecture."[1]

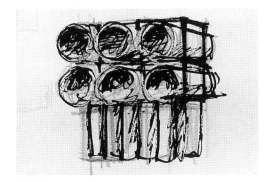

Hans Hollein, *Architecture*, 1958

1. Hans Hollein, *Retti Candle Shop*, Vienna (1964–65)

The first project built by Hans Hollein, the *Retti Candle Shop* in Vienna (1964–1965), made him world-famous overnight, and although it was only a small project, it had enormous impact. With a wealth of ideas and fanatical attention to detail, Hollein put into practice and brought to the public eye basic principles of his overall approach to architecture: a concept of architecture as a magical, sacred, ritual art form, sensual, physical, as well as erotic.

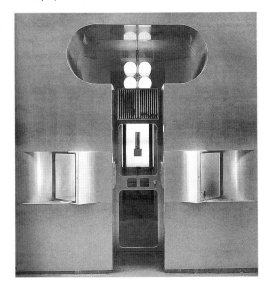

Hans Hollein, *Retti Candle Shop,* Vienna, entrance and façade detail

Opposite page:
Coop Himmelblau, *Funderwerk 3,*
St. Veit on the Glan, 1988–89

Hans Hollein, *Retti Candle Shop*, Vienna, 1964–65, interior view towards the entrance

It is a mixture of architecture and interior design, full of contrast and inner tension, implanted in a Baroque building on the *Kohlmarkt* in Vienna. Styled to perfection, it presents an interplay of organic, flowing, rounded and austerely geometrical shapes, rectangles, triangles, semicircles, cubes and prisms, anthropomorphic scale and technological abstraction, cool and warm, sensual colours, the bluish gleam of aluminium on the outside, and inside tactile orange shantung wall coverings and terracotta-coloured carpeting.

The two shop windows follow a principle which is particularly erotic. In contrast to common practice, they do not present themselves and their wares directly to the viewer, but coquettishly turn away; they conceal before disclosing, and then not with an expansive display but by focusing on a single point. The viewer looks more closely as a result. As with the shop windows, the door and the fanlight above it are also made up of rounded and rectangular shapes which flow into one another or are juxtaposed. The elliptical fanlight leads into a bulbous, kidney-shaped hollow on the inside.

Candles suggest warmth, fire, passion, romance, sacrifice and altars, and lend themselves to elements of colour and design. Hollein leaves the appropriate scope for association: here male and female principles meet and pervade each other. Entering the shop is like gently penetrating a womb-like interior through a narrow passage which then opens out in a rhythmic sequence of expansion and contraction.

Two horizontal axes, a vertical and a right angle, are all that are required. For a moment, the two mirrors at the far end seem to stretch the narrow room into infinity. Faced with the phallic symbolism of the candles, the shelves, for their part, turn slightly away from the viewer. There is no counter to separate sales personnel from customers.

Elegance, extravagance and exclusiveness are what the customer is expected to associate with the consumer good "candle", which is raised to a festive, solemn, ritual status. Ten years ahead of his time, Hollein presents himself here as the trendsetter of post-modern shop design.

2. Hans Hollein, *Abteiberg Museum*, Mönchengladbach (1972–1982)

With the *Abteiberg Museum* in Mönchengladbach, Hans Hollein presented the first major building project which he had designed in every detail from beginning to end. Its opening in 1982 turned this provincial city on the Rhine into a mecca of architectural tourism, and even in the mid-'90s this building has lost nothing of its attraction. After Alexander von Branca's *Neue Pinakothek* in Munich had tremendous effect, it was above all Hollein's museum that triggered off a series of post-modernist museum building projects in a decade that saw a boom in museum architecture hitherto unparalleled.

It was here for the first time that Hollein had the opportunity to realize his principles of erotic

Hans Hollein, *Museum Abteiberg*, Mönchengladbach, 1972–82, façade detail

architecture on a grand scale. The *Abteiberg Museum* stands simultaneously inside, on the side, and atop the very same hill, and is thus a complex body of architecture within as well as upon the earth. It addresses all the senses, both long and short range, the outward senses as well as the inward senses, of which the latter are all too often forgotten when it comes to perceiving the interior of bodies.[2]

The visitor approaching from the old part of town first sets foot on the roof of the museum, turning it into a pedestrian precinct and meeting place. Meanwhile the shed roof clad in titanium zinc shelters the other exhibition areas, a visible reminiscence of industrial architecture. Next to the tall office tower the visitor descends into a second tower, small, narrow but striking, leading to the cellars, caverns, crypts, treasure vaults of contemporary avant-garde art, which are announced with a playfully solemn gesture. The building has a showy, theatrical side, with such effects demonstrating its affability, cheerfulness, and even its vanity. Nonetheless it also has its secrets, hidden temptations and surprises which entice the visitor to go in search of adventure and discovery. It is clear that the outside was built first, progressing inwards from its sensual outer surfaces, followed then by a building process from the inside out.

The greatest care has been taken to compose the interior of the museum as an ensemble, and that represents the essentially erotic element of Hollein's art. With this building he has shown himself to be a trendsetter. A decade before the

emergence of fluid concepts of space in media form, Hollein had already designed rooms that flowed into each other. Not that Mies and Le Corbusier had not already propagated concepts of open space, but with Hollein we see for the first time that colourful transition from one amoeba-like room to the next, such as have become familiar through computer graphics and special animation software, those psychedelic effects which cry out for aural accompaniment. Holleins' interiors are like those fluid pictures which are generated on the computer without any reference to real models, and at most to associative images in the mind and body.

Within the *Museum Abteiberg* the visitor is confronted again and again with new, unexpected perspectives. Large, small and medium-size rooms alternate with intimate alcoves. There is a predominance of curving lines, the likes of which would have delighted Antonio Gaudí. And there are relatively few right angles.

Hollein tries to ensnare the visitor in an enhanced spatial feeling directly accessible to the senses, in which the additional historical, mythical, religious and erotic dimensions play an essential part. In addition to this he has always had a theatrical affinity to death and burial, the very opposite of vibrant eroticism. Thus begins the interplay between Eros and Thanatos. Hollein celebrates joyful funerals, as probably, in Europe at least, only the Viennese can, with all the magnificent pageantry of their "pompes funèbres" in Vienna's Central Cemetery. All this is based on the Austrian Catholic tradition, but also on a propensity for the irrational, for mysticism of the kind found in Viennese lore that celebrates the quasi-erotic attraction between morbidity and decadence. But then, as one born after Freud and Musil, Hollein evades the heaviness of these themes with playful irony, dissolving them in his optimism.

A further element is the fascination with the "labyrinth", a form closely associated with secrecy and the search for knowledge. Here too we find a light-hearted approach: think not of the classical, rigid labyrinth, the kind that tolerates no intersection of paths, which one enters with rising apprehension, and at the end of which a great secret lies in wait, or perhaps a confrontation with the realization of death and nothingness. Instead consider playful labyrinths, luring the visitor into a building and a bewildering array of settings. Thus the Eros–Thanatos theme is staged in an architecture of the senses, using building mass, materials and special effects.

Hollein's structure offers long perspectives, but also various intersections at which the visitor may decide to go straight on, follow a diagonal or turn off and embark on a new adventure. There are staircases and galleries at various heights constantly opening up new vistas, as well as vaults in which provocative examples of art are ritually and solemnly laid out so that they look like the tomb furnishings of Tutankhamen. All of this has something extremely theatrical about it, in that the architecture and the exhibits are involved in an interplay of bodies, each providing a backdrop for the other.

Eroticism depends on communication. Hollein has thus based his whole design concept on the principle of encounter: the open spaces, the tight passages, the intersections of paths in the labyrinth are all potentially places of encounter. The beautiful cafeteria is integrated into the exhibition area, but even that is like a theatre behind glass into which one sees and is seen. Then there is a classroom for painting, a lecture hall, and an audio-visual theatre. In the theatrical manner he employs to turn the mutual attraction between bodies into architecture, Hollein shows his mastery of the game, the interplay of concealing and revealing, of light and dark and of changing colours.

One extraordinary feature of this museum design is its use of light and colours. The clever arrangement of fluorescent tubes in clusters according to the amount of light required and the space to be illuminated obviously owes a debt to artists like Dan Flavin. The effects echo the resident exhibits of Pop-Art and Op-Art. The lighting design has a function which goes far beyond the playfully decorative, whether it be

Hans Hollein, *Museum Abteiberg*, Mönchengladbach, 1972–82, spatial impression

daylight or artificial light, skylights or ceiling lights, or even the fragmented reflection of the built or natural surroundings in windows and aluminium or zinc plated façades. According to Freud, mirrors are symbols of the psyche. "Mirror, mirror on the wall, who is the fairest of them all?" is only a naive fairy-tale query. Hollein's approach is more clever, less direct, and refracted, ranging from narcissism to the art of seduction. He bends light to control atmosphere and applies colours to embrace a variety of historical and contemporary quotations,

issues which are mirrored, evoked, and constantly alluded to. Here, too, the tactile senses come into play, and materials take a leading role in forming the building complex as a whole. All of its parts come togehter to stage a work of architectural eroticism, which, although fully aware of the problem of post-modern authenticity, derives its own identity and authenticity from that very same awareness.

Hans Hollein,
Pierhead Building, Düsseldorf docks on the Rhine,
Visions for Europe Competition, 1994

3. Hans Hollein, *Pierhead Building*, Rhine Docks, Düsseldorf (1994)

Hans Hollein has never given up on the guiding principle of his younger years, one that he has since exercised on many occasions: that architecture and eroticism are one and the same, that architecture is perhaps even the final domain of eroticism. In 1994, alongside Norman Foster, Dominique Perrault, Romuald Loegler, Hans-Ullrich Bitsch, Niklaus Fritschi and Matteo Thun, he took part in the architects' workshop "Visions for Europe", whose exhibition travelled to various European cities and participated in the 1995 Venice Bienniale.

The task set for this workshop was the design of a series of individual but highly compact building complexes along a promontory in the disused Rhine docks in Düsseldorf. To create his "Vision", Hollein was given the pierhead building at the end of the promontory, which, as a "mixed-use building" with apartments, offices, studios, a café and an observation platform, was to round off the projected design. What he succeeded in creating was an architecturally sensuous sculpture that offered solutions which were both technically and visually innovative.

The building combines female and male principles, oval and phallic shapes. The design and construction of the convex façade dispenses with beams, supports and walls, whose functions are adopted by an independent membrane. According to the interplay of clouds and sunshine, an electronically controlled sunblind veils and unveils the interior like a foreskin. The building, which hangs over the water at the dock's end, is accessible from a lift that runs diagonally and conveys a completely new form of room dynamics. Instead of being divided into storeys, the one large room allows many arrangements on a variety of levels. Hollein writes:

> "What has become relevant for my work over the past few years is a new view of tectonics—I no longer use supports and beams, walls and ceilings as constituents layered vertically one above the other, but dynamic diagonals, dissolving into a supporting shell and an independent membrane. The "façade" vanishes, leaving a single, homogeneous body, a continuous surface. This surface is spherical: even the elements, the materials from which they are made, are not reduced to two-dimensional (or polygonal) shapes, but are genuinely spherical in form, curved in all directions—both the stone and glass surfaces of the outer skin, as well as the inner walls are made of plasterboard."[3]

From Hollein's design it is evident that sensuality is always seeking to keep abreast of the times in its choice of forms, materials and room layouts. Building on ancient organic shapes, modern technology is perfectly capable of ensuring body mass and transparency in equal measure.

4. Santiago Calatrava, *Tabourettli Cabaret Theatre*, Basle (1986–1988)

"The meticulousness with which the assembly structure is undertaken is another indicator of an understanding of the building as an organism in progress,

Hans Hollein, section of the *Pierhead Building*, Düsseldorf

Santiago Calatrava, *Tabourettli Cabaret Theatre*, Basle, 1986–88

more than as a finished form in which the constructive process is a marginal problem to the generating idea."[4]

With our second architect, Santiago Calatrava, we enter a more abstract department of erotic architecture. Calatrava is a Catalan who sees himself influenced equally by Renaissance artists like Leonardo and Michelangelo, the French architect Viollet-le-Duc, who earned great merit in the 19th century by restoring important works of medieval art and architecture, as by modern architect-engineers (Maillart, Menn, Candela and Prouvet), and avant-gardists like Alvar Aalto and Constantin Brancusi. He has created a form of civil engineering with its own artistic mode of expression that effectively operates as a challenge to engineers and architects alike. It is a suitably original and sensual means of revitalizing a language which has become sterile in the modern age, and at the same time of eroticizing technology and the apparent brittleness of the engineer's art. And, of course, among his ancestors there is another Catalan who also knew how to combine architecture, sculpture and engineering know-how into monumental works of art, a designer Calatrava has chosen to emulate: Antonio Gaudí.

Using an ingenious mixture of organic and physical shapes and abstract construction features, Calatrava works according to principles which, in terms of our theoretical model, we define as erotic. He draws inspiration from nature, plants and animal skeletons as well as human body shapes and movements. In his work we repeatedly find porous, shell-shaped anchors, perforated by taut cables, with spanning elements mounted parallel to them. The combination of eroticism and power, the critical factors of simultaneous veiling and unveiling, and of connecting and dominating are revealed, only to be immediately hidden again. This occurs, for example, when the different forces emanating from one point and supplying force to swivel joints are balanced out and redirected into shapes, forms which seem to suggest frozen dance figures, so that the whole structure is then held in an almost magical state of suspension. Again and again, the tension becomes visible between the nerves and skeleton of Calatrava's constructions and the protective outer skin which envelops them. And as an engineer-architect who was awarded his doctorate at Zurich's Eidgenössische Technische Hochschule (ETH) in 1981 for a dissertation on "The Foldability of Framework Constructions", Calatrava can fold walls and roofs with the skill of a couturier.

We have chosen his alterations to the *Tabourettli Cabaret Theatre* in Basle (1986–88) as an illustrative example. The main challenge involved in this commission consisted in re-designing the interior of a 16th-century house, a structure located in the old part of the city and protected by a preservation order. Its historic fabric had to be transformed to accommodate an especially physical and sensual art form, cabaret, a small but upbeat form of theatre. Calatrava makes allowances for this in his choice of materials, construction details and the sequence of rooms: "The order of the different rooms and the experience of space and materials are the most important features."[5]

Santiago Calatrava, *Tabourettli Cabaret Theatre*, Basle, 1986–88, staircase

The elements to be designed were the cloak-room, lobby and stairway, a foyer to be used as a meeting place in the intermission, and the auditorium. The cloakroom and the staircase are constructed in steel and glass. An existing medieval drawing room was transformed into the foyer, in which a kinetic, folding wooden coat rack with mirrors was installed. The hall was altered so that three existing pillars could be dispensed with, a radical change that required suspending the ceiling from other construction elements. The solution was to transfer half of the ceiling's weight onto the steel stairway, thus giving it the complex task of distributing a 211-ton load onto the foundation while providing a flight of stairs up to the cabaret theatre and a connecting platform between the auditorium and the foyer.

For the theatre's interior, Calatrava designed his own furniture, tables, chairs and lamps, and married them to the structure using his erotic sensibilities. The erotic features, according to our definition, include the choice of materials and matching colours, the careful way in which materials with a somewhat visually aggressive appearance are put together, the peaked ceiling elements whose points and loads are elegantly and cleverly distributed, and the sensual use of leather in conjunction with steel chair legs.

Among the most erotic elements in theatre and dance are the arousal of the senses, the evocation of anticipated pleasure and the sensitization of the body by means of movement and tension, facial expression, body language and costume. This can be achieved by hinting at an exchange of physical contact, by delaying the moment of contact, and by keeping the other at a distance. An analogous technique in Calatrava's work is the confrontation between a Gothic stone wall with its rough sensual charm and the steel-and-wood constructions in the auditorium. In addition there is the encounter and contact, without actual penetration, of materials used in the construction of tables and chairs: the prancing physical lightness of table legs and chair legs, and, the most ingenious example of all, the construction of a stairway which is also a bridge, a gleaming metal body which nimbly shrugs off its own massiveness and whose weight and wantonness are concentrated on a single spot, on a shining egg made of chrome steel, without placing any strain on the old structure of the house:

> "The stairway designed by Calatrava thus acts in a twofold capacity as a new distributive element, and as a bearing solution to the frame of the building as a whole (...) As with other works by Calatrava, the interplay of forms and stresses is refined and virtuosic, and the result always exciting."[6]

Even the sculpturally folded shutters on the windows follow the erotic principle of partial disclosure and sensually exciting concealment.

5. Santiago Calatrava, *La Ciudad de las Moreras*: Museum and Culture Quarter in Valencia (draft design, 1992)

"What interests me is breaking down barriers. I strive to create a context, and not so much to do what my contemporaries do. I understand my activity rather as a projection towards the future."[7]

Calatrava has produced such an impressive oeuvre since 1982, one that is both experimental and practicable, that points the way forward while setting its own style, that of all the world's architects it was he who reigned as the rising star of the '80s and '90s. In his building Calatrava achieves a successful and fortunate synthesis of his three talents as sculptor, architect and engineer. All his buildings and interior installations are sculptures that expose the construction elements and thereby raise construction itself to an art form. It is in exploring and using the principles of construction that he creates his own style. He not only manages to coax poetry out of them, but as he progresses from project to project he also drafts what is actually a poetics of building in steel, glass and concrete.

During these processes his thinking and drafting is less dominated by theory than spontaneous association, and he builds on graphic ideas to which he adds his own personal stamp:

> "In his work, nature not only appears as a conceptual analogy, but also as a symbolic image that tries to express the existence of life in structures. His romantic affiliation is especially evident in his return to nature as the beginning of creation, a hidden feeling that underlies the rational structure."[8]

Calatrava has the ability to see and think predominantly in analogies: he derives functional organic shapes from plants, animals, and human beings and is able to transfer them by analogy to technical constructions. In so doing, however, he avoids making the mistake which Frei Otto made throughout his life, which was to concentrate on looking for the best ways of putting nature's principles to technical use—e.g. how can dragonflies' wings be modified to make lightweight girder constructions?—and thus to create a poetry of minimalism which, in spite of all its aesthetic qualities, ultimately remained one dimensional. In contrast, Calatrava's work is becoming progressively more multidimensional because he succeeds in incorporating symbols, fantasies and cultural contexts into his designs. In addition to the skeletal forms and sculptural, dance-like elements already mentioned, there are two more important features relevant to this topic, elements which Calatrava sets free to lead lives of their own: roofs and bridges.

Within a single decade Calatrava has developed into perhaps the most important builder of roofs and bridges in contemporary architecture. He consistently succeeds in coaxing roofs and bridges to take on ever new shapes, from skeletal structures in the form of pouncing cats and blossoms folding and closing to musical instruments such as harps. Such graphic themes never turn into a prosaic "architecture parlante",

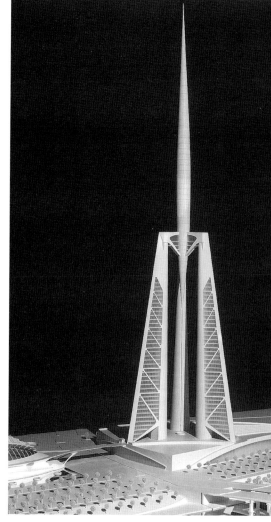

Santiago Calatrava,
La Ciudad de las Moreras,
model, 1992

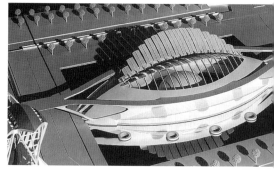

Santiago Calatrava,
La Ciudad de las Moreras,
model of the cultural centre, 1982

however, because Calatrava always manages to find a synthesis of sensuality and abstraction, whereby he is constantly playing with metaphors of movement. He has stated that he has been interested in problems of foldability and kinematics ever since his student days in Zurich. It is from that time that his architecture derives its dynamism and flowing characteristics.

Opposite page:
Santiago Calatrava, *BCE Place*,
Toronto, 1987–92

Very often in the case of his bridges and railway buildings, Calatrava puts his architecture at the service of transport, at the heart of movement and flow as one of the main features of a century of mobility. Using glass and steel or glass and concrete, particularly impressively in the case of *BCE Place in Toronto* (1987–1992) and the *Satolas Rhône-Alpes Railway Station* in Lyon, Calatrava succeeds in creating whole forests of steel palm trees and immensely sensual roof-bridge constructions shaped like blossoms. They are characterized by an ongoing organic process, but also by a mathematical, musical rhythm that is augmented by transparency, lightness and a poetry of light and shadow. In both cases it has the effect of making the passerby feel lighter on his feet, more cheerful and buoyant.

Anyone familiar with this square in Toronto the way it was before Calatrava used bridges to roof it in knows that it was a draughty, unfriendly place. Pedestrians blown about by the down drafts from surrounding skyscrapers hurried grimly across it—especially in the winter months—in order to pass it by as quickly as possible.

Incorporating Heritage Square into the project has turned it into a bright and friendly place. The subtlety and the philosophical complexity with which the architectural styles of various epochs are pervaded by Calatrava's forests of steel and his interplay of light and shade make it a real pleasure to pause there and enjoy it.

Erotic in a narrower sense, however, are the designs Calatrava has drafted for centres of culture. In 1992, for example, he drafted *La Ciudad de las Moreras*, the city of mulberry trees, for Valencia, a masterplan comprising a museum and art-and-culture quarter which offers a tribute to the vitalizing power of eroticism. Calatrava describes the project as follows:

"The location of the science museum generates a close link with the Turia River and the future communications tower. This has led to the creation of an avenue or boulevard as an urban organizational element for the unit, with the museum arranged on a parallel axis to the avenue and the riverside. Platforms on different levels with a profusion of trees serve as plinths and transitions between the river and the building. A long glassed arcade groups all the areas of public access and is used for exhibitions. A series of terraces are established for thematic exhibitions, constituting the functional structure of the building. Aside from the museum function as such, there is a cultural zone, situated on a platform which continues the communication tower plaza like a plinth course. It includes auditoriums, a restaurant, a library, etc. The structure of the science museum is based on concrete arches which sustain the metallic structures of the glass façades and the roof."[9]

In the draft for the tower, the aerial-topped phallic shape of its upper reaches seems to hang in the air among the three sail-shaped entrance wings, the ground plan of which clearly circumscribes a vaginal form. Both the draft and the model show a path linking the phallic principle of the tower to the vaginal shape of the art and culture building, and then encompassing it and leading to the science exhibition centre beyond. In the centre of this vagina stands—in the form of an egg, the primeval cell of all life, of all creativity—the auditorium building. Like protective pubic hair on the mons veneris, the roof unfolds in an arc.

Again Calatrava has succeeded in avoiding the directness of "architecture parlante" although his symbolism is unmistakable. Masculinity and femininity are united, art and culture are attributed the function of the germ cells of cultivated humanity. In its structure the exhibition building combines the elements of skeleton, bridge, folding wall, folding roof, as well as the trees of the forest made of concrete pillars and steel supports. Sketches showing only the bare minimum in construction features and load distribution resemble the drawings of Salvador Dalí from his erotic-surrealistic period in the 1920s.[10]

6. Coop Himmelblau, *Hot Flat*, 1978

"This project is dedicated to building speculators who are always talking about economy but always have the economy on their side. This is a project for architects who are always talking about ideas but build only surrogates. It is dedicated to the city planners who reduce "I" to the latest results of some statistics. And to those acrobats of taste who sit on the councils. This is dedicated to all who see architectural freedom as a consumer good."[11]

The last two examples in our survey of contemporary architecture are to be found at the opposite end of the erotic scale, which, at least in the case of the leading French theorists of the '70s and '80s, from Bataille to Foucault and Baudrillard, also includes aggressive sexual metaphors. According to Georges Bataille:

"It is only because we are human and because the shadow of death hangs over our whole lives that we have come to know the savage and desperate power of eroticism."[12]

Coop Himmelblau's draft project *Hot Flat* from the years before Deconstructivism (1978–1984) shows this very different face of eroticism in its architectural form:

"The *"Hot Flat"* is a city apartment building for five to ten families. One of the principal concerns was

to make each apartment as large as possible as cheaply as possible. We found a model for this in large factories which have been renovated and made habitable. Another fundamental concern we had was shaping and directing attention to the connections and transitions between the private sphere (the apartment) and the public sphere (the city)."[13]

A violent symbol of deflowering and penetration dominates the building's peak at the level of the golden section, where a girder-like element of glass and steel, a full two storeys in height, stabs right through the building at an angle. A leaping flame of glass springs from one end like a torch and cuts through the apartments on the upper floors. This act of rebellion and provocation, this blazing signal of passion and impatience is Coop Himmelblau's reaction to the desperate plight of cities: slums, cramped conditions, oppressive heat, dirt, high rents, criminality, brutality, couldn't-care-less attitudes and so on. Various layers of meaning and symbolism overlap and complement one another in the process.

According to statements made by Wolf Prix and Helmut Swiczinsky,[14] however, they implied the erotic layer deliberately. Giving eroticism such an insistent aesthetic value is a by-product which, as Coop Himmelblau's career in the '80s has shown, always involves risk—especially the risk of being perverted into a trendy doomsday fascination.

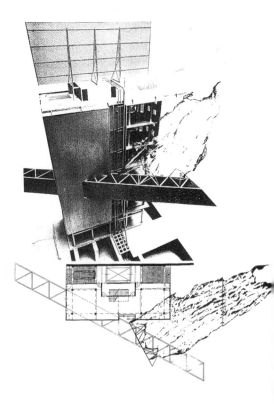

Coop Himmelblau,
Hot Flat,
design sketch, 1978

Hot Flat is an impatient, aggressive example of erotic architecture. Just imagine, however, that someone actually had the courage to build such a house: it would become the main architectural attraction of any city and the relatively high costs of erecting such a bold design would practically pay themselves off as a result. As a genuinely avant-garde project it was in fact ten to fifteen years ahead of its time, but on the strength of its draft plans alone it played an important part in paving the way for Deconstructivism. Zaha Hadid, Coop Himmelblau and Eric Owen Moss in Los Angeles are among those architects whose drafts and buildings most rigorously followed the example first established by projects like *Hot Flat*.

Hot Flat is a lasting monument to the *Sturm und Drang* (Storm and Stress) period of these Viennese architects. During the '80s Coop tended to work more as "building" architects than as theoretically oriented designers. But in comparison to other members of the Viennese avant-garde of the '60s and '70s, they managed to salvage a surprising amount of their impetuous, passionate and demanding vigour, as well as their aggressively erotic connotations and layers of symbolism, and apply it to their built repertoire.

7. Coop Himmelb(l)au, *Art Museum,* Groningen: The Deflowering of Post-Modernism (1992–1994)

"Whoever marries the zeitgeist soon finds herself widowed."

That was the snide comment the Amsterdam newspaper *Volkskrant* issued after the opening of the *Art Museum* in Groningen at the end of October 1994. In the face of considerable opposition, Museum Director Franz Haks commissioned four designers to create a major avant-garde attraction for a port in north Holland on a shoestring budget of slightly less than US $30 million. The fruit of this joint project was to rise up out of the water of a canal situated between the railway station and the city centre.

Architect Alessandro Mendini spearheaded the project, and successfully recruited Michele de Lucchi, Philippe Starck, a rising star on the international design scene, and the American painter and sculptor Frank Stella for his team. But Stella's draft—a complicated, spiralling roof construction reminiscent of a snail's shell, similar to the one he suggested for a museum of modern art in Dresden—turned out to be both technically and financially impracticable. Stella's flop was a windfall for Coop Him-

Coop Himmelb(l)au / Alessandro Mendini, *Groningen Art Museum,* 1992–94

melb(l)au, who seized the oppotunity to land their first involvement in a spectacular museum project. The *Volkskrant* diatribe, witty though it may have been, missed the point: the project had nothing to do with claiming the zeitgeist as ally. In fact, one of the most original features of this building is that, paradoxically, it trails behind the zeitgeist. The resulting building is a post-modernist collage, and even Stella's roof would not have changed that. But now the overall effect is broken up by a deconstructivist top storey, upsetting the carefree balance of its candy-coloured, Disneyland appearance. A "petit four" architecture, pasted together from a post-modernist assembly kit of quotations and set pieces, would presumably lose its colours within ten years in Groningen's harsh climate. Or it would simply be worn down by the hordes of visitors and degenerate into another tiresome example of throwaway architecture. If it were not for the muddled, provocative, completely contradictory aesthetics of Coop Himmelb(l)au's contribution, the museum could very well blend into the sad milieu of clichéd post-modernist pastiche.

In all fairness, it must be said that the museum's post-modernist quotations refer not so much to examples in architectural history as to the history of Groningen and to the function assigned to the interior of each part of the project. Michele de Lucchi's ground floor, for example, which is devoted to the archaeology and history of the city, is built of the same brick characteristic of Groningen's built fabric. Walking past large proscenium-like display cases, which are draped in shadows, the visitor embarks on a city tour presented in a variety of scenes and epochs from the Middle Ages to the 1950s.

Mendini alludes to the industrial site, the canal and harbour, in his aluminium-wrapped rotunda, while Starck stages a veil dance using vases, chinoiseries, and arts and crafts. For this purpose he has created an impressive array of glass cabinets, whose semi-transparent curtains wind their way in graceful curves, now concealing, now revealing, and—as if by analogy to the gently swirling steps of Chinese dancers—offering new insights and intimations as the perspective changes.

What is more, Starck is a master of irony par excellence: In one of these delightful high-tech cabinets he has installed an aquarium in which goldfish swim around pieces of Chinese porcelain salvaged in 1985 from the "De Geldermalsen" (1752), a ship that sailed the route to China for the Dutch West India Company. Two other polished aluminium cabinets recall high-tech versions of a sutler's waggon from the Thirty Years' War, reconceptualized and constructed using cutting-edge forms.

Coop Himmelb(l)au / Alessandro Mendini, *Groningen Art Museum* exhibition hall, 1992–94

As the centrepiece, the section of the building contributed by Mendini connects the disparate parts facing the canal and railway station and assembles them into the right-angle shape which dominates Groningen's historical quarter. Bow-shaped ship fragments penetrate his windowless Disneyland tower on an east-west axis above the main entrance. It looks like the storeroom for a stage set, but instead of lighting and stage props it houses a depot and subterranean offices. Mendini reserved the box-shaped building to the rear for contemporary art.

The drawbridge over the canal connecting the museum to the station area and the city centre is at once witty and useful. When the halves of the bridge are lifted, their underside reveals "Männeken Pis" performing the act for which he is famous in magnificent Delft tiles.

Coop Himmelb(l)au's contribution breaks with the aesthetic conventions established on the site, forcing the viewer to see the entire project from a fresh perspective. Coop crush Alessandro Mendini's chocolate box, whose windowless exterior is decorated in the style of

Paul Signac's pointillistic paintings. Automatically the viewer thinks of coloured gift wrapping.

The deconstructivist part of the building attacks the post-modernist candy-box architecture and steals the show. Coop Himmelb(l)au mobilize Deconstructivism's entire repertoire of principles, materials, and conventions and violate them, reversing the familiar and pressing it to perform new functions. This is expressed in asymmetrical forms, shapes piercing one another, cutting through one another, and pervading one another, all indicating a metaphorical layer which is violently sexual. The effect is enhanced by paths, rooms and perspectives crossing one another, as well as the creative use of unusual construction principles to infringe upon aesthetic boundaries.

This is expressed in the articulation of the building's interior: ramps, sloping staircases that turn off at odd angles, galleries, suspended ceilings, asymmetrical windows, floating platforms, jutting ledges, and rooms interpenetrated by sharp corners. This cacophony of disparate effects embodies the boldness to establish an

aesthetics of force, even of brutality, and—by normal standards—of apparent ugliness. It is a boldness which eyes this pretty post-modernist ensemble, made out of a do-it-yourself Disneyland kit with all of its cleverly conceived details, then jumps it from behind and rapes it.

The room layouts are strangely unfamiliar: steel girders and joists intersect at acute angles, while staircases and catwalks with perforated metal floors cross the rooms high up in the air. From the outside the whole thing looks like an exercise in tilting a cube; standing it on one of its points and splitting it open, so that its fragments are set in motion, revealing partial views of its exciting insides, but only enough to arouse curiosity. Here again the architects are following a process of reversal in that they make what is according to traditional teaching a weaker construction element penetrate a stronger one. Viewers familiar with the work of Coop Himmelblau's Wolf Prix and Helmut Swiczinsky see that the graphic ideas and the aggressive construction gestures of the *Hot Flat* era (1978 onwards) live on in this project.

Coop Himmelb(l)au / Alessandro Mendini, *Groningen Art Museum,* façade, 1992–94

Since the museum's opening, the interior layout has proven to be an attraction and an inspiration to visitors and museum staff alike. Like most experimental buildings, though, the structure does have its share of problems. Embarrassingly enough, during the museum opening water dripped onto the floor right in front of Queen Beatrix's feet, right at the time when she was making her introductory remarks. To be sure, there have been considerable difficulties involved in sealing such extreme forms of architecture so that they are watertight. Other drawbacks involve the compatibility of form and function. Early on in the building process the design team jettisoned its original plan to exhibit art from 1500 to 1950 in a certain section of the museum. The Old Masters were just not matched with dynamic, flowing interior layouts such as those that Coop Himmelb(l)au had created. Such great difficulties arose, in fact, that the curators decided to use the complex of rooms designed by the Viennese group for the most modern art exhibits instead.

Breaking with age-old conventions is, however, programmatic to Frans Haks' concept of museum life. Architecture, art and kitsch, publicity and design, various taste factors and preferences should be allowed to permeate and fertilize each other; old dividing lines, which have now become obsolete, should be abolished. If all of this is to be taken seriously, one can only agree with the critical Dutch voice at the opening symposium which warned of a "swatchification of architecture".

Here the post-modernist "anything goes" of the '80s is yet again forced to celebrate success tinged with irony. Its colourful idyll faces a radical challenge from Coop Himmelb(l)au's Deconstructivism, one that introduced the troubles of the present to its candy-coloured dream world. Coop makes the multicultural character of modern cities evident, reflecting within the museum a colourful ensemble—or perhaps one should say hotchpotch—of exhibits, from city history and Old Masters to chinoiseries, arts and crafts, to design and art of the '80s, a verit-

able microcosm of the contemporary heteropolis. The design principle "form follows emotion" instead of the modernist credo "form follows function" applies to all of these exemplary illustrations of contemporary erotic architecture. Hollein, Calatrava and Coop Himmelb(l)au are involved in every aspect of design work: they have not only drafted and built architecture, but also create furniture, art objects, glassware and a variety of other consumer goods, some of which have been acclaimed as pioneering works. In all of the buildings presented here the erotic is far more than a mere aesthetic drafting principle. Alongside visual features, haptic, tactile qualities, colours, shapes and materials play a major role. However impressive architecture may be from the outside, its practical value is determined by qualities within. In very different ways this applies to the works of Hollein, Calatrava and Coop Himmelb(l)au: the achievements of these designers testify to the fact that eroticism cannot be reduced—or committed—to any single image.

Prelude: Vathek and the Palaces of the Five Senses

"Vathek, ninth Caliph of the race of the Abbassides, was the son of Motassem, and the grandson of Haroun al Raschid. From an early accession to the throne, and the talents he possessed to adorn it, his subjects were induced to expect that his reign would be long and happy. His figure was pleasing and majestic; but when he was angry, one of his eyes became so terrible, that no person could bear to behold it; and the wretch upon whom it was fixed, instantly fell backward, and sometimes expired. For fear, however, of depopulating his dominions and making his palace desolate, he but rarely gave way to his anger.

Being much addicted to women and the pleasures of the table, he sought by his affability, to produce agreeable companions; and he succeeded the better as his generosity was unbounded and his indulgencies unrestrained: for he did not think, with the Caliph Omar Ben Abdalaziz that it was necessary to make a hell of this world to enjoy paradise in the next.

He surpassed in magnificence all his predecessors. The palace of Alkoremi, which his father, Montassem, had erected on the hill of Pied Horses, and which commanded the whole city of Samarah, was, in his idea far too scanty: he added, therefore, five wings, or rather other palaces, which he destined for the particular gratification of each of the senses.

In the first of these were tables continually covered with the most exquisite dainties; which were supplied both by night and by day, according to their constant consumption; whilst the most delicious wines and the choicest cordials flowed forth from a hundred fountains that were never exhausted. This palace was called The Eternal or Unsatiating Banquet.

The second was styled, The Temple of Melody, or The Nectar of the Soul. It was inhabited by the most skilful musicians and admired poets of the time; who not only displayed their talents within, but dispersing in bands without, caused every surrounding scene to reverberate their songs; which were continually varied in the most delightful succession.

The palace named The Delight of the Eyes, or The Support of Memory, was one entire enchantment. Rarities, collected from every corner of the earth were there found in such profusion as to dazzle and confound, but for the order in which they were arranged. One gallery exhibited the pictures of the celebrated Mani, and statues, that seemed to be alive. Here a well-managed perspective attracted the sight; there the magic of optics agreeably deceived it: whilst the naturalist on his part, exhibited in their several classes the various gifts that Heaven had bestowed on our globe. In a word, Vathek omitted nothing in this palace, that might gratify the curiosity of those who resorted to it, although he was not able to satisfy his

The moated *Château Azay-le-Rideau*, Loire, 1518–29

own; for, of all men, he was the most curious. The Palace of Perfumes, which was termed likewise The Incentive to Pleasure, consisted of various halls, where the different perfumes which the earth produces were kept perpetually burning in cencers of

Fonthill Abbey,
where William Beckford
lived from 1796–1844

gold. Flambeaux and aromatic lamps were here lit in open day. But the too powerful effects of this agreeable delirium might be alleviated by descending into an immense garden, where an assemblage of every fragrant flower diffused through the air the purest odours.

The fifth palace, denominated The Retreat of Mirth, or The Dangerous, was frequented by troops of young females beautiful as the Houris, and not less seducing; who never failed to receive with caresses, all whom the Caliph allowed to approach them, and enjoy a few hours of their company…"[1]

William Beckford's *Vathek,* published in 1786, grew out of the spirit of the caliph's palaces so prevalent in English, continental and oriental sources at the time. The architectural vision that Beckford's prose conjures in the mind's eye is one of *châteaux de plaisance* and palaces reflecting a yearning for power, beauty, nature, wealth, and the joys of hunting and love.

France, with its aristocratic lifestyle, its luxury, its architecture and fashion, set the trends in Europe at the time of the late Baroque and Rococo (*c.* 1730–1780). Voltaire's observation, "civilization creates luxury and man adapts quite naturally to it",[2] is particularly appropriate to the age. It was then that the English park and

Opposite page:
Georg von Dollmann,
Linderhof Palace, 1874–78

landscape garden, with all its classicistic, romantic and exotic architectural styles, reached its peak.

This was a time long before the word 'sex' was invented, and a time when no one spoke openly about eroticism. Eros, Amor and Cupid were nevertheless seen everywhere, depicted as winged cherubs, as sculptures, ornaments, pictorial motifs, as naked hobgoblins out to pierce marriageable young men and women with their fiery arrows, and set them aflame with desire. The term 'summer residence' was, of course, a euphemism for a retreat where the nobility concerned themselves with eroticism and sexuality, where sensual pleasures were of primary importance, albeit as elements in a broad palette of subtly aesthetic refinements integral to a tradition of living and loving marked by frivolity, a blaze of colour, a sensuality and an imagination such as have never before and never since shaped European culture.

At that time life revolved around *plaisirs*, including not only the fine arts, architecture and garden design, music, courtly feasts and theatre, but also philosophy, hunting, love—notably the love for one's mistress—and culinary delights. Louis XIV had pointed the way for others by

interpreting life—and by choreographing his own life—as a perpetual feast in constantly changing settings.

This was preceded in the 16th century by the Renaissance, imported to France from Italy by Francis I, and the subsequent rebuilding of the almost 300 castles and palaces along the Loire and its tributaries between Orléans and Angers. Two centuries earlier, battle-hungry French knights fighting in the crusades had discovered the civilizing blessings of a refined lifestyle[3] and began to make their spartan and cheerless castles—characterized by "donjons", the keep or central tower of the stronghold—a little more comfortable. Carpets to cover the cold, damp walls and floors constituted the greatest improvement.

At that time it was not Paris but the Loire valley, with its fine wines, sensuous breed of people and bucolic charm which was the political centre of France, and as such it developed into the crucible of French culture and identity. With the châteaux *Blois* and *Chambord*, which were more than just grandiose symbols of the king's pomp and power, Francis I set new standards in the patronage of literature, art and science:

"During his reign, the court gave up the last relics of the Middle Ages. Whereas women had until then led an existence on the outskirts of a purely male society, they were now integrated into courtly life and thus upgraded from women to ladies. At the same time the men—in their new roles as courtiers—turned into gentlemen."[4]

To compensate for his military losses in Italy, Francis I contributed more to culture and the arts than almost any prince before or after him. He summoned Italian artists like Leonardo, Serlio and Primaticcio to his court to work together with French architects. The result was a genuinely French Renaissance style which was made manifest in a variety of châteaux that share certain salient characteristics:

"Of particular importance are the compact buildings and the palaces with several wings: The majority are three-wing complexes with a *'corps de logis'*, the main tract, and protruding wings which enclose the the *'cour d'honneur'*, or main courtyard. Inside there are suites of rooms

and galleries, important aids to propagating power as well as an appropriate setting for courtly festivities. The compact building type was most popularly employed as a hunting lodge, regularly serving at the same time as a *'maison de plaisance'*. Situated in wooded areas rich in game, they were often surrounded by water. It is not surprising that amorous affairs were frequently conducted in the seclusion of such lodges, some of which even passed into the possession of the king's mistress. Most of these castles consist of a plinth, the ground floor and the *'bel étage'*.
Under the saddle roof there is a further full storey, whose dormer windows are the main features of lordly symbolism. The fireplaces are primarily decorated with sculpted forms illustrating the claim to power; images important to the overall artistic impression, but also symbols of royal dignity such as portals, arches and stairways. The rooms within the castle are arranged in a fixed order, forming *'appartements'* made up of *'salle'*, *'chambre'* and *'cabinet'*."[5]

The kitchens and bathrooms in these castles bear witness to the fact that here sensual pleasures reigned supreme. *Chenonceaux, Azay-le-Rideau* and *Amboise* are all characterized by that amorously playful intimacy whose primary purpose is amusement and pleasure. Leonardo da Vinci himself was the spiritus rector of a number of royal festivities between 1516 and 1519 for which he fitted out the château at *Amboise*. Whereas bathrooms remained rather rudimentary,[6] cooks were busily performing extraordinary and exquisite culinary feats in their palatial, superbly equipped kitchens.

A site nestled in the bosom of nature—surrounded by woods, water, and gardens—contributes just as much to this impression as the architectural design itself, a brilliant conception that expresses gaiety, even elation, in the ornamentation that decorates stairways, towers, portals, especially the putti and amoretti.

With the spread of courtly culture and the rise in the status of women, who, incidentally, were responsible for running the castles while their menfolk spent time travelling on diplomatic service or in battle, there was also an increase in the demands made on the buildings' interior design. Tapestries and other wall hangings, floor coverings, ceiling reliefs, frescoes, pictures, furniture, and upholstered furnishings all underwent enormous refinement in the course of time and became increasingly feminine. Much of the erotic ambience discernible in some of these buildings can be ascribed to the taste of cultured, aristocratic mistresses:

"This feminine space of artifice and intrigue became an architecture of its own in the châteaux of the Loire. Though based on fortresses, such structures as Henry IV's Chambord were in fact caricatures of the defence. Their turrets took on bowed out, circular shapes in accordance with

Chambord,
Loire,
first half of the 16th century

The *Château of Chenonceaux*, Loire, 1512 onwards

their courtly domestic function and provided no ramparts from which to defend the castle. Their roofs turned into collages of chimneys, each leading to a circle of warmth and comfort inside, and their many gables reiterated the reality that this was really a series of homelike spaces, and not a single defensive structure. Rising like a mirage in the middle of an artificial forest, it was a compact agglomeration of physical comforts and sensual moments so complex that one could easily get lost in its rooftop labyrinths and endless little rooms that opened up on to one another around the central ceremonial halls buried deep inside this fantastical structure."[7]

The most famous of all paramours, the beautiful and intelligent Diane de Poitiers, was the mistress of Francis I and—after his death—of his son Henry II. Her beauty was legendary even when she was over forty, an age at which women usually looked old and worn-out at that time. She preserved her youthful appearance with—among other things—a programme of fitness training, as a keen horsewoman and swimmer. Diane ruled over *Chenonceaux*, which earned her the deep-seated envy of Henry's wife, Catherine de Medici, who was a plump, domineering schemer. When in 1559, at the age of only forty-one, Henry died following a jousting accident—a splinter from a lance had stuck in his eye and caused a fatal infection— Catherine banished her hated rival to the decidedly cheerless castle at *Chaumont*.

For decades Catherine, who lived until 1589, maintained her place among the movers and shakers of French power politics. She extended *Chenonceaux* and in 1580 added a two-storey gallery to the bridge over the Cher, a structure that Diane had originally begun building. Her plans to extend the castle into an enormous three-winged construction with an annexe on the opposite bank of the river, however, remained unrealized. Nevertheless, she gave her three sons sumptuous banquets at *Chenonceaux*, earning the castle its label as a *château de plaisance* in the modern sense, since these were occasions which earned it a reputation which has been widely discussed, one that could at the very least be described as suspect:

"Particularly during the reign of Henry III these banquets turned into real orgies, at which it is said the women serving at table dressed in men's clothes, but with their breasts exposed, and the king himself dressed up as a woman."[8]

But it was Diane de Poitiers who ordered the famous garden of *Chenonceaux* laid out to the northeast of the castle. Her fame and beauty have survived the centuries, partly due to the painting of *Diana the Huntress* (*c.* 1550), ascribed to Luca Penni. Thus with Diane the contradictory view of woman as a creature of nature on the one hand and as a work of art on

the other, as a virgin and as a whore, a view derived from the late Middle Ages, reaches the peak of its validity:

"It is to this period that the seemingly contradictory images of the woman as part of nature and as artifice, as virgin and as a whore, belong. The space of the woman becomes the space of the gar-

Luca Penni, *Diana as Huntress, c.*1550

Courtly drinking bout at the time of Catherine de Medici, etching after a painting by Bernard Amsterod

den, something natural to which man must return by dint of sexuality but at the same time a force which he has caught, walled and domesticated. Within that constraint the female space is luxurious, organic in its blossoming, rounded and intertwined in its shape, and attractive to all senses. The woman is a rosebush, the garden itself; she is landscape, the part of nature that man has recreated."[9]

The emancipation of the royal mistress stands in stark contrast to that of all other women, considering that it is she who is able to have the garden laid out, an erotic space which thus also becomes a place of seduction and the perennial pleasures of love.

This and the fact that Henry II even went as far as to put a tax on all bells rung in his king-

Anonymous French master,
Festivities at the Valois Court, 16th century

dom in order to raise enough money to satisfy the extravagant demands of his beautiful mistress certainly did nothing to detract from Diane's glory. In fact, such accounts have helped to heighten it, and in 1847 Gustave Flaubert wrote a literary monument to Diane and to the dreams of countless tourists who even now seek her timeless charm:

"In Diane de Poitiers' chamber we saw the large four-poster bed belonging to the King's concubine, covered in blue and cherry red damask. If it were mine, I would find it difficult not to lie down in it sometimes. There is more charm to be found lying in a bed belonging to Diane de Poitiers than to resting amidst tangible reality. Did someone not claim that in these matters the source of all pleasure was only to be found in the imagination? And so, provided that one understands something of these things, one can grasp the strange, historical lust—a savouring of the 16th century—to lay one's head on the pillow of Francis I's mistress and to toss and turn on her quilts."[10]

The château *Azay-le-Rideau*, begun in 1518 on an artificial island in the River Indre, competes with *Chenonceaux* for the reputation among historians and tourists as the most beautiful castle on the Loire. Its many towers, its pronounced Renaissance style, the amorous cherubs on its staircase, and its playful decorations display that buoyant Renaissance spirit which we tend to appreciate as the vital, erotic side of humanism. The fact that this building was also accompanied by intrigue and scandals cannot ultimately be attributed to the architecture itself. The man who had it built, Gilles Berthelot, was treasurer to Francis I, and because he was frequently away in the service of the king, he left supervision of the construction work to his wife, Philippe Lesbahy. Evidently, however, his fondness for opulent architectural trimmings led him to embezzle considerable sums of money. His financial exploits caused him to fall from grace, and in 1528 Francis confiscated the castle.

Two hundred years later princes all over Europe, not least in Germany, were doing everything in their power to emulate Francis I and Louis XIV. According to Friedrich Karl von Moser's 1755 *Teutsches Hof-Recht*:

"There is probably hardly a sovereign in Germany who, apart from his normal residence, does not own one or more summer seats, hunting lodges or country houses."[11]

The names alone of these residences bear witness to their purpose.[12]

Each summer residence in a 'locus amoenus' was dedicated, in the words of an art historian, to the pursuit of "pleasures and lustful relaxation".[13] But for academics it is obviously still

difficult to see these castles as testimonies to an erotic architecture in spite of the fact that all the requisite architectural ingredients are present. Friederike Wappenschmidt describes the 18th-century trend away from residences which had taken on the dimensions of palaces towards≠ the smaller *châteaux de plaisance* and ultimately even more private and individual love nests. Genuine eroticism, of course, is nurtured within a sphere of intimacy:

"Courtly art, the arts of Western civilization and those of far flung lands served a representative function, at the centre of which were residences which had taken on the dimensions of palaces and where princes exercised their power and flaunted their wealth. The splendour increased from room to room. From the vestibule, one's gaze climbed the towering staircase, and from there it trailed the triumphal procession of Apollo's entourage set in the stone balustrade right up to the ceiling canopy glorifying the lord of the house and his dynasty. The vestibules and large halls were linked by suites of rooms which led from antechamber to antechamber into the audience room and the state bed, where the prince publicly laid himself to rest and arose refreshed in full view of the entire court. After the bedroom and halls follow picture galleries and smaller cabinets with exotic exhibits displaying the prince's taste and conception of life and the world, but above all, the understanding of art among the artists working under his patronage."[14]

The connection between eroticism, power and architecture reflected so vividly in the castles on the Loire is no less obvious here, although this Rococo variant is less direct and less exhibitionistic. This shift occurred during the course of the 18th century, when the 'monde', or fashionable high society, indulged itself in the dream of Arcadia, of an eternal spring and everlasting youth. Taste at court became more feminine under the spell of the Rococo. Wappenschmidt takes the view that the *châteaux de plaisance* were small and charming syntheses of Baroque art forms in which colours were the decisive emotional factors:[15]

"Architects and decorators used their mastery of colour to fulfill the proprietors' wishes to imbue interiors with their ideas of dignity and atmosphere. They were familiar with all the colours of the rainbow, the effect of light and shade, the way in which colours came to life in sunlight or candlelight and died in dusk and darkness."[16]

Such visual delights meant to fire the imagination are complemented by an architecture of the senses which, starting with garden layout, works its way inwards using sculptures, fountains, flights of stairs and architectural façades to achieve an interpenetration of natural and artificial space that draws on all the senses, the hap-

Salomon Kleiner, *Pommersfelden Palace*, staircase,
etching, 1726

Leopoldskron Palace, built by Fürsterzbischof Leopold Anton Freiherr von Firmian, 1736-40
below: *Temple of Venus* in the Wörlitz gardens, 1765–1808

tic and tactile as much as the olfactory, offering
the fragrance of flowers to the nose and sweet
birdsong to the ear in parks and aviaries and
castle chambers.

The parks especially offer a wealth of architectural features and fragments which incorporate sensual or erotic symbolism. They are oases
of aesthetic craving and erotic fancy: summer
houses, pavilions, pseudo-medieval fun castles,
hermitages, small temples, artificial ruins or
their fragments, all underscoring the playful
nature of the culture and displaying a multitude
of regional and individualistic features at the
same time. For in most cases design was also a
question of the search for identity. Here a yearning for the Middle Ages and antiquity finds
theatrical expression.

The interplay of castle and grounds offers
itself as a magnificent natural stage upon which
fêtes champètres could be staged. Pathways and
stairways, often flanked with ideally beautiful
male and female sculptures to lend an air of
antiquity, led into the interior of these *maisons
de plaisance*, where decoratively dressed figures
paraded up and down the staircases, each attracting the gaze of the opposite sex while admiring
his or her own theatrical presentation.[17]

One needs only to look at the fashions of the

time, portrayed for example in François Boucher's depictions of Madame de Pompadour, whose impact as an archetype has survived to this day. Such prototypes clarify the connection between the skin of the flesh and the second and third skins of fashion and architecture. The fall of folds in dresses or robes, the variety of strategies for veiling and at the same time accentuating parts of the body, especially of erogenous zones such as the breasts and hips, all of these aspects are reflected in the organic curves of stairways, foyers and banqueting halls, which were often designed as quasi-uterine spaces. The visitor's entry into them can be seen as an initiation, as breathing life into an architectural shell, whereas his lingering within the building is accompanied by multisensory enjoyment, clearly demonstrated in the magnificent stairway at Pommersfelden, built in 1726 by Salomon Kleiner.

The tendency towards a synthesis of art forms is continued in the architecture and decoration of the interior through the careful coordination of the daytime and nighttime effects of the colours adorning the floors, walls and ceilings. The same degree of care is taken with their painted and sculpted ornamentation, in the stucco motifs, the carved wainscoting, the wood and marble panels, marquetry on furniture, in the furniture itself, in painted cabinets, some with mirrors, and in the design of the porcelain. Poetry, laughter, merriment, temptation, elegance and convenience are the order of the day. That applies to everything from the kitchens to the rooms used for representative purposes and the boudoirs with their resplendent beds of state. Stairs and corridors behind concealed

James Wyatt, *The Island Temple, Fawley Court,* Buckinghamshire, England, c. 1771

François Boucher,
Madame de Pompadour,
oil on canvas, 1756

doors, drawing rooms with passages running round the outside so that refreshment could be served unobtrusively; all of these measures emphasize the desire that developed during the course of the century for intimacy and discreet eroticism, a wish which interior designers were able to fulfill.

Undoubtedly the French sense of ceremony shaped many of these principles and room arrangements. Particularly within the German cultural sphere, however, the principles of musical composition played an important part, with the erotic context of the music of Mozart and his contemporaries representing a high point in the development of Western culture. Thus the mid-18th-century *châteaux de plaisance* of continental Europe bear witness as never before to a lifestyle which was erotic through and through.

Eroticism may not have been of central importance in the park and garden architecture of the British Isles except in conjunction with a propensity for exoticism in which it played a significant role. What is expressed by such architecture, however, is a longing for fantasy and surrogate worlds, for unprecedented variety and originality.

The 18th-century English aristocracy owned palaces, castles and parks, while the lower nobility and the upper middle classes, 'upwardly mobile' and becoming wealthier all the time from empire trade, was possessed at the very least of large gardens, country houses and country seats of style and splendour, the architecture of which tended to follow relatively strict conventions.

The garden architecture of the 18th-century English aristocracy, however, was where fantasy and a spirit of experimentation could be set free. It hosted the eccentric tendencies so fondly cultivated at that time by noble cranks who, with all their 'whims' and 'oddities', could celebrate its triumphs, and where, circumstances permitting, they could recreate the far off fields of Arcadia on a cool and rainy island.

Indeed it is a nostalgic fascination for antiquity which serves as a model here, promoted in particular by the the educational journeys or 'Grand Tours' undertaken by the nobility and upper middle classes to visit Italy's classical ruins and see its magnificent landscape painting. Claude Lorrain's pastoral scenes with bridges, temples, towers, solitary, mysterious buildings, and shepherdesses are not only the models for budding master painters like Joshua Reynolds and John Constable, but also come to life in the design of landscaped gardens and parks. It is the English who invented the profession of the landscape and garden architect. These designers, whether working alone or collaborating on large building projects, manipulated nature imaginatively, civilizing it while at the same time shaping it according to aesthetic principles. It is this which has since distinguished English gardens and parks so strikingly from their austere, courtly French counterparts:

"It was Kent who, above all, formulated the ideal of the picturesque garden as a circuit walk, with buildings, statues, cascades, and other 'incidents'

The Pineapple, Dunmore Park,
Stirlingshire, Scotland, 1761

The Gazebo, Alkerton Grange,
Gloucestershire, England

gradually revealing themselves to the spectator at different angles and in different combinations."[18]

William Kent, Capability Brown, William Chambers, Nicholas Revett and John Vanbrugh are some of the masters who gave form to such aesthetic tastes as the "Gothick" and the "Picturesque", the nostalgic imitation of Virgilian antiquity as well as more exotic types of garden architecture, such as Moorish, Egyptian, and Chinese historical styles.

Here allegorical motifs from literature, mythology and politics play as prominent a role as an appetite for exploiting the world's treasures played in power politics and high finance in the voyages of the discoverers, the founding of colonial empires and the emergence of the large trading conglomerates like the Hudson Bay and East India Companies. In literature this technique had already found expression in Elizabethan times in the works of William Shakespeare and especially in the plays of Christopher Marlowe, which make it possible to trace—as never before—how a language takes possession of the world and establishes new

areas of experience, thoughts and concepts. The terms 'Nature', 'Sentiment', 'the Sublime', 'the Picturesque' and 'Taste' are among the key utterances of the age. Landscape and garden architects as well as the builders of follies and pleasure pavilions added their contribution to creating aesthetically "good" taste even through mere architectural quirks and whimsies, terms which ultimately express the underlying sense of the French loanword 'folly'. What they all have in common is imagination, even fantasy:

> "Follies and eye-catchers, gazebos and belvederes, temples and pagodas, dairies and bath houses, menageries and aviaries, sham castles and artificial ruins—there is scarcely a country house in England, Ireland, Scotland or Wales that does not have its quota of garden buildings. (...) Legends cluster around such buildings and their very names intrigue: the Treacle Eater at Barwick Park, the Needle's Eye at Wentworth Woodhouse, the Jealous Wall at Belvedere in Westmeath, the Whim at Blair Atoll."[19]

In a large garden or park it was common to find several of these buildings, which—as described

above—served the most varied purposes. A classical sense of harmony and proportion was accompanied by a quest for diversity to cater to a variety of moods, so that alongside the serenity of Elysian Fields in the Virgilian or Arcadian sense, as created by William Kent at Stourhead, Wiltshire, there was often also a place for the bizarre and grotesque. This suggests that concealed beneath the measured geniality of a mind under the stabilizing sway of classicism there was an undercurrent which was unpredictable, rough-edged, and far from tranquil, turning the thrill of creepiness into a fascination with fear.

It was after all the age of the rakes and libertines, cynical lechers for whom women were merely objects of lust, men who unscrupulously destroyed the lives of others as long as it offered a modicum of satisfaction to slake their thirst for sadistic and licentious pleasures. How else could the gothic novel with all its "maidens in distress" being chased by libidinous monks have attained such great popularity if there were not at least a little de Sade lurking in most?

Thomas Wright, *The Menagerie*, interior, Horton, Northamptonshire, England, *c.* 1750

House—still in use as the private residence of Lord Burnham—demonstrates a far more blithe and joyful eroticism. By no means does it allow any frivolous digression of thoughts to the orgies of Beckford or the Earl of Rochester. For a long time the flexible double standards of the British served them well, and this is confirmed by the apparent contradictions of the 18th century, precisely because they are not really contradictions but the sophisticated expression of a complex culture.

Even if in most cases follies and pleasure pavilions allude only remotely to eroticism, they are certainly buildings which express longings and pipe dreams, and as such are instructive examples of an architecture of the senses. Its appeal promoted an erotic ambience and encouraged erotic encounters in a broader context. Orangeries are an excellent example dating from about the middle of the 18th century onwards. Anyone who thought anything of them—

Just like the princes on the European continent, the British nobility and the upper classes had from time immemorial also been keen on hunting. But openly indulging in keeping a mistress and even building her a castle as a love nest was usually regarded as exceeding the British aristocracy's moral sensibilities. And it was certainly the height of frivolity to allude to this by means of an architecture laden with erotic symbolism:

> "The charming shell grotto that the second Earl of Halifax built for his mistress in the gardens of her house at Hampton Court: alcoves representing Dusk on the west side and Dawn on the east, each equipped with a couch and a miniature fireplace, while much use was made of stalagmites and cowrie shells for their almost too obvious male and female symbolism.
> Sir Francis Dashwood went further still with his Temple of Venus at West Wycombe, which he built on a mound and designed to have wide open wings supposed to represent a pair of legs, flanking the oval opening to a cave."[20]

A *Temple of Venus* that Colen Campbell designed in 1720 for the garden of *Hall Born*

Stourhead, Wiltshire, England,
Neo-Palladian stone bridge, 1785 onwards

selves strove to set up his park as a status symbol, and to cultivate what at that time were exotic fruits was an expression of lavish extravagance, one that called to life the colour, the fragrance, the shape and the taste of distant continents in the garden outside pseudo-gothic pseudo-castles.

Such sensuality, coupled with the same exquisite feeling for colours and shapes, is also reflected in the interior of many follies and pleasure pavilions, and it is there that numerous sculptures of naked Dianas and other mythological beauties are to be found, giving the word "pleasure" an erotic connotation.

English Romanticism, a yearning for perfect harmony between a nature which is cultivated but not subordinated as in France, and buildings which, as a synthesis of forms, please the eye and serve the well-being of body and mind, finds its most effective realization in gardens like the one at Stourhead, a landscape which slowly matured over a period of thirty years:

> "Barbara Jones has aptly described it as 'achieving a balance between intimacy and space so just that one wonders if serenity may have a mathematical constant'."[21]

If garden architecture of the English Enlightenment produces to a certain extent miniature versions of antique temples, the Acropolis in Athens or the Forum in Rome, it is taking into account a whole panoply of reasons for choosing its particular models: the ennobling effect of following classical example; finding beauty from observing mathematical principles, a realization pleasing to the eye at first glimpse from a distance; in its function as a place of meditation, contemplation, conversation, or, in the case of larger structures, from time to time as a banqueting hall for entertaining guests, as a tea or music pavilion, or as a place of romantic, amorous encounter.

The idea of the *châteaux de plaisance* did not die with the end of the Baroque, but in the 19th century the tendency turned more and more towards privacy, as when the Bavarian King Ludwig II turned his daydreams into private

Villa Stonehaven,
Texas, 1985–90

architectural fictions.[22] But this point in time already marks the incipient growth of those surrogate and epigonic qualities which escalate into a kitschy eclecticism in the 20th century as seen, for example, in the creations of Texas multimillionaires, which are no more than distant echoes of the originals even if the idea of the synthesis of art forms is never actually abandoned. Even the erotic element in architecture takes on a surrogate quality, displayed for example by the hotchpotch of a Game Room at *Stonehaven* or by the ceiling in that very same residence, an imitation of a *château de plaisance* painted from a postcard between 1985 and 1990.[23]

Angela Krewani

*"I trace the print of your body with my hand
Like the map of some forbidden land
I trace the ghosts of your bones."*[1]

An architectural model conveying the very opposite of the lightness of the Baroque *châteaux de plaisance* is provided by a major author of the French Enlightenment, Donatien Alphonse de Sade, whose writings have made him popularly known as the founder of sadism. De Sade's erotic nightmares are always closely associated with architecture: they take shape in castles, country houses, in monasteries, in underground torture chambers and gardens. In terms of literary history they continue the tradition of the chivalrous novel, in which against the background of a castle or pleasure gardens the figures are tangled up in playfully erotic adventures, which, however, invariably end with a scene of jollity and general happiness. Just like in de Sade's texts, here the world is reduced to a love den, albeit a light-hearted one.[2]

Architecture in de Sade's work always means places of torture and suffering, in contrast to the street, which is a place of refuge, as demonstrat-

Rochester Castle,
Kent, the keep,
1226–39

Opposite page:
Bernard Tschumi, detail of *Folly in the Parc de la Villette,* Paris, 1987–91

ed in the novel *Justine*. Here the largest enclosed space in which the action takes place is the remote monastery of Sainte-Marie-des-Bois, in which a handful of men execute their reign of terror.[3]

The most detailed literary description of an architectural complex presented by de Sade is to be found in his fragmentary novel *The 120 Days of Sodom and Other Writings*. Silling is a castle inaccessible to the outside world, to which four libertines withdraw with a number of selected victims to spend the next four months indulging in their meticulously prepared excesses. The remote location of the castle already constitutes a contrast to the Baroque *châteaux de plaisance*, which were guaranteed accessible at all times:

> "To reach the place one had first to get to Basle; at the city you crossed the Rhine, beyond which the road became steadily narrower until you had to abandon your carriage. Soon afterward you entered the Black Forest, you plunged about fifteen leagues into it, ascended a difficult, tortuous road that, without a guide, would be absolutely impractible. (...) Five full hours are required to reach the top of the mountain, and there you come upon another extraordinary feature which, owing to the precautions that had been taken, became a new barrier so insurmountable that none but birds might have overcome it: the topographical accident we refer to is a crevice above sixty yards wide which split the crest into northern and southern parts, with the result that, after having climbed up the mountain, it is impossible, without great skill, to go back down it. Durcet had united these two parts, between which a precipice fell to the depth of a thousand feet and more, by a fine wooden bridge which was destroyed immediately as the last of the crew had arrived, and from this moment on, all possibility of communication with the Château of Silling ceased."[4]

The remoteness of the place is matched by the appearance of the castle, which is itself built in such a way as to make access extremely diffi-

The chapel of *Rapottenstein Castle,*
Lower Austria, 12th century

cult. Surrounded by a high wall, it towers up high on a rock and is further cut off from the outside world by a moat, so that the seclusion of the stronghold certainly suggests analogies to the inner and outward isolation of totalitarian states. It was with this in mind that for his film *Salò o le 120 Giornate* Pier Paolo Pasolini removed the castle to the remote republic of Salò, which Mussolini had founded shortly before the end of World War II.[5] Angela Carter goes a step further and interprets the seclusion of the castle and above all the lack of any possibility to escape from the terror as a metaphor for the world.[6]

The building is realistically drawn: in the centre are the main rooms, alcoves and niches set aside for the orgies. The private quarters of the libertines are on the second floor, as are the bedrooms of the victims. At the back of the

Conway Castle, view from inside a round tower towards the watch tower

as a setting for these erotic fantasies. The following long sequence of excerpts is intended to demonstrate to what extent and with what precision of detail de Sade's erotic imagination concerns itself with the architecture of the rooms:

"From the gallery you moved into a very attractive dining hall provided with buffets shaped like towers which, communicating with the kitchen, made it possible to serve the company its food hot, promptly, and without the help of any waiters. From this dining hall, hung in tapestries, warmed by heating devices, furnished with ottomans, with excellent armchairs, and with everything which could make it both comfortable and pleasing to the eye, you passed into a large living room or salon. (...) Adjacent to this room was an assembly chamber intended for the storytellers' narrations. This was, so to speak, the lists for the projected jousts, the seat of the lubricious conclaves, and as it had been decorated accordingly, it merits something by way of a special description.
Its shape was semicircular; set into the curving wall were four niches whose surfaces were faced with large mirrors, and each was provided with an excellent ottoman; these four recesses were so constructed that each faced the center of the circle; the diameter was formed by a throne, raised four feet above the floor and with its back to the flat wall, and it was intended for the storyteller; in this position she was not only well in front of the four niches intended for her audience, but, the circle being small, was close enough to them to insure their hearing every word she said. (...) Steps led down from the throne, upon them were to sit the tools of debauchery brought in to soothe any sensory irritation provoked by the recitals. (...) At the back of each niche was a little door leading into an adjoining closet which was to be used at times when, having summoned the desired subject from the steps, one preferred not to execute before everyone the delight for whose execution one had summoned that subject. (...) On either side of the central throne an isolated column rose to the ceiling; these two columns were designed to support the subject in whom some misconduct might merit correction."[7]

De Sade's association of architecture and eroticism, however, points beyond the level of order-

ing scenes according to the architectural layout and actually structures the form in which eroticism appears: all erotic actions follow a strict set of rules which govern the overall "performance" within the given architectural form. In certain formations in fact it becomes indistinguishable whether the arrangement of figures is designed to spotlight eroticism or to comply with the architecture; for example when the participants are required to take up strictly defined positions in the room which they are not allowed to leave. In this context the architectural structure and its observance are prerequisites for erotic pleasure. The palimpsest-like layering of eroticism and spatial arrangement thus defines the type of eroticism. *The 120 Days of Sodom and Other Writings* does not describe an eroticism of intoxication and overstepping limits, of surrender and the loss of self, but propagates instead the joy of observing mechanical rules and adapting to strictly defined structures:

Alter do Chão Castle, stairs through the interior of a defensive wall

castle are the utility rooms and the kitchens, the cellar rooms being used exclusively for torture.

The literary picture reproduced here accurately reflects the exterior and interior architecture of many castles and citadels. Even the torture chambers in the cellar are based on cellar architecture of the Middle Ages and the Baroque. De Sade's precise knowledge of such architecture should make us aware of a biographical fact which is ignored when the texts are discussed: the Marquis de Sade spent most of his life in prison and the majority of his texts were written in a dungeon.

The relationship between architecture and eroticism is established in a variety of ways. One aspect of this relationship is the close link between erotic scenes and the architectural layout, a link already clear in the introductory descriptions: all occupants of the castle are given quarters which are presented in detail, while the main rooms are reserved for the various erotic "projects"; they fulfill all that is required

Almodóvar del Rio,
Cordoba,
14th century

"At exactly six, Messieurs shall pass into the assembly chamber heretofore described. They shall each of them repair to their respective alcoves, and the following distribution shall be observed by the others: upon the throne shall be the storyteller, the tiers below the throne shall be occupied by sixteen children, so arranged that four of them, that is to say, two girls and two boys, shall be situated directly opposite each niche; each niche shall have before it a like quatrain; this quatrain shall be specially allocated to the niche before which it is placed, the niches alongside being excluded from making any claims upon it, and these quatrains shall be diversified each day, never shall the same niche have the same quatrain."[8]

Another aspect of de Sade's eroticism is the architecturalization of the human body, which runs diametrically counter to the anthropomorphosis of architecture otherwise so often mentioned. The remodelling of human bodies as architectural objects is demonstrated just as clearly in another work of de Sade's: *Justine, Philosophy in the Bedroom, and Other Writings* reports on the initiation of a young girl into the world of debauchery. As there are fewer figures involved here, the reduction of architectural form to the human body is all the more obvious: the presentation of the rooms as the stage setting for the action and the choreography of the orgies to fit into that setting are no longer important since pleasure is derived exclusively from the strictly mathematical and architectural arrangement of the bodies and the observance of the merciless rules of sexual behaviour. The bodies form living tableaux of eroticism.[9]

The reflection of architectural principles is not confined to de Sade's use of bodies as spe-

cific construction elements in his arrangement of the orgies but is extended to individual bodies. In her analysis of de Sade's writing, the English author Angela Carter points out that de Sade describes the female body in the terminology of ecclesiastical architecture, "as if it were a holy place. The female opening is, for him, a shrine, a place of adoration".[10] Without at this point having exhaustively examined the relationship between architecture and eroticism in de Sade's works, we can, however, already discern a consistent architecturalization of the human body and of human eroticism: in de Sade's texts architecture becomes a model for eroticism.

In a wider sense, as a metaphorical link, architecture contributes to a theory of eroticism. In *The 120 Days of Sodom and Other Writings* de Sade hints at a connection between configurations of eroticism and architecture and the act of narration. In the creation of filigree designs and constantly changing patterns, a congruence is achieved between eroticism, narration and architecture. And their underlying structure, made up of threads which can be spun ad infinitum, makes it possible to compare two dramatic settings of architecture: one the erotic arrangement of bodies, the other built in stone.

An additional aspect of de Sade's texts concerns the denaturalization of the human body and its transformation into a pleasure machine, devoted only to seeking and providing satisfaction. Seen in the context of the history of the human body and its representation, it becomes clear that de Sade's mechanistic materialism makes its appearance at a point in time when in medicine the concept is also beginning to gain a validity in its own right.

In this respect, such conceptualizations of the body anticipate a mechanistic understanding of the human body which dominates the whole of the 18th and 19th centuries. In the 20th century it is especially in France that conceptions of the body arise which describe it using metaphorical references to mechanisms and machines. Such approaches are primarily directed against the practice in psychoanalysis of setting up hierarchies in which the body and its organs are interpreted as functions and effects of mental structures.[11] The counterpart to the body in psychoanalysis is a body which is mechanically and dynamically interested in experiencing pleasure and which infiltrates all constructs with a cultural connotation. Deleuze/Guattari conceptualize it as follows:

"It functions anywhere, sometimes non-stop, and then again with interruptions. It breathes, gives warmth, eats. It shits, it fucks. This It (...) Everywhere there are machines in the truest sense of the

Richard Rogers / Renzo Piano,
Centre Pompidou,
escalator

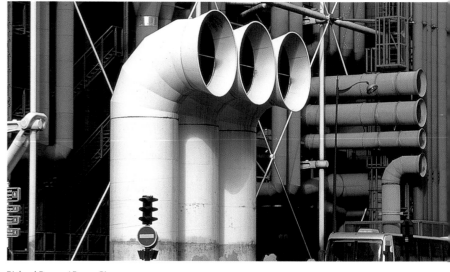

Richard Rogers / Renzo Piano; *Centre National d'Art
et de Culture Georges Pompidou*, Paris, 1971–77,
construction detail with escalator

Richard Rogers / Renzo Piano,
Centre Pompidou,
air conditioning exhaust vents

word: machines of machines, with their clutches and gears. An organ machine coupled up to a source machine: the current produced by the latter is interrupted by the former. The breast is a machine for producing milk, and connected up to it is the mouth machine. The mouth of someone without an appetite wavers between an eating machine, an anal machine, a speaking machine, a breathing machine (asthma attack)."[12]

In these admittedly very divergent and scarcely systematic conceptions we see a countertradition to the prevalent views of the body as a homogeneous system of instruments subject to the control or the mechanism of the psyche.

It is as architectural analogies to this literary and philosophical dramatization of the human body that we see the iron and steel architecture of the 19th century, whose lack of outer skin focuses attention on the construction of the members, the way they are held together and the functions they perform. Such architecture no longer tries to hide its skeleton under a skin or to deny it. Now it is no longer the façade by which architecture is judged to be aesthetic but the construction itself which is represented in an aesthetic context. The most outstanding example of this is the Eiffel Tower.

A contemporary continuation of the architectural exposure of the body in the sense of de Sade's materialization is to be found in the high-tech architecture of Richard Rogers, Michael Hopkins and Norman Foster. Numerous buildings by these architects give the impression of mechanistic materialism, this time via the me-

dium of architecture. Irrespective of their functions, their inner workings, their cultural and regional contexts, these buildings are largely subordinated to the functional aesthetics of a machine. Stripped of specific meaning, they mainly demonstrate their own function and its dynamics, openly presenting itself to view.

Here there is no erotic game of concealment and disclosure, of withdrawal and intimation, even the protective skin covering function is missing from some of the buildings of Rogers and Hopkins. Their eroticism is to be found in the interplay of mechanistic energies and intensities: the distinction between outside and inside no longer exists, and everything which is displayed on the outside is in fact an inside. In a metaphorical sense these machine-like buildings represent de Sade's tortured bodies, whose structure is also openly exhibited. The analogy is confirmed by the terminology used which refers anthropomorphically to the "skeleton of the load-carrying construction" and the "outer skin of the façade".[13]

In architecture the machine images of high-tech architecture reach their climax at the historic moment when, as a result of computerization and digitalization, machine processes begin to be obscured from view. Thus architecture acts as an agent recording this loss of technical potential and at the same time preserving it as a museum piece, a potential which at the beginning of the century had been manifest in the form of turbines, grain elevators and chimneys.[14]

The prototype of a newer form of machine aesthetics in architecture is represented by the French *Centre Pompidou* built by Richard Rogers and Renzo Piano. As an icon of machine aesthetics, standing out against the context of the medieval quarter in which it is located, the *Centre Pompidou* has certainly become one of the best-known buildings of the 20th century. It is also the most frequented building in Paris, with seventy million visitors in only ten years, more than the Louvre and the Eiffel Tower together.

It was actually with some reluctance that Rogers and Piano took part in the competition. The French government invited entries for a cultural centre in Paris, and for Rogers and Piano it went against the grain to set up a monument to a centralistic presidential system which was so highly autocratic.[15] In the words of the architects themselves, their draft pursues the idea of democratic communication and functional variability:

> "It is our belief that buildings should be able to change, not only in plan, but in section and elevation. This is a freedom which allows people freedom to do their own thing, the order and scale and grain coming from a clear understanding and expression of the process of building, and the optimization of each individual element, its system of manufacture, storage, transportation, erection and connection, all within a clearly defined and rational framework.
> This framework must allow people to perform freely inside and out, to change and adapt in response to technical or client needs, this free and changing performance becoming an expression of the architecture of the building—a giant Meccano set, rather than a traditional static transparent or solid doll's house."[16]

Interestingly enough, in their comments on the *Centre Pompidou*, Rogers and Piano break not only with traditional humanistic ethics but also with politically motivated values. In principle they are praising a building each individual part

of which they grant a life and a momentum of its own as well as "a right to self-determination". With this they are approaching conceptions of a body devoid of organs and determined by its own momentum, as advocated by Deleuze/Guattari:

> "All we say is that the identity of effects, the continuity of species and the total number of all bodies devoid of organs on the level of consistency can only be achieved by an abstract machine which is capable of covering them and even outlining them; in other words by structures which are capable of supporting the desire, of taking more effective care of the desires and of continuously securing their connections and links."[17]

In the case of the *Centre Pompidou* it is the main body of the building, torn open and swelling up, which turns its insides out and surrenders to the intensity of its surface. The other high-tech buildings of this generation offer no form of privacy either; they are not granted any inhibition threshold which assigns the body a system of values. Mercilessly the function of the organs is displayed to the viewer: "it is possible to see even the most private functions displayed on the outside".[18] The colours of the brightly painted pipes and ducts signify their functions, and like huge, transparent intestines hanging out of the body, an escalator transports visitors into the interior of the *Centre Pompidou*.

In these buildings, like in de Sade's texts, there is no erotic game of concealment and disclosure, of withdrawal and intimation. Like the figures in the novels, the individual parts of the building have to submit to the dynamics of mechanical desire. In this sense the *Centre Pompidou* is then no longer a mark of architectural democracy but—as mentioned above—an expression of mechanistic energies.

Once the eye has become accustomed to this fact, contemporary architecture reveals how little the body and its metaphors are bound by cultural, religious or ideological systems of values.

Richard Rogers,
Lloyds Building,
London, 1976–86

It appears that architects are trying to break with cultural codification in order to arrive at a "direct self-articulation" of their buildings which is not dependent on systems of signs and symbols. The fact that a number of architects concentrate on the ability of an architectural body to articulate itself may stem from an underlying fear of the body disappearing, a fear which has dominated the last two decades of our century.

In view of the trend to proliferation in the media, which spares neither bodies and body constructions nor architecture, a renaissance of the body has also been developing, a growing concentration on the importance of the body, in literature and philosophy as well as in certain

Alfredo Arribas, *Torres de Avila Nightclub*, Barcelona, 1990, entrance, exterior view

branches of architecture. It is against this background that the manifestos of the Viennese architects *Coop Himmelblau* repeatedly project the elements body, eroticism and architecture onto one another, propagating metaphors of physical intensity:

"Some one-eyed people
confuse this poster-like sensitivity
with brutality. Let 'em.

Because incongruous aesthetics
is political aesthetics.
And these aesthetics call:
a spade—a spade
a whore—a whore
lipstick—lipstick
lies—lies
power—power
power hungry—power hungry
and architecture—architecture.

It is never make-up
on the façade of mediocrity
because it creates counter pressure.

The tougher the times,
the tougher the architecture."[19]

At first, cursory glance the architects Coop Himmelblau appear to continue de Sade's erotic brutality. Some of their manifestos, which admittedly read like erotic texts, display a phallic aesthetics of piercing, tearing open, ramming through, in short, of deflowering. On closer examination, however, this apparent phallocentricity turns out to be superficial, and it becomes clear that Coop Himmelblau are concerned with a non-hierarchical, intensive physicality which breaks away from the familiar clichés of sexuality.

In contrast to de Sade's mechanizations, the architects of Coop Himmelblau reflect on the

phallic position of power never questioned by de Sade. Their aesthetics of penetration reverses the phallic position, always allowing the weaker, lighter element to bore its way through or rip open the stronger element. By resorting to an aesthetics of brutality and subordinating it to the purpose of differentiation, they go beyond de Sade's rationalizations—and in so doing they prove themselves to be romantics in disguise.

Their approach denies the unshakeable validity of a traditional system of rules in favour of an individualization and redefinition of the construction principles in architecture. Accordingly, the erotic aura of Coop Himmelblau's architecture stems from the reversal of symbolic structures of power and the attempt to arrive at deeper, revised levels of meaning by the redefining and recoding of construction elements.

A further similarity between de Sade and Coop Himmelblau is revealed in their deconstructivist intentions. With Coop Himmelblau we encounter common clichés concerning architecture and technology which they then proceed to undermine. Even the materials which they used in the '80s with a gesture of improvisation similar to that in the early houses of Frank Gehry rebel against consumer aesthetics. They are actually inverting architectural clichés when their materials give the impression that they have been gathered on a scrapyard.[20]

In de Sade's work it is also possible to observe the dismantling of contemporary patterns of thought which are still common even today, in particular the subversive criticism of the claim to universality, of the all-embracing rationality of the Enlightenment and its antifeudal naturalism. The derogation of the family and the debasement of the idea of romantic love, which has left such an indelible stamp on our emotional lives, are already to be found in de Sade's early works. By the use of subversion and deconstruction as well as fantasies of erotic brutality, both de Sade and Coop Himmelblau demand a reformulation of prevailing patterns and world views.

While it is the mechanistic body in the spirit of de Sade which is propagated in the fantasies and high-tech architecture of Coop Himmelblau, the Spanish architect *Alfredo Arribas* captures the ambience of de Sade's fictions. His interiors and their furnishings revive de Sade's castles, monasteries and torture chambers. Alfredo Arribas is one of those young Spanish architects who have shaken up the architectural scene in Spain, which mostly follows international trends.

With his nightclubs, schools and boutiques, Arribas managed within five years to attain international recognition. The frame of reference for his interiors and his conversions is not only architectural tradition but also literature, films and new developments in the media. Contemporary popular culture in particular is something he employs as a foil to his constructions.[21]

The references to de Sade are to be found primarily in his nightclubs and cultural centres, in other words in buildings which from their very function imply an invitation to playful dreaming and imaginative experiment. The erotic effect of Arribas' architecture is derived from the "staged" innuendoes and room structures which appear to give tangible form to de Sade's texts: the iron staircases behind wire netting, gates leading down into mysterious uncharted basements, the struts across iron doors and mirrored walls reminiscent of prisons or de Sade's castles, locations cut off from the outside world where deadly orgies took place.

The entrance to his *Torres de Avila*, converted into a nightclub in 1990, is made to look like the entrance to an underground torture chamber. The old walls of the tower have been additionally reinforced with iron struts that stretch upwards, the doors are iron frames with steel gratings. A sort of trap-door connects the top of the stairs with the interior of the building. Customers are left to speculate about the possibility of the trap-door being nailed shut or sealed off, leaving them imprisoned inside. In the nightclub itself yet more associations are suggested by the bareness of the walls, masonry that dates to the Middle Ages.

Arribas charges the brightly polished surfaces with allusions to the repressed potential for sensuality in our culture, which he integrates into a happy world of pleasures and consumerism, thus giving the latter an ambivalent image. The ambiguity of sensual potential and carefree consumerism is also echoed in the materials Arribas chooses. The hard, shiny surfaces of polished steel and chrome in concert with the pellucid elegance of glass walls and the transparency of steel gratings create an architectural situation which is fascinatingly indeterminate.

What is clearly shown in comparison to the *Centre Pompidou* and the manifestos of Coop Himmelblau is how various the architectural

Alfredo Arribas, *Torres de Avila Nightclub*, Barcelona, 1990, interior view of the entrance

references to de Sade's texts can be: on the one hand, the machine aesthetics of a body ripped open and charged with energy, and the deconstructivist impetus of phallic shapes. On the other, the lustfully creepy game with set pieces and allusions to sadomasochistic fantasies. It

becomes evident that although de Sade's writings may not have become part of the literary and philosophical canon, their strategies and metaphors of sexuality and sensuality have had an intense influence on artists and—as we have seen—on architects.

*"People are firmly convinced that there is close con-
nection between bathing and lust; an old belief
which contributes to the mystery of these public institutions."* [1]

Louis Aragon

On what can this "old belief" to which Aragon
refers be based? No doubt to some degree on
the mystery of the naked body or the eroticizing
effect of scanty clothing, in other words on the
breaking of taboos which many cultures have
set up around the unclothed body and genital
areas. It also has some relationship to the myth
of the life-giving, life-saving, and sometimes
even death-bringing power of water, the element from which we all originate, and even the
pleasant sensation of plunging into water and
surfacing again, relaxing the body, allowing it to
unwind and enjoy its weightlessness.

Aragon's "old belief" also results from the
visual delights of voyeurism (a male domain,
although nowadays more and more frequently
shared by women), which explores bodies and
their nakedness—whether one's own or of
others—lets itself be aroused by them, and
excites erotic fantasies in one's head and that
well-known tingling sensation in the nether
regions. It derives from wishful thinking about
all the things one could get up to with other
bodies in a mixed bath, erotic practices which
in other ages and other cultures were indeed
performed in the bath and enjoyed to the full.
Thus it is difficult to separate the description of
sensual bathrooms from a cultural history of
bathing, and so for our purposes the two will be
combined.

Here we shall stick to the definition that outlines sexuality as the natural and eroticism as
the culturally refined aspects of human sex life,
both of which shape to the mutual sexual attraction of human bodies. The two areas can merge
into each other, partly overlap, and be combined. Which one dominates is a question of
emphasis, although it is clear that eroticism is a
reflective process in the mind whereas sexuality
is a physical instinct, a "gut reaction". Concerning bath culture, the aspects relevant to our
theme are erotic bathing practices on the one

hand, and on the other the eroticizing aura of
the bath itself, its material quality, its design and
its special facilities.

The human foetus leaves the safety and comfort of the amniotic sac, is born into the world
and is bathed. This washing is at the same time
a ritual act. Bathing marks the beginning of our
lives on earth, even if some people, for whatever reason, have only ever bathed when they
were children. Religious rituals and eroticism
are closely related in many cultures. In our cultural tradition, however, this realization has
been obscured and supplanted by the fact that
whether we have particularly religious inclina-
tions or not, our thoughts and deeds have for
two thousand years been thoroughly saturated
with the ideas and values of a religion which
makes the one half of humanity—the women—
responsible for the sin in the world and to this
day obliges its male priesthood under threat of
being defrocked, in Catholicism at least, to
renounce sexual pleasure. Even compensatory
fig leaves in the form of female saints and worship of the Virgin Mary cannot cover up the fundamental hostility of Christianity towards pleasure and eroticism.

That explains why the cohabitation of bathing and eroticism has such a hard time in our
culture and why it constantly has to fight against
suppression. Historically, polytheistic reli-
gions—such as on the Indian subcontinent—
have adopted an essentially different, more
hedonistic attitude, which nowadays, however,
has given way to gruff official prudishness. All
this has an effect on the architectural forms and
features given to baths.

If in our public and private baths we are
today just beginning to approach the norms
applicable to the bath culture of Roman times,
that casts some light on what has been lost in
the meantime. For in terms of architecture,
hygiene, therapeutic effect, luxury and eroticism, the Romans carried the art and the joy of
bathing to an excess which has never been surpassed since (as verified by a number of sources,
e.g. Strabo, Pliny the Younger and perhaps
best of all in Ulrika Kiby's detailed and vivid
historical survey[2]). The public thermal spas, the
most gigantic example of which was built by the
emperor and mass murderer Caracalla
(211–217 AD) and measured 337 x 328 metres,
were laid out as cultural centres and structures
of prestige:

Sebestyén Hegedüs / Isidor Stark,
Gellért Baths,
Budapest, 1911

Wood engraving based on a drawing by F. Thiersch,
reconstruction of the *Tepidarium* in the *Baths of Caracalla,*
Rome, *c.* 1890

Opposite page:
Karl Hocheder, *Müller's Public Baths,* swimming pool,
Munich, 1896–1901

Knossos, *Palace of King Minos*,
fresco with blue dolphins,
Crete

"In the halls decorated with mosaics and marble, costly sculptures and opulent wall hangings there was an army of experts and servants attending to the guests' every need. There were libraries and reading rooms, halls for concerts and entertainments, refreshment rooms and shops for traders."[3]

Enormous windows—even at this time already made of glass—and a daily water consumption of 10,000 cbm were further indices of luxury, whereby the technical standards of the cold, warm and steam baths were constantly being improved. For our purposes it is important to note that the artistic and architectural decoration of both public and private baths with colours, sculptures and precious materials, with visual, haptic and olfactory stimuli indicated a tendency to turn bathing into a multisensory experience and a synthesis of art forms. Realistic, erotic wall paintings and statues were intended to set the mood, to lend stimulation and inspiration. We again encounter these athletes of antiquity with bodies tempered by sport at every turn in the 1990s, particularly in cosmetics commercials, the only difference being

Della Venere nella Conchiglia,
fresco,
Pompeii

that they are made to act with less conviction than in classical times.

The private baths in the villas of wealthy Romans were scarcely less opulent than the public ones. Baths as luxurious centrepieces were simply part and parcel of the living standard of noble houses, whereby a single room was never deemed sufficient—there were always dressing rooms, restrooms, ointment rooms, hallways, pools in the shade and pools in the sun, too. Pliny the Younger describes such a bath in the villa of one of his friends in Etruria. There was always an interplay between functional architectural shape and its erotic decoration with accessories such as fountains, sculptures, and paintings:

"A large friendly room for undressing is followed by the cold bath with a spacious pool lying in the shade. If, however, you wish to swim in water which is not so cool, there is an artificial pond in the courtyard, and right next to it is a fountain in which you can cool off when the lukewarm waters are no longer to your taste. After the cold bath comes the centre room which has plenty of sunlight; even more so in the warm bath, which appears to spring forward to capture your attention. Here there are three sunken baths, two of which are exposed to the sun while the third is out of the sunlight but still well lit. Above the changing room is the room for playing ball games which is big enough for several parties to play different games simultaneously."[4]

It is clear from this that even private bathing was a complete "bathing experience", as widely advertised today, including the pleasures of communal bathing and play. As far as the erotic aspect is concerned, the playful elements were probably more highly rated than the doctrine of sexual performance which is preached to us by at least some of today's advertising, while the latest advertising campaigns nowadays actually tend to turn to hedonism or even irony.

Compared with the luxurious and refined decadence of the late Roman Empire, bathing customs and erotic pleasures degenerated more and more during the course of the Christian Middle Ages into a state of joyfully coarse barbarism. Monks in early Christian times were not averse to the idea of building baths for the sake of cleanliness, warmth and health, and so monasteries were often built near thermal springs. But one should not imagine particularly voluptuous bathing sessions there, at least not with any great regularity. St. Augustine, who gave his name to the holy order of Augustinians, saw it as a considerable favour and an exception when he occasionally allowed the nuns of the convent in Hippo to take a bath:

"Neither washing the body nor the use of the baths should be undertaken regularly, but is only per-

Bathing scene on a
medieval calendar vignette

missible at the customary intervals, that is once per month."[5]

For many holy men and women, however, physical uncleanliness gradually gained the status of a religiously motivated ideology:

"Baptism, Christianity's ritual bathing, which of course is intended to benefit the soul rather than the body, was often the only bath in the life of a devout Christian. Out of inner conviction Caesarius von Heisterbach, a pious monk, avoided all contact with water for washing or bathing. He reports that he once scared off an impetuous and ardent admirer who had fallen passionately in love with him by showing her his body caked with dirt and crawling with lice.
For St. Elizabeth a bath amounted to no more than the dipping of one foot. And she even had to be persuaded to go as far as that. Bishop Reginald of Liège was also proud of the fact that he did not allow water to touch his body. St. Augustine issued the urgent instruction to bathe only once a month. St. Hieronymus on the other hand advised strongly against bathing altogether. He especially warned virgins against contact with bath water since they might perceive their naked bodies and thus do harm to their souls. If, however, they should take a bath against his good advice, then they should preferably do so only in the dark of night with the shutters tightly closed."[6]

The secular and courtly population happily indulged in the amusements offered by bath houses, which mutated more and more into cosy places of sexual pleasure until the terms bath house, pleasure house and brothel became almost synonymous. To the strains of invigorating music, men and women frolicked naked in the warm water of large wooden bathtubs, tightly arranged in rows and spanned with a board covered in fine linen and damask. Here there was feasting, singing and lovemaking. From an architectural point of view, all that was required for this purpose were simple wooden houses, the depiction of which in woodcuts testify to a similarity with the bath house culture which has survived in Scandinavia and Japan.

In the bathtub the women wore only something to cover their heads, or sometimes a bath dress which was open at the back. Men bathed in the nude. The bath maids were scarcely distinguishable from prostitutes, and the bathkeeper's trade, which involved being a bath attendant, a barber and a surgeon all at the same time, became more and more disreputable. To heighten the enjoyment he frequently offered the sexual favours of "beautiful whores and bath maids"[7] as a package deal, so to speak. And even the high clergy was not averse to massage and other services of gentle womanhood. And so during the Council of Constance in 1417, there were 1400 beauties on hand for the amusement of the illustrious guests, including 700 "bath maids".[8]

During the course of the Middle Ages, however, the culture built up around private bathing died out almost completely, at least as far as permanently installed baths were concerned. Even in castles and palaces—with few splendid exceptions—there were soon almost only bathtubs which were carried into certain rooms and laboriously filled with hot water. One reason for this, of course, was that bathrooms with

running hot and cold water, something which had been perfectly familiar to the Romans, remained an unattainable luxury right into the 20th century. In castles, guests were welcomed on arrival with the offer of a bath. After jousting tournaments the combatants enjoyed carousing in warm baths and having their bumps and bruises nursed. The architectural aspect of bathrooms was of practically no significance any more since baths became mobile, as it were, and withdrew into the living quarters, to where servants carried the tub and jugs of hot water.

In his *Parzival* (*c.*1207) Wolfram von Eschenbach describes such a medieval mobile bath, one which was offered to guests. In the morning a wooden bathtub was set up by the bed and the maids poured hot water into it and sprinkled fragrant rose petals onto the surface. When the guest awoke, he climbed into the bath and chastely dressed, fair young ladies hurried to his service, to wash and oil his body and to tend his wounds and bruises. Although this was a source of great pleasure to the guest, chivalrous discipline and decorum forbade any further exchange of potentially erotic caresses, and the young ladies were obliged to leave the room again before the knight climbed naked out of the bath.[9]

There is a chaste eroticism implied here, embedded in that courtly romanticism in which almost everything takes place in the mind and in coded allusions.

Ever since antiquity, however, bathing has granted painters and sculptors the opportunity to celebrate one of their favourite motifs—the representation of the unclothed male or female body, in the bath most commonly the female nude—without immediately being made to feel the censure of worldly or spiritual powers. Often they were also able to refer to the myths of antiquity, and the esteemed reader will recall that it was the gods who were always showing off their potency, contrived erotic situations, impregnated the daughters of mortals and thus called into being dynasties of heroes, the stories of whose great feats are brimming over with murder, incest, rape and the bloodiest of crimes.

But for the artist it is time and again the myth of the beau-

Sir Lawrence Alma-Tadema (1836–1911),
Caracalla's Baths,
oil on canvas

Draft for medieval water and steam baths for both sexes, from the *Göttinger Bellifortis* by Konrad Kyeser

tiful woman which appeals most: Venus Anadyomene, Claudia Schiffer, Cindy Crawford. Or heroes and athletes with muscular bodies tempered by sport. That is of course precisely what has interested painters at all times but especially during the Renaissance and the 19th century. It is just that women would never have dared to paint let alone talk about what they were repressing and perhaps thinking with guilt-laden consciences, whereas under the pretext of artistic portrayal the men could at least enjoy Susanna in the bath or the beautiful Bathsheba. For it was not only King David's blood pressure which rose at the sight of Bathsheba taking a bath.

The eternal voyeur inside men is always demanding new visual food for erotic fantasies. In the bath it was possible to portray the female anatomy particularly effectively and to start the fantasy of the observer working voluptuously. Nowadays nude photography as an art form has taken over those functions to a large extent. It is the architectural layout of such pictures which provides both the pretext and the background, whereby it is noticeable that in many of these paintings—an exquisite example being the work of Sir Lawrence Alma-Tadema (1836–1911)—it comes to a marked interplay between bodies of architecture and architectures of the body. Both were idealized, exaggerated, depicted in a state of festive euphoria. Caracalla's thermal springs serve Alma-Tadema as a monumental pretext for a bath scene.

Another bath motif to arise since the discovery of thermal springs in Greece and the resulting hydrotherapy, but one which particularly in the Middle Ages and in the Renaissance appeared in numerous forms with an erotic connotation, was the Fountain of Youth. There is no doubt that this is one of the most beautiful and touching pipe dreams which human beings have ever nurtured, particularly at a time when the ageing process was quicker and more dramatic and the average life expectancy was hardly more than thirty years.

The Fountain of Youth painting by Lucas Cranach the Elder (1546) is one particularly impressive testimony to this myth. On one side of the picture the old women are carted, dragged, and wheeled to the spring to bathe, decrepit, burdened, and worn-down. They step into the water, which rejuvenates them rapidly to become sexually attractive, buxom young girls, and as such they step out of the Fountain of Youth on the other side, proceed to a tent where they dress up in splendid robes and are then accompanied by handsome cavaliers to a festive banquet with dancing and games and to amorous rendez-vous: paradise, aurea aetas, the land of milk and honey, El Dorado, cosmetic surgery, the fashion, jewellery and cosmetics industries are some of the stages in this myth, appearing in ever new pupations. Its promise has since provided a livelihood for an industry with a multibillion dollar turnover. The hope for beauty and lasting youth is one which hardly anyone can seriously resist. As times change, bathroom design is constantly adapting to these fundamental yearnings, supporting and nourishing them.

In the 16th century the plague, syphilis and church precepts of morality put an end to public baths. The interconnections are unmistakable. And of course the fact that germs multiply quickly in warm water is one reason for medicine of the 16th and 17th centuries to develop theories which result in washing and bathing being reduced to a minimum. Presumably it was not even so very difficult to make it plain to people that water entering the body

Advertising for Davidoff, *Cool Water*

through apertures and through the membrane of the skin had the effect of destabilizing the harmony of body fluids. In 1655 Réaudot put forward this theory:

"Except for urgent medical reasons, bathing is not only superfluous but also very harmful to people's health. (...) Bathing has a destructive impact on the body as the water which finds its way in makes it susceptible to the effects of the deleterious properties of the air. (...) Limp bodies are also the frailest and do not live as long as firm bodies. Bathing fills the head with vapours and is an enemy to nerves and sinews because it causes them to grow so tired that one is never plagued by gout after taking a bath; it kills the foetus in the mother's womb even if the water is warm."[10]

Thus hard times set in for the erotic side of bathing, at least as far as the lower classes were concerned. The fact that the pleasure of taking a bath could never be fully separated from the pleasures in and around the bath is demonstrated even by pictures of the Vatican baths and of course from royal courts. The famous paintings by an anonymous master of the Fontainebleau school *Gabrielle d'Estrées and her Sister Taking a Bath* (1592) and *Portrait of Diane de Poitiers Bathing* (c. 1550) document the withdrawal of bath culture into the private, courtly sphere.

They document how the wooden tubs are decked out with precious fabrics, and how, by the use of heavy curtains, the tub can be converted into a *chambre séparée*, a place of carnal lust drenched in eroticism. And when Gabrielle suggestively twiddles the nipple of her sister's breast, it is more than just a frivolous allusion; it holds the prospect of erotic games and pleas-

Lucas Cranach the Elder,
The Fountain of Youth, 1546

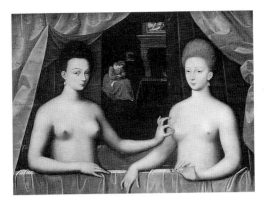

Anonymous master of the Fontainebleau school,
Gabrielle d'Estrées and her Sister in the Bath,
1592

sensual splash. It was between 1718 and 1721 that Max Emanuel, Elector of Bavaria, commissioned his architect, Joseph Effner, to build the Badenburg as a "petite maison" in the grounds of his Nymphenburg summer residence. Apart from the bathing hall with its 6 x 9 metre pool, it has several bedrooms and a palatial banqueting hall with a large balcony.

The depth of the water in the "swimming pool" amounted to no more than 1.45 metres, so that scarcely anyone ran the risk of having seriously to swim. Above the water level, the walls are faced with Dutch tiles. The ceiling paintings show bath scenes from mythology. The console is used for serving drinks and depositing bath utensils. From the gallery which ran around the room at a safely splash-proof height, the elector and his guests could watch beautiful young girls at play in the water. If one can believe the lustful paintings of Adrian van der Werff documenting life at the elector's court in Munich, there were some lively and indeed erotic goings-on in the pleasantly warm water of the pool there.[11] For the middle classes and the aristocracy of

ures of a lesbian or heterosexual nature, even if the official interpretation sees it as an allegory of pregnancy. In three-quarters profile she is looking more towards the viewer, however, than at the object of erotic stimulation.

When Louis XIV had a drawing room at La Roche-Courbon equipped with a bath recess, he became one of the inventors, so to speak, of the "living-room with pool". But in accordance with the spirit of the times, which was hostile towards bathing, the bath was small and modest, and although the opulent wall coverings and pictures were sensual, their motifs were only moderately erotic. But under the influence of the Sun King, the age of *plaisirs*, of gallantry and of keeping mistresses reached its zenith, an age when life was enacted as a sequence of feasts charged with eroticism. Any European ruler with serious regard for his reputation simply owed it to himself and his position to possess a number of mistresses and at least one "summer residence", whereby the term describes only euphemistically what it was understood to mean in the Baroque and Rococo ages.

Then of course baths were a must, even if they were not used for personal hygiene or for the relaxing effect of the water but as places in which to take a swim or as showpieces, in view of the fact that it was the custom of the day to take a "dry bath", or in other words to stifle the evil smells of bodies and wigs with generous doses of powder, make-up and heavy perfume, and that under their voluminous gowns and heaving bosoms respectable ladies as well as coquettish courtesans wore flea traps everywhere on their skin. As a rule, the sculptures and the paintings on the walls and ceilings of such grand bath houses celebrate nakedness and erotic games, often in the form of mythical masquerades.

Not all of these baths served exclusively as bombastic showpieces. According to what is told about the "Badenburg" in Nymphenburg Palace, the bath there was indeed used for a

Château La Roche-Courbon,
Louis XIV's living room with bath recess, 17th century

Joseph Effner, *Badenburg* in the park at *Nymphenburg Palace*,
Munich, interior, 1719–21

the 18th century, taking the waters at a spa
came into fashion as a replacement for the old
bathing halls, and the fact that this did not only
involve passively sitting in water for up to ten
hours per day is borne out by the tradition of
making acquaintances of the opposite sex, who
became "escorts" for the duration of the cure.
Magnificent hallways, pump rooms and bathing
facilities, such as for example in Aachen, Karlo-

vy Vary, Baden near Vienna or Bath in England,
underline the altogether therapeutic relationship
between architecture, bath culture and eroticism. These spas were the scene of a carefully
planned symbiosis of garden design, exterior
and interior architecture.

Public bath culture was thus given tremendous impetus and the result is to be seen above
all in the late 19th and early 20th centuries in

all the splendid thermal baths, spas, public
baths, hotel baths, those "temples of bath
delights",[12] which, under the banner of public
health and for the most part also from the point
of view of their interior design, strove to make
bathing into what it had once been: sensual
enjoyment shared with others. Among the many
good examples—too many to mention here—
are *Müller's Public Baths* (*Müllersches Volksbad*)

in Munich, *Friedrich's Baths* in Baden-Baden, the *Public Baths "Am Plärrer"* in Nuremberg, the *Neptune Baths* in Cologne and—unforgotten to this day and praised to the skies for its luxury and its unsurpassed atmosphere—the *Gellért Baths* in the hotel of the same name in Budapest.

What these baths have in common is that, in contrast to the Roman thermal baths and today's leisure centres, the emphasis is placed almost exclusively on the architectural realization of the interior. It was the major concern of the architects—today one would call them designers—to create a harmonious ambience by balancing colours, shapes, materials and accessories. Even if it was not possible to capture the indulgence in luxury of the *Gellért Baths*,

it was at least important to conjure up an intense feeling of well-being. Frescoes and sculptures depicting bathers, and often putti and amoretti in the Baroque tradition contributed just as much to this sense of well-being as the creation of intimate places for relaxation by means of curves, recesses and grotto-like cavities. The achievement ethic of today's leisure-orientated society was still completely alien to the baths of the turn of the century, as were hosts whose job it is to constantly make sure that leisure is consumed in the form of organized games.

Swimming baths, even new luxury thermal baths, are no longer anything unusual. Swimming has become a mass sport, and in order to survive against tough competition, in Germany at least, the baths try to outshine each other

Women's bath in Turkey,
from *Mœurs, Usages, Costumes des Ottomans*,
Paris, 1812

with their choice of activities and attractions and theme-park exoticism. Here the senses are exposed to inflated stimuli, a flood of constantly changing impressions. Whether this has very much to do with eroticism is an entirely different matter; indeed, erotic accessories are scarcely permitted other than in the design of private pools, mostly in Florida and California. Commercialization always tends to undermine and destroy authentic experiences. That does not mean, however, that even today the fascination of eroticism in the pool cannot be newly discovered by each and every one of us, just as Lady Mary Montague described it in 1764 in her "travel letters" upon visiting a women's bath in Turkey, and nor does it mean, as the following quotation shows, that one's erotically appreciative gaze must be confined to the opposite sex:

> "The girls were walking about, moving with that majestic grace which Milton bestows upon the progenetrix of all humankind. Many were of the same shapely build as a certain goddess painted with the brush of a Guido Reni or a Titian. Most of them with dazzling white skin, adorned by nothing more than their beautiful hair, which hung down over their shoulders in plaits, braided either with ribbons or with pearls—they were perfect images of the Graces."[13]

In view of the fact that at least in northern latitudes private baths and their interiors are more important for our theme, I should like to leave the subject of public baths at this point and from here on limit myself to modern private baths and consider the part eroticism plays or could play there.

Le Mont-Dore, spa hotel,
first-floor lobby

If one disregards the baths of antiquity and the creations of court architects in the Renaissance and Baroque eras, modern bath design begins with the upper middle classes of the 19th century. There was no room for eroticism in the private showers, rented bath tubs and hydrotherapeutic oddities of the lower classes. For the members of the bourgeoisie, however, it was quite a different story: as they gradually took over a number of powerful political functions from the aristocracy, they assimilated the latter's chivalrous code of virtue in order to be able to accuse the nobility of decadence, i.e. a decline in morals. Or expressed the other way round, for religious and power-political reasons, which indeed may not have been obvious to the individual, the European middle classes of the 19th century developed their own specific morality and a sense of shame which is marked by guilt complexes and a deeply defensive attitude towards any form of nakedness.

Although the bourgeoisie feudalized itself, as Erich Küthe called it,[14] the taboos which they set up stop at nothing, and the bathroom is no exception. Even here are pictorial and sculptural depictions of nakedness no longer possible. But as this is a place in which eroticism is always at least potentially, latently present, it withdraws into the materials, for example into precious polished marble floors, sensuously shaped washing basins, carvings, heating stoves, dressing tables etc., and into fragrant essences, lavish sponges and other such bath ingredients.

At the end of the 19th and the beginning of the 20th century, designers and architects like Charles Rennie Mackintosh, Josef Hoffmann, and Eileen Gray, as well as a number of lesser known architects, built exquisite private baths which even today have lost none of their charm. The only thing they have in common is a high degree of individuality, reflecting the personality of their owners as seen through the eyes of their

Claudio Silvestrin, bathroom
in a private residence converted from what was once a
pilgrims' hostel, Provence, 1990s

architects. During the history of private baths since the 19th century, the concept of the bath integrated into the living room has been the exception rather than the norm. But for individualists, and not only the particularly rich, it has attained popularity as a very private gem, a showpiece of their houses and apartments, proving that it is certainly not an invention of recent years as clever advertising executives would have us believe.

Culturally eroticism becomes visible in the multisensory interplay among shapes, colours, bodies and light, and is integrated into a network of cultural communication. In terms of style, however, bathrooms tend to be characterized by a greater heterogeneity and a greater variety of overlapping elements and influences than, for example, kitchens, living rooms or bedrooms. This is because of their individuality. The physical experience of these bathrooms is complemented by sensibilities which can be touched off by interiors, decor, fittings, colours and accessories.

It was not until the 1970s and '80s that there was a really significant surge of development in bathroom design. It was then that Dieter Sieger and several other designers began to concentrate their energies more intensively on it and to put designer baths on the mass market. In the process they came across a number of long-term issues. Firstly they discovered that there were many millions of bathrooms in old houses which were in need of renovation; alongside

new building projects, these help to fill the design order books, for nowhere in the house is the demand for modernization greater. Secondly, as a result of a long period of continuous peacetime, generations of well-to-do heirs who can afford to invest far more in their bathrooms than their parents were able to are crowding on to the scene. And thirdly, Sieger and others hit upon various topics of public discussion which strongly influence consumer behaviour and the decision to buy, albeit indirectly: these factors include leisure, recreation, fitness, health and a shift in status symbols.

Here there is a connection with the currently topical "body discussion" and the body cult of the '90s, which is establishing itself more and more firmly in philosophy and the social sciences in opposition to a development which derives from modernism towards a steadily growing depersonalization, abstraction and scientification. These ideas have gained greater currency through French poststructuralists influenced by Lyotard, Baudrillard and Derrida, whose work examines these issues in conjunction with the change of paradigms from analogue to digital culture, from material to immaterial aesthetics, leading to a "disappearance of reality" as Virilio calls it. Thus the body rebels and is not prepared to allow itself to be abolished so easily.

What significance does this have for bathrooms and eroticism? First and foremost it indicates a heightened awareness of sensuality, both

Dieter Sieger,
Dornbracht bathroom fittings, model *Obina*,
1993

Simon Ungers / Tom Kinslow, bathroom in the private
residence of Lawrence Marcelle, New York, 1990–92

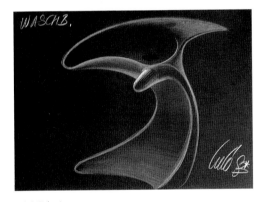

Luigi Colani,
draft for a wash stand,
1983

Manfred Wolff-Plottegg,
bathroom in a private apartment,
Graz, 1984

are always accompanied to a certain extent by the Eros–Thanatos motif, and it goes without saying that there is nothing that can prepare the body more intensively for tender caresses and physical love than a shared bath. The combination of bath and eroticism means employing shapes, colours, light, fittings, furniture, bath tubs and wash basins to create a sensual ambience. And for the toilet it means banishment from the bathroom! Ideas about what constitutes a sensual ambience can, however, never be reduced to a single or even a handful of common denominators; too various, fortunately, are the individual conceptions on this point.

So an intellectual may well feel turned on by that cold stainless steel technicality which the two young New York architects Simon Ungers and Tom Kinslow installed in a new house in New York state belonging to the author Lawrence Marcelle. The bathroom in question is one reduced to the bare necessities which is normally produced for prisons. Someone may derive great sensual stimulation from a bathroom like the one which the architect and minimalist Claudio Silvestrin built into a house in the Provence which at one time served as a shelter for monks on pilgrimages, and now hosts New York art collectors and their pictures. The bath tub, weighing 700 kg and hewn out of a single block of chalky sandstone, embodies the extremely sensuous archetypal shape of a fruit or egg cut open, the material texture of which, in conjunction with the techniques of condensation and reduction, can have an erotic effect on certain people. For others it may be bulbous, sculpturally amorphous fittings like Sieger's *Obina* which trigger off key erotic stimuli.

on and around one's own person. The bathroom is a place of the most intimate encounter with one's own body and one's own nakedness, possibly also with that of the person with whom one is living, not counting the sex act itself. It is a place of destigmatization for the body, a place of body care, of body culture, of body love in a narcissistic sense, but also a place of privacy and intimacy. It is for this reason that mirrors are so important in the bathroom, and all the cosmetics and all the oils, essences and herbs. This is something the people of the ancient world already knew all about. But even the venerable, but nonetheless sensuous old bath utensils already mentioned, like natural sponges, play an essential part.

The bathroom is where "bodiliness" is celebrated. Bathing means crossing the border between inside and outside. It opens the pores, and the soul, to indulgence. Water and bathing

Philippe Starck, *Teatriz Restaurant*, passage leading to the toilets, Madrid, 1990

Luigi Colani was the first to create organic shapes for bathroom design, forms which in the '70s were new, startling, moulded to match the body's contours and of an almost natural sensuousness. Furthermore he was the first modern designer to single out and highlight the bathroom as a field for erotic recreation. In the late '70s and early '80s Colani also designed freestanding washbasins and double washbasins in shapes which were organically curved and at the same time extraordinarily ergonomical.

Just as with erotic architecture generally, an erotic bathroom should play with surfaces, layers, materials, visual and haptic stimuli, with the symbols and functions of sexual attraction between bodies, skin, and interiors. Add to this

the lighting design and, to round off the multisensory experience, the olfactory component of fragrances.

If there has been so much talk recently from interested parties about "bathrooms for living", "the bath(room) experience" and about "joy and pleasure" in the bath,[15] technical journalists should comment critically on such slogans and analyse the degree of reality they contain rather than repeating them without reflection; for the industry, of course, is only interested in sales. The pie-in-the-sky world propagated by advertising and the reality of people's lives are as different as chalk and cheese, or to be more precise, they are different bathroom realities. If these slogans mean no more than turning one's

bathroom into a fitness centre or a domestic recreation area, it can be no more conducive to eroticism than if there is no division between bathroom and living area. For even when eroticism is only a question of personal ambient, it requires intimacy, unless we are talking about exhibitionists.

Taking a bath in privacy is an activity with erotic connotations, and as such it is also of growing importance in the media, of course. For the arts, moving images in ever changing guises, from the silent movie to the computer, are probably the most significant and momentous invention of the 20th century. The crucial scenes of many feature films take place in the bathroom since it is in such a setting that action and symbolism can be presented in a form which is visually impressive and charged with erotic tension. The excerpt on which I should like to comment is taken from the three-part TV film *"Der Erfolg ihres Lebens"* ("Her Life's Success"), which was broadcast in Germany by ZDF in 1990 and which deals with the chequered career of a fictitious female fashion designer.

A bath scene in the middle of the second episode, carefully worked out to the last detail, is in many respects a critical and realistic comment on the increasingly optimistic promises made by the manufacturers of bathroom materials and furnishings about "bathrooms for living" and "the bath(room) experience". Here the designer bath is highlighted to perfection as part of a landscaped living area styled by interior designers, an open-plan room concept in which the areas for bathing, living, eating and cooking merge into each other. Every accent is placed with meticulous accuracy and the materials, the furnishings, the accessories in the form of flowers, lamps, vases, plants, sculptures are impeccably matched in textbook fashion. The beauty and functionality are flawless and yet just as sterile as the set-up in the broken-down marriage which unfolds before the viewer's voyeuristic eyes.

Solange, the wealthy but somewhat unrefined wife of Erik, an intellectual who is in love with the fashion designer and protagonist of the film, emerges naked from the bathwater like Venus, as a maturely sensual beauty. Every movement breathes erotic enticement, but the promise comes to nothing as she performs an antistriptease in front of her husband: she dresses slowly and deliberately and even gets him to zip up her dress, only to let herself be undressed again later by her lover.

The couple conducts a verbal duel, which also contrasts precisely with the open-plan layout of the room; both are extremely careful not to leave themselves open to attack, not to drop their guard. Simultaneously they feint and

Public Baths "Am Plärrer", Nuremberg

thrust, needling each other with their pinprick attacks to lure their opponent out of defence and then to finish him or her off. What is presented to the viewer is the reversal of pie-in-the-sky advertising scenarios in the real world, but also the reversal of the old myths in the context of the emotional frigidity of modern relationships which have long since lost all vestiges of eroticism. And what then is the point of the carefuly styled bath landscape?

One conclusion which can be drawn from the film excerpt with regard to our theme is that a reduction of interior design to functionality and aesthetic perfection alone is too one-dimensional. Something more needs to be added. For years now, Dieter Sieger, one of most successful bathroom designers of our time, has had an effective name for it, even if it does contain perhaps a little too much pathos: "design with soul". What is meant is emotional appeal, that quality of design with which it is also possible to identify in terms of feeling. There is no doubt that harmonious, elegant and perfect surfaces are part and parcel of good architecture and good design, but emotional depth is necessary too.

One man who has found an outstanding

solution of his own to the question of eroticism in the bathroom is the architect, painter and sculptor Wolfgang Meisenheimer, who is a professor of architecture in Düsseldorf, Germany. For years Meisenheimer worked as a sculptor and painter on the theme of "body landscapes", and as an architect he has always advocated an "architecture of the senses" in both theory and practice. This means that it is necessary to cultivate not only the long-range senses of seeing and hearing but also the close-up senses of touch, taste and smell, and to pay attention not only to the outward senses but also to the senses within in order to feel thoroughly at home. For the architect it means then that he or she has to build a house from the inside outwards and that the interior of a house, just like the insides of the human body, can look very different from the exterior, the face, the façade.

It was by following this principle and his own personal ideas about key erotic stimuli that he also built the bathroom in his home in Düren. To reach it one has to climb a narrow staircase which deliberately forces the body into contact with a fur-like wall-covering. But this is only a prelude in preparation for the uterine

cavity of the bathroom, in whose water one is reborn every day. Meisenheimer thinks it necessary to have the immediate physical sensation and not to experience it with the eyes: to walk around the outside of the bathroom first, feeling the fur on the walls before entering through a narrow sliding-door. And then inside everything is completely different: here light-coloured tiles dominate, with concave walls of mirrors which magnify the room enormously and indulge the visual senses. Above white mosaic tiles, a domed roof light bulges upwards so that even without windows it is bright and cheerful in Meisenheimer's bathroom.

Wolfgang Meisenheimer has found a holistic approach to the theme of eroticism in the bath, one which sprang from his temperament but which was also the result of careful deliberation and a precision job of architectural planning. The cultivation of living styles for the future should not shy away from placing greater emphasis on bathing, to borrow ideas from the bath culture of the ancient world or even from Asia, and openly to make baths—from their architectural exterior as well as their interior design—into places of sensual enjoyment.

"The Prince longed to be with her and he searched about the tower to find a door, but in vain. And so he rode home, but her singing had so touched his heart that every day he would go out into the wood and listen. One day, as he stood there hiding behind a tree, he saw a witch appear and he heard her call out, 'Rapunzel, Rapunzel, let down your hair!'

Thereupon Rapunzel lowered her braids out of the window and the witch climbed up to her. 'If that is the ladder that will take me up there, then I too shall try my luck,' he thought. The following day as it was growing dark, he went to the foot of the tower and called, 'Rapunzel, Rapunzel, let down your hair!'

At once her tresses came tumbling to the ground and the Prince climbed up to her." [1]

Lebbeus Woods, *D-QUAD.OAN:*
Biomechanical and Biodynamic Towers, 1987

Lebbeus Woods, *QUAD.150 (Timespace Overtaken):*
Protomechanical Towers, 1987

The fairy tale is as simple as that. At first climbing the tower brings Rapunzel and the Prince much joy, then much sorrow, but then finally twins and a happy end. It would rather twist the picture if one were to say that the tower is the most common and thus least outstanding of all erotic architectural symbols, because it stands out if nothing else. With regard to high-rise buildings, Hans Hollein's ironic view puts it in a nutshell: a sinewy arm with a clenched fist, a sinewy penis, power and potency. But apart from the obvious phallic symbolism, the tower shows itself to be a fascinating architectural topic because of its variety of possible shapes, historical forms and functions. Just consider how many different towers there are: lighthouses, watch towers, peel towers, prison towers, observation towers, drilling rigs, church spires, bridge towers, television towers, office towers, ivory towers, and finally women's harem and love towers, which brings us back to our theme. The dynastic towers of the aristocracy in Bologna, Florence

Opposite page:
The Temple of Khajurâho, India,
reliefs with figures of gods and women

Lebbeus Woods,
Biodynamic Ring and Tower, 1987

Lebbeus Woods, *D-QUAD.9M,*
with groundshields, 1987

and San Gimignano stood not only for strong fortifications but also for power, potency, strength and beauty. [2]

Erotic symbols in architecture immediately call psychology and psychoanalysis onto the scene, but the annoying thing about such discussions, if they are not conducted by academic specialists, is that amateur psychologists in the fields of art, architecture and literary studies normally know nothing but Freud, the Grand Old Man whose psychology of sex they carry around with them as their fetish and their bible. That is about the same as persistently trying to base arguments in contemporary physics and

Hans Hollein,
project for a skyscraper in Chicago,
1958

Hans Hollein,
project for a skyscraper in Chicago,
1958

chemistry on the scientific knowledge of the turn of the century. Günther Feuerstein has put together in concise form the sexual symbols applied to architecture which are to be found in Freud's work. This includes among other things the identification of human being and house; pillars, columns and legs as phallic symbols. Where a building's openings—archways, doors, windows—are supposed to symbolize female orifices, even the most well-disposed reader

begins to have doubts, or at least it becomes clear that such a symbolism cannot be reduced to a 1:1 basis:

"The female genitals are symbolized by all objects that share their characteristics of being able to envelop a hollow space which can enclose something within itself: Like, for instance, by wells, mines, caves, by vessels and bottles, by cases, cans, trunks, boxes, bags and so on. (...) Some symbols are more related to the womb than to the female genitals, like cabinets, ovens, and, above all, rooms. The room-symbol meets the house-symbol, so that door and gate become symbols of the genital orifice."[3]

As this sort of interpretation seems to lack differentiation and to be too closely bound up with the circumstances of Freud's life in Vienna, and since we lack specialized knowledge about a modern psychoanalysis of architecture, this book will for the most part have to manage without a psychoanalytical dimension.

The association between sexuality and power, verbosely formulated in complicated theories by psychologists and philosophical theorists, is given its clearest architectural manifestation in the shape of a tower. But there are also other attributes to be seen, especially in the case of skyscrapers: success, joie de vivre, ambition, fame, fashion, a high-altitude euphoria, a pioneering spirit among civil engineers and outstanding achievements in technology.

Scarcely anywhere is the mixture of architectural origins—cultic and sacral on the one hand, erotic and sexual on the other—more in evidence than in the building of towers, as Hans Hollein himself is also quick to emphasize. In addition to their phallic appearance, towers often derive their erotic aura from their function and their architectural ornamentation and decoration. Whereas Egyptian obelisks and Germanic and Celtic rock steles serving

cultic purposes symbolized the link between heaven and earth, the great variety of phallus-shaped Islamic minarets is not part of some cult of the senses—in spite of the often almost textile sensuality radiated by their faïence outer shells or their painted architecture built in glazed tiles—but serve a religion which strongly emphasizes morality. The church spires of Christianity, a religion which only in the Baroque and Rococo periods overcame its fundamental hostility towards pleasure, are an early attempt to incorporate a spiritual rather than earthly, sensual symbolism into its architecture.

It is different in the case of the places of worship on the Indian subcontinent, such as the

John Portman, *Peachtree Center Plaza*, Atlanta, drafted in 1967, completed in 1975

Minaret
of a mosque
in Thichma

famous Hindu temple *Bhuvaneshvara* in Orissa, whose ornaments and pictorial scenes incorporate into the basic tectonic form not only pictures of animals but also representations of gods, maiden-gods and pairs of lovers. *Khajurâho*, the 16th-century Khandariya temple and the largest and most important example of *Chandella* architecture, is particularly rich in ornamentation, depicting gods, goddesses, crocodiles and lovers. The sculptural effect is underscored above all by the wealth of *absuras*, god figures, which adorn the outer walls and are set on consoles and depict maiden-gods called *surasundarî*. The tower of the temple is decorated with gatekeepers, handmaidens, gods and goddesses, dancing Shivas, with their many arms, seated Parvati, governesses, hair braiders, bathers and numerous other figures related to this religion, all testifying to a sensuous religiosity.

It would be totally wrong, however, to draw the conclusion that Hinduism today is a religion particularly tolerant of sensuous pleasure and eroticism. The Indian film industry, for example, which is bigger than Hollywood's, puts out new love stories every day but not even kissing is allowed in them, let alone scenes of undisguised eroticism. In a puritanically inhibited society, the only outlet for bottled-up desire is to be found in the film characters' tight-fitting clothes, which mainly show off voluptuous female forms, and of course in visiting temples which are no longer

consecrated, like *Khajurâho*, and which under a veil of religious symbolism depict in no uncertain terms the love life of the gods, especially of Shiva.

But these examples of sculpted architecture have nothing to do with pornography in the Western sense of the word. Indeed in his book about the *Khajurâho* temple, Louis Frédéric, one of the greatest connoisseurs of Asian art, writes:

"Throughout the course of Indian history, woman has always been an object of adoration, and sexual union was regarded as one sacred act among many, to be performed in a religious spirit, no matter what form it might take. Here the sexual act is an act of union between two inseparable principles of the universe, by its very nature an act of creation. The man performing it feels on a par with the deity. The woman who participates in collective sex rites is equally aware of her involvement in the grand cosmic game of creation. There is no hint of subjugation, but a profound sense of equality, of sharing in the performance of a divine duty."[4]

The *Khajurâho* temple is completely covered with sculptures, not all of which are exclusively devoted to representations of eroticism, however; they also depict scenes of everyday life, animals fighting, battles, dancing, deities, plants and floral ornaments. Architecturally these sculptures perform no important load-bearing function, but they have a profound influence on the architectural face, the façade of this building. The implication is that the stone effigy testifies to the presence of the deity:

"The Hindu notion is that erotic ecstasy is a symbol of mystic union, of the infinite lust of the indi-

vidual soul as it is united with the universal soul. According to the 'Chândognya Upanishad': 'Just as a man forgets the whole world in the arms of the woman he loves, so that everything within him is turned outward, so it is that in the act of union with the omniscient being inner and outer worlds become one.' This is precisely the message which is being eternally repeated to us by the erotic sculpture of the temple."[5]

The statues of the gods find their complement in free-standing sculptures of mythical creatures which, although not an integral part of the architecture, adorn the individual platforms of the temple. These *shârdûla* represent tiger-like monsters, each of which is tearing at the flesh of a man or a woman, most probably as a symbol of the power of physical desire.

The inner rooms of the temple as well as the circular ambulatories of the sanctuaries are free of directly erotic figures, but the female body in all its variety of forms is nevertheless to be seen sculpted in masterly fashion in scenes of everyday life, thus becoming an integral part of the interior design.

There are also many monastery and temple towers in Thailand and Burma which display an extraordinarily sensual splendour. It is only permissible to talk of erotic architecture, however, when it is accepted that—isolated from the original religious context—the aura of sensuousness emitted by the object and the associations of the individual perceiving it must complement each other in order to create an erotic impression, and to have an erotic effect on a variety of viewers observing one specific architectural form.

The Temple of Khajurâho, India,
temple of love

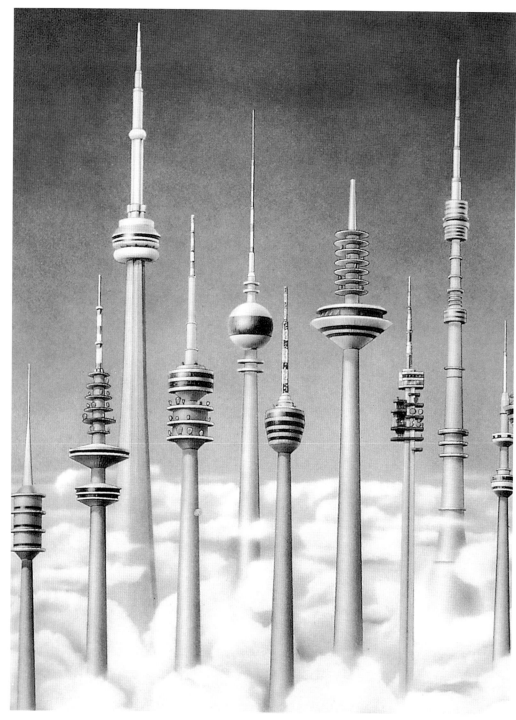

York was not the pseudo-aesthetics of the straight-lined, sterile stiffness of the Rockefeller Center, the poetry of New York is not the poetry of a wretched ice box into which those despicable European aesthetes would like to lock away the unstomachable remains of their young, modern sculptures! No! The poetry of New York is as old and as powerful as the world; it is poetry which has always existed. Its strength, just like the strength of all other poetry, lies in the extremely gelatinous, paradoxical nature of the maniacal carnality of its own reality. Every evening New York's skyscrapers assume the anthropomorphic shapes of the motionless figures out of Millet's Angelus Bell, multiplied, inflated to gigantic proportions and transported back into the Tertiary period, ready to perform the sexual act and to devour each other like swarms of praying mantises prior to mating."[6]

The box-like modernism of the late '50s to the '70s deprived the skyscrapers of much of their sensuality, however. The skyscraper's trinity of plinth, shaft and head was destroyed; it was often beheaded and thus it degenerated into a featureless shaft, whereby this smooth, functional form grew longer and longer and then simply broke off at some point, suggesting that it would have been possible to go on building until it really did pierce the clouds. Park Avenue and 5th Avenue in New York offer a rich source of material to illustrate this point.

It is not until the advent of Post-modernism, much maligned in an arrogant, moralizing tone by European critics, that the shafts are given back their features, that they are again provided with curves and ornaments, with hips, breast-

Advertising for Bosch electronics, *The Comparative Heights of Television Towers*, Toronto 549m (third from left), Berlin 212m (extreme left)

Nils-Ole Lund,
The Fashion of Architecture,
1986

Nowadays the purest form of phallic symbolism is to be seen in the television towers which are shooting up all over the world, the various tops of which would be a suitable subject for a "phallological" study, in spite of the fact that it would probably never occur to anyone to ascribe a particularly erotic effect to these towers. This proves the extent to which eroticism is a question of imagination and of the emotional associations triggered by the objects perceived. Purity of form is by no means enough, otherwise television towers would have to be counted among the most erotic architectural structures of all.

Office towers on the other hand, skyscrapers, have always had an erotic flair, probably as a result of their greater complexity and their prominence in the cityscape. Salvador Dalí testified to this as early as 1937 in his typically eccentric manner:

"In that misty state midway between waking and sleeping before I finally fell asleep in this my second night in New York I could make out the irreconcilable contours of the pictures I had seen during my first day, which were still going round and round in my mind. No, a thousand times no! The poetry of New York was not what they tried to persuade us it was in Europe. The poetry of New

works and galleries, that the architecturally playful nature of high-rise blocks is revived and thus given a new aura of eroticism. This, however, has a lot to do with the game of fashion, its narrow mentality and decorative quality and its rapid change.

Nils-Ole Lund has taken the fascination of tower blocks in both its erotic and its fashion senses and, with subtle satire, has made it visible in the form of superb collages:[7] the *Chrysler Building* as a bizarre headdress on an enigmatically cool beauty in his picture "An Architectural Hat" (1979). In *Clean and Cool* (1976) he depicts the *World Trade Center* in the spirit of an "ice cream technique of blonde love," an impersonal, cool shaft on smooth female skin. In a series of collages entitled *The Fashion of Architecture* (1986) it is Philip Johnson and Helmut Jahn he has set his sights on. And in *Architectural Call Girl* (1987) his sharp criticism is aimed at the prostituted character of interchangeably smooth, anonymous, modern office architecture.

The return to functional boxes and "container architecture" observed in the early '90s augurs well only up to a certain point, although in the case of Helmut Jahn and William Pedersen surfaces are roughed up with constructivist details. Jahn at least is developing new glass technologies for buildings' outer skin which, when vapour-coated with ceramic layers, can seem to take on the texture of a fabric, create three-dimensional effects, be dyed in different colours and even change its colour according to the light intensity, all helping to give the boxes a surface charm hitherto unknown. In the context of this, Matteo Thun's suggestion to drape the façades of tower blocks with alternating outer skins according to the change in fashions, users and seasons seems logical and convincing.

In Botho Strauss's novel *The Young Man*, the tower is proclaimed as the post-modernist habitat:

"It was a tower built in pink granite coated with a glazing the colour of bronze; a slender building which climbed a good hundred and fifty metres into the sky and widened out gently at the foot into a plinth, reminiscent of the bottom end of a tree-trunk. This building had nothing in common with the bulky rectangular blocks, the merciless Corn-flakes boxes of a previous high-rise epoch. It had to have an exhilirating effect on anyone looking at it. People felt it to be beguilingly weightless and intimately bound up with the air. It played with any light which fell on it; it picked up even the faintest gleam from the sky and made something out of it. (…)
We were greeted by a fresh current of motionlessness and leisure, as though we had set foot on the shore of a different time, an everlasting daylight drowsiness. It was now around midday and there

Charles F. Johnson,
house in Arizona desert

were only very few people to be seen. They were easily overlooked in the spaciousness of the lounge and reception area, they were swallowed up by the white leather armchairs, they were almost faded over by so much artistic lucidity, or they lingered far off among the glittering lights down in the garden of the atrium, access to which, from the hall, was down a long marble stairway. There on could see a piazza roofed over with glass, a complete little city area with boutiques and a shopping arcade, a sauna, a cinema, restaurants and a travel agency.
The square itself was lined with towering bamboo shrubs, among which a powerful waterfall poured over a rock ledge, making a rushing sound, but not

thundering. Not far from it was a frozen pond which served as an ice rink. So this was 'Tower City'. Here all the walls were faced far above head height with honey-coloured marble, streams of polished brass flowed along balustrades and hand-rails and up and down lamps, and fountains and long flower beds with bizarre, ghostly white shrubs were enclosed with colourfully illuminated ribbons of cut glass."[8]

This new eroticism in architecture is clearly characterized as synthetic and feeble and caricatured as an object of cultural satire. It is also personified in the formerly vigorous and ener-

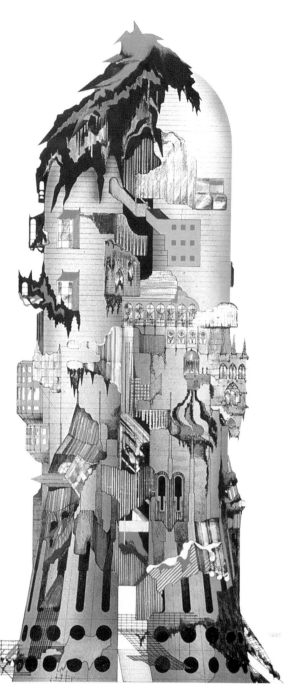

In terms of erotic association and aura, the counterpart of the tower is the cave: at least from the male point of view it is mysterious, organic, uterine, asymmetrical, bizarre, orgiastic, and suggests warmth and security, cosiness, a place to hide, embryonic life, mystery and sexual enjoyment. In a cave one is cut off from the outside world, focused on oneself or one's partner, suggesting concentration, an ivory tower mentality, but it also means that one cannot see what is going on outside, except via some sophisticated system of mirrors.

The generous donor of a library extension for the University of British Columbia in Vancouver demanded in the '70s, for example, that the view down an avenue of plane-trees and across the bay should be preserved. So the clever architect, Richard Henriquez, set the building underground and with the aid of an enormous mirror opened up a view of the sea, visible even at a depth of six metres. But soon the original idea was watered down and reduced and finally destroyed by a new building which, for cost-saving reasons, was put on top of the old one.

In the age of electronic media, of course, the view from the window can be replaced by media windows in the form of simulations, animations and television pictures from all over the world, a technology common to all those

undergound headquarters of military command. Instead of the human eye, it is camera systems which look out on the world. But the simple fact that the view from a window is one of the oldest motifs in traditional panel painting proves that in the long term the cave dweller's emotional life is not good: he needs daylight and a view out into the open in order not to waste away as a ghoulish wreck.

There are other points of view, however, and not only those expressed by potholers. In the late '70s and early '80s, during a phase when he was drafting architectural projects inside mountains and making extensive use of natural elements, Peter Cook, the indefatigable experimenter, propagated his project *Hilltop Academies*. With this project Cook leaves the imagination ample room to visualize in the interior of his cavernous mountains palaces, laboratories, dwellings and factories.

Thus it is clear that such architecture can be made very attractive, and that architects can imagine numerous alternatives to the usual military installations to fill the insides of mountains. Cook combines this with references to Bruno Taut's and Wenzel Hablik's fantasies of crystalline alpine architecture as well as to the provocatively erotic language of shapes used by Finsterlin in Cook's drafts *Lump* and *Prepared Landscape*.

Peter Cook,
Arcadia: Trickling Towers Metamorphosis,
1979

getic actor and author Ossia, who lives in the luxury of this post-modernist tower and under the influence of the "anything goes" attitudes of the '80s, degenerates into an emasculated wimp:

"He read out a few episodes from his collection, drafts of Pat as a comic character. If I understood it correctly, the whole thing was set out like a sort of lecherous ride on a ghost train, during which a "sweet young thing" was constantly frightened and molested on all sides. The first sensuous heart in a joke world of grotesque faces from which there was absolutely no escape, a hopeless world of erotic stultification. People doddering from thrill to thrill and showing off their prematurely decrepit sexuality like blowing into those paper party hooters so that they unfurled in each other's faces. (...)"[9]

Peter Cook,
Lump (Mound), 1973–74

Ferdinand Cheval, *Palais Idéal*, cave, 1879–1922

half Stone Age cave and half rustic family home, and alludes to the loam-built pueblo and adobe architecture of the native Americans, can be planned and built to become an organic constituent of its natural environment by making use of Nature's sensuous aura and, with a clever eye for detail, underscoring and even heightening it.

It is only right that this chapter should close with an ingenious example of architectural obsession that unites all of the erotic symbols architecture has employed to date—towers, caves, sculptures, genital, phallic and uterine elements—an architectural dream come true, the apotheosis of eroticism and pansexuality: Ferdinand Cheval's *Palais Idéal*, which this country postman erected between 1879 and 1922 in the South of France after having spent ten thousand days planning, building and modelling it with his own hands. Peter Weiss has written an essay about this project, "Postman Cheval's Great Dream", which turns psychological analysis into a literary work of art:

"But these images fade again; all that remains in my dream is the building instinct, all that remains is the urge to decorate, to melt down and remodel. Art history, geography, ethnography become empty concepts. This is my own, my innermost world. A village in the South of France. A country postman. The outside world falls into oblivion. All that exists is the dream. All that he holds faith with is the dream. And here his absolute certainty. Only the inner voice. The living core. The convolutions of the brain. The intestines. The heart. The lungs. The breathing. The gushing. The pulse. The organism with its stirrings. The genitals. The search for soft members, to feel them, to fondle them. Breasts, hips, wombs. To snuggle up to them, to thrust into them. The inner world, I surrender myself to it. I am now in it, it engulfs me. I landed in here through some archway, some orifice or other, into the interior of thoughts, into the interior of impulses. (...) Things which have only just escaped from the intestines and entrails as impulses are already developing further in fairy tale variations. What was only just oozing out as excrement now stands as the architecture of a magical

realm. You are on the inside of the body, enclosed in the cells and tissues, cloisters open up before your eyes, columned halls, ladder-like networks, chambers and steps, such as are to be found under the microscope in a laboratorial world."[10]

A trained architect could probably never have dreamt up such a universe of erotic architectural symbols. It just had to remain the prerogative of a country postman to capture the visions of his dreams and desires in loam and stone. As a visit to Hauterives and the surrounding countryside shows, Cheval made use of the potato-shaped fieldstones which are found strewn all over the landscape there, which are normally used for building garden walls and houses and which in his hands mutate into a cosmos of architectural sculptures, just as they do in Peter Weiss's imagination:

"Sometimes the foundation is made of spherical blocks of marble, or porphyry, sometimes of rectangular blocks of tufa or a skillful assemblage of river boulders. The boldly tossed arches, full of airy grace, are made of slag, a very light material which comes either from coal stoves or from the locomotive of Saint-Vallier. There are garlands and friezes made of mussels, rosettes of fossils, bouquets of oyster shells which a nephew brought from Marseilles. For the restoration work, the spherical sandstone rocks which Cheval used were, unfortunately, nowhere to be found."[11]

There is no doubt that he was an architect with a natural gift which came from deep within, for all the proportions and dimensions of his *Palais Idéal* are unremittingly consistent, although he spent half of his life, precisely forty-three years, working on the building. We have no difficulty in making out the influences of medieval castle architecture and local architectural styles as well as the exotic fashions of late 19th-century colonialism which Cheval would have discovered in magazines of the time. A contemporary architect like Gaudí, however, and the Catalan-Moorish tradition upon which he based his work, were completely unknown to Cheval. His work is indeed the inner being of a naively ingenious eccentric turning itself inside out; it is an ideal world, a dream world, a fairy tale world, the genius of which lies in the fact that here a person with an enormously strong and individual hand succeeded in combining an eclectic variety of statements into a single deliberate style which is motivated by the psychology of sex, and in erecting for himself and for posterity a unique monument of erotic architecture.

A lot of people feel compelled to convert their perfectly normal houses into cave dwellings. A number of the original residents on the *Weißenhof* estate in Stuttgart, that prototype of modernism, could no longer bear the sober white paint and the functional layout of their new apartments. They followed their den building instincts and redesigned the flats in blatant contrast to the external architecture, even erecting pitched roofs on top of the flat ones.

In Nils-Ole Lund's fantasy—as to be seen in his collage *A Nude in a Decorated Setting* (1976)—such caves are ruled by strong, sensual women with dark or red hair, ready to receive a partner of either sex for loveplay in an atmosphere charged with eroticism.

An example in Arizona, built by the architect Charles F. Johnson, shows how a house which is

"Ettore travels to live. He seeks out life like a wild boar seeks truffles. He tracks it down to the most mysterious and unlikely places. He scents it out like a rabbit hunter at the burrow and courts it, to be seduced by life and to seduce it himself, if it is at all possible to seduce life." [1]

As a rule, erotic architecture fantasies are marked by a pronounced vitalism that often reaches beyond the mere imagination into the realm of the fantastic, where it becomes possible to build what is generally considered impossible. At the time of the French Revolution, for example, Claude-Nicolas Ledoux managed to coax the ground plan of a house of pleasure, where the young "citoyen" was to be prepared for the duties and pleasures of matrimony, into a phallic shape.

Such fantastic buildings can even be realized today without causing offense in the eyes of moral watchdogs, as Stanley Tigerman has proved. His *Daisy House* (1975–78), located on the shore of Lake Michigan, whose windows all face the lake, presents itself to the visitor as an elegantly curved, cedar-panelled building. Its erotic wit only becomes fully apparent when one looks at this building's ground plan and axonometry. The plan shows that the building is erected in the shape of male genitals, with the male and female principles mixing in the windowed living area. Tigerman, a proponent of paneroticism, allows the slit-like front door to open directly into the kitchen, obviously an erotic-culinary allusion, for with him, as with many others, the way to the heart goes through the stomach. [2]

In 1959 Nicolas Schoeffer, another architect with a finely tuned erotic sensibility, included in his proposals for a cybernetic city a sexual leisure center shaped like a woman's breast. [3] Generally, however, the oldest profession in the world presents itself publicly in a discree manner, one that is not discernible in luxury establishments, but rather as a dreary assortment of sexshops, porn-cinemas and strip-show bars (now that peep-shows have been all but done in). Lacking any hedonism, these establishments disfigure the station and character of entertainment districts in Europe's urban centres.

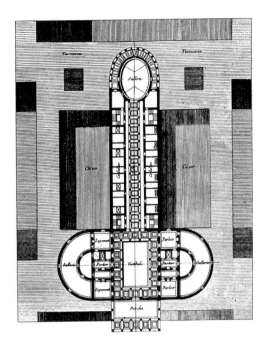

Claude-Nicolas Ledoux,
ground plan for a house of pleasure
in the Ideal City of Chaux, 1785–89

When architects and artists work on erotic architecture fantasies, the results can be sorted into a handful of distinctive groups. Either they attempt prosaic erotic symbolism (breasts, vaginas, phalluses), otherwise known as "architecture parlante", or they abstract the forms and arrive at a sensual and erotically allusive sign language, a form of expression that moves away from Euclidean geometry towards organic shapes, lines and bodies. Realizing such fantasies usually depends upon good interior design (cf. the chapter *"Staging Interiors"*).

One of the few people to give genuine impulse to an organic, hedonistic and erotic sign language in 20th-century architecture was

Ettore Sottsass, *Laughing-Gas
Station*, 1972, detail

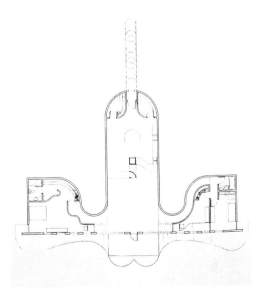

Stanley Tigerman,
Daisy House,
ground plan

Stanley Tigerman,
Daisy House,
Lake Michigan, 1975–78

Opposite page:
Massimo Iosa Ghini,
comic strip, 1983–85

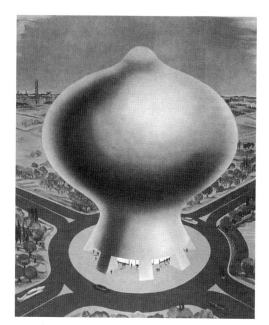

Nicolas Schoeffer,
Cybernetic City, Sex Leisure Centre,
1959

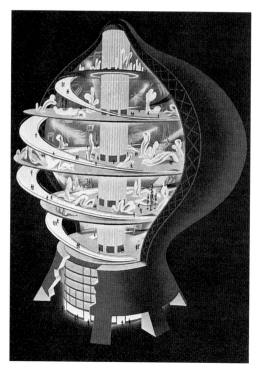

Nicolas Schoeffer,
Cybernetic City, Sex Leisure Centre,
1959, sectional view

Hermann Finsterlin, who drew his inspiration from nature and the erotic play of human bodies.[4]

In the years after World War I Finsterlin worked as a revolutionary artist, one of the most theoretical among the members of the *Gläserne Kette* (Crystal Chain). As a proponent of the "synthesis of the arts" theory, he formulated alternative utopian plans to battle the sobriety of emerging modernism. His bizarre, fantastical designs are plantlike, organic, crystalline structures, a declaration of war against the drawing board mentality of modern architects, whose

work he contemptuously called boxes *(Wohnkisten)* and coffins *(Sachsärge)*. He preached down-to-earth living in harmony with nature. *"Wohnlinge"* (possibly a humorous translation of the English dwel-ling) is what he named his only seemingly absurd residential building drafts for which he even received a number of commissions in the years after 1919. But, being an architect of fantasy, he did not know how to realize them, for his plans, like his skills, lacked a solid foundation in reality. The construction elements visible in his plans, like stairs, openings, windows, platforms, and curvatures, are not connected in any logical fashion.[5]

Like many of his contemporaries, Finsterlin preferred to see secular buildings as sacred, and worked to develop shrines, cathedrals of art, exhibition halls, research stations, theatres, as well as places of worship. Stemming from Art Nouveau, his forms in all their abundance are rooted in organic and mineral structures: crystals, corals, snails' shells, ammonites, and bones. But that is just one side of the story—the other is usually played down: Finsterlin was undoubtedly almost addicted to eroticism and sex, and he turned his erotic fantasies into architectural fantasies as no one before. A comparison of his pictures and sketches shows how the crystalline, organic sweeps and entwinements of structures hide the embraces and sexual acrobatics of lovers. Erotic (day)dreams and experiments are abstracted to produce organic body architectures.

Frank Lloyd Wright's late works show a certain affinity to Finsterlin's drawings, and if you compare Finsterlin's sketch of an exhibition hall dated 1917 with Jørn Utzon's Sidney Opera House (1956–73), an astounding resemblance becomes apparent. It is not especially daring to predict that Finsterlin's career as an inspiration for built architecture has yet to begin, because Computer Aided Design, new materials and new technologies will make shapes possible which at his time could indeed only figure in erotic dreams.

Aesthetically speaking there are a host of similarities and parallels between

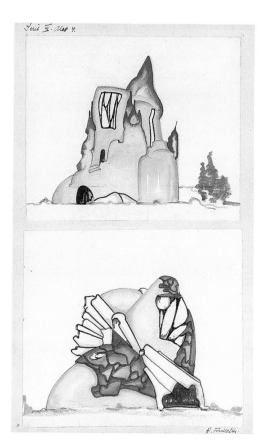

Hermann Finsterlin,
Architectures,
watercolour, 1920

Ettore Sottsass, *Temple for Erotic Experiences,*
1972

YOU'LL BE MINE, HONEY, YOU DON'T BELIEVE IT YET.
MISTRUSTFUL AND AUSTERE YOU INTOXICATE ME WITH PERFUMES TO MAKE ME LOSE YOU.
COME ON, BE TEMPTED BY THE MERRY-GO-ROUND, DON'T BE AFRAID, THE FIRST TURN'S FREE.

YOU'LL KNOW WHEN IT'S TIME, WHEN HE KNEELS AT YOUR FEET IN THAT DAILY ACT OF HUMILIATION.
YOU'LL OPEN WARMLY AND WRAP HIM IN THE BIGGEST TIP OF HIS CAREER.

TAKE HER, NO ONE EVER COMES DOWN HERE.
JUST HER AND THE MACHINE, ONLY CURDLED LIQUIDS, MEMORIES OF BECKONING BODIES.
DON'T WAIT FOR THE BLEACH TO EXPIATE, FEEL HER, NO ONE WILL COME DOWN AND
YOUR ODORS WILL MINGLE WITH THOSE OF OTHER UNKNOWN LIVES.

Roberto Baldazzini / Lorena Canossa,
Interiors

"WHY" YOU WONDER, EVERY TIME THE BELL RINGS.
"NEVER AGAIN" YOU PROMISE YOURSELF AS YOU LIFT YOUR SKIRT.
YOU'RE HIS INSTRUMENT, THE KEYBOARD ON WHICH HIS FINGERS PRESS
INTENSE EMOTIONS AND A TENDER FAINTNESS.
AND HIS RHYTHM BECOMES THE THUMPING OF YOUR HEART.

YOU'RE POSSESSED, EVERY FOLD OF YOUR SKIN HAS BEEN PUNISHED FOR A BLAME
YOU WON'T ADMIT.
YOU KNOW THE LAW OF THE FLESH, NOW YOU'LL KNOW THE LAW OF BLOOD.
THE ROPE TIGHTENS, IT'S TOO LATE TO DEFEND YOURSELF AND TOO EARLY TO ASK FOR MERCY.

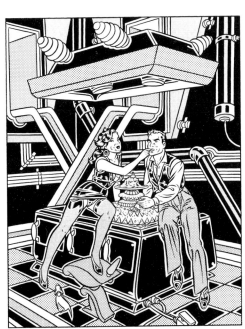

YOU LOVE HIM.
WHAT WOULDN'T YOU GIVE TO FEEL HIS SIGH ON YOUR SKIN.
WATCH IT, HE'S SMELT THE TRAP, HE'S GOING ROUND YOU WITH SUSPICION.
YOU MUST BE MORE CAUTIOUS, CONCENTRATE ON THE FINAL GOAL.
YOU LOVE HIM, AND THE THOUGHT CATCHES YOU BY SURPRISE LOOSENING YOUR BELLY.

WHAT COULD BE SWEETER THAN HER MOUTH?
LICK SLOWLY, ABSORB EVERY FLAVOR AND SWALLOW IT.
HE'LL PENETRATE YOU RED-HOT.
LET HER SATISFY YOU, SHE KNOWS YOUR TASTES WELL.

YOU'RE SOFT AND SMALL, YOU FILL MY HANDS.
LET ME LOOK AT YOU, LET ME READ ON YOUR SKIN THE BODIES THAT YOU'VE STROKED.
LET ME READ IN YOUR EYES, THE EYES THAT HAVE SEARCHED YOU.
THAT'S THE ONLY WAY SHE'LL BE MINE, MINE AT LAST.

Massimo Iosa Ghini, *Bolido Nightclub*,
New York, 1988

Hermann Finsterlin and Lebbeus Woods, but in all other respects the New Yorker is cast from a different mould. In his unpublished notes and papers, Finsterlin states: "Today we have the unprecedented situation that the two youngest pillars of the cultural triangle, science and technology, seem to be completely devouring the most ancient one, art, as a cancerous growth consumes a healthy organ".[6]

Woods, on the other hand, fights for the holistic idea of "universcience", in which engineering and technology, the biological sciences, physics, media studies, philosophy, poetry, art and architecture intermingle, complement and cross-pollinate each other in ever changing correlations.

It is particularly Woods' towers that exhibit organic and phallic-erotic shapes, as in the project *Centricity* (1988–89).[7] These vital, budding tower forms employ thinly veiled erotic symbols and associations, no matter whether they seem youthful, energetic and just about to burst, or exhibit clear signs of ageing.[8]

Occasionally the towers seem to be copulating, producing buds and offshoots. In the *Berlin Project*, towers grow downwards into uterine cavities before turning around, penetrating the

surface and flinging their fertilized idea-projectiles all over the city and the surrounding countryside. Other drawings depict science towers and experimental laboratories in which fantastic technical shapes hang like female organs. In interviews Woods not only admits to this architectural and artistic sublimation of erotic fantasies, but particularly stresses the view that new technological worlds have to be erotic and emotional if humankind is to avoid becoming completely intellectualized, thereby negating its own sense of body. Woods' approach supports a demand for erotic architecture fantasies, since this would improve the sensitivity and the sensuality of architecture in increasingly technical environments. Woods' ideas may in fact bridge the gap between high-tech and ecological architecture. Influenced by the war in Bosnia, changes in his personal life as well as series like *Zagreb Freezone* (1991–92) and *War and Architecture* (1993–94), the open eroticism in his work has given way to violent, aggressive, dynamic, penetrating shapes and architectural projectiles, all of which contain destructive powers which reveal anarchic qualities and at the same time try to give impulse to a new start, a new jagged aesthetics, one that rejects the

hypocritical "cosiness" of the old bourgeois architecture.[9]

When in the early '70s Ettore Sottsass, one of the most creative and artistic designers in the world, picked up on the old traditions of drafting temples of pleasure, he did it in the spirit of pop culture, out of a mixture of rebelliousness, humour, satire and irony, joie-de-vivre and protest against a "consumismo" as well as against the mass production industry's monopoly on design. Using explicit symbolism he lays bare the double standards often displayed by church and state, and combines the severe nobility of classical elements with openly sexual symbolism. His *Temples of Sexual Experience* (1972) mean exactly what their name implies. Beyond humour and directness, Sottsass' architectural-erotic sketches offer alternatives to the built world of double standards. They form a counter-world of sensory gratification, of leisure, of exuberance, of satisfying natural needs, of celebrations, of the bizarre, which makes our present architectural reality seem all the more dull. Here architecture becomes part of sex play, makes visible in its structural design what it is that drives its creator.

Parallel to his drawings Sottsass published programmatic texts, which combine the creativity of unusual metaphors with socio-political criticism.[10] Indicative are titles like *Counterdesign*[11] or *How to Protect Beauty from Dust and Piranhas.*[12] Their aggressiveness, humour and wealth of unconventional ideas are characteristic of Sottsass' ironic, radical designer image of the late '60s and early '70s. His opposing stand-

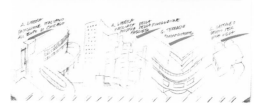

Massimo Iosa Ghini,
comic strip,
1983–85

point to profit- and turnover-maximizing industrial design is a rebellious anti-design:

> "Counterdesign is an anger, or better, a boredom or perhaps desperation or a pain or simply the result of the awareness of what's going on in the acts and the talk that goes on around DESIGN, seeing that this design is becoming an increasingly difficult and dedicated and consumed, pumped and flattered affair and is used mainly for everybody's business (...)
> Counterdesign is not a formula but a way of being aware, a way of knowing or feeling that the way the mechanism works is not the ideal."13

While Sottsass combines painting, comic strips and serious architectural design, Roberto Baldazzini and Lorena Canossa take a satirical potshot at Sottsass' *Art Déco* cum *pop-culture* turned *post-modernism*, at Roy Liechtenstein's *American modernism*, the Barbarella Cult and other comic series in their multifacetted Comic-Satire *"Interiors"*.

Their *Majestic Hotel* is filled with sex-machines, the architecture is laden with sex-symbols, the heroes are a sado-masochistic couple, and the underlying text is dripping with sarcasm and irony, expressing the Italians' delight in poking fun at the American way of life, its myths and its symbols.14 In the end frustration prevails when it is revealed that everything is just the daydream of an author who is sitting in a futuristic coffee shop, indulging in his high-tech reveries. The American culture of consumption, overloaded with sex-symbols, presents itself as a sterile surrogate world, containing nothing more than dreams and mirages. The architectural wit of *Interiors* stems from the dovetailing of European and American traditions of art, comics and architecture.

The same—taken one step further into real design for chairs, eyeglasses, kitchens, nightclubs, futuristic, even utopian fantasy architectures and city planning—can be found in the ingenious designs of Massimo Iosa Ghini. He takes up the dynamic tradition of *Art Déco*, of the Futurists and Raymond Loewy's streamline culture of the '50s and integrates it into his philosophy of *Bolidismo*.

Bolidism adopts elements of sweeping or even aggressive movements like curves, circles and ellipses, and weaves them in powerful yet supple convolutions and penetrations. Massimo Iosa Ghini's personal style is characterized by his ironic quotes, his optimism, an abounding joie-de-vivre, energy and strong mixed colours. Iosa Ghini takes up Edward Hopper's symbol-laden existentialism with its atmosphere of impending doom, and by adding aspects of the fantastic, turns it into a bright futuristic world. Formally speaking, its eroticism derives from dancelike movements of penetration, from phallic and bud-like shapes, and creates an atmosphere from the visual qualities of strong colours, the tactile qualities of the materials used, and ultimately their combined energy and elegance. The resulting tensions and field of energy are continually rising and falling, intensifying and fading out. On a subliminal level, the world of the classic Hollywood movies of the '40s and '50s is evoked and like a dream world reaches out into the everyday lives of all those who are sensitive to it.

Ghini once said of his fantastic design entitled, *Home in the Year 2000*: "This will be a home which is at the same time interactive, fun and functional." Fashioned on the futuristic manifestos of Sant'Elia and Filippo Tommaso Marinetti, Maurizio Castelvetro wrote contributions for a Bolidist Manifesto, which begin as follows:

> "Bolidism was inevitably propelled by its compulsion to act with no other plan than that of adhering with enthusiasm to the innovative and frantic rhythm of the XX century, optimistically awaiting a more organic and mythical XXI century.
> Bolidist action is triggered by THE EXALTATION OF LIFE, a search into the positive shapes it embodies, in the anguished awareness of the numerous obstacles which kill expression.
> Life as an exciting arm wrestling match with death

that endures for thousands of lifetimes: how fascinating!
> Thousands of symbols, traditions, fashions, experiences, ruthlessly centrifuged and continuously bandied about everywhere around us.
> A multimedial projection of millions of lives and billions of experiences which has caused and is causing an exponential acceleration of consciousness and knowledge, the effects of which still have to be calculated.
> It is just this perceptive SIMULTANEOUSNESS which we are experiencing more and more every day; the Goddess of the XX century to which the Bolidists concentrate their production.
> *Bolidist production is the personal synthesis of the following elements: BOLIDIST SPEED— BOLIDIST TENSION—BOLIDIST FORM."*15

Massimo Iosa Ghini, who, while still at school, compulsively produced utopian comic strips, the successors of which were published in the '80s in avant-garde magazines, did not stop at fantastic sketches and designs. In the New York nightclub *Bolido* (1988), he not only installed his well known *Memphis* furniture line, but also amalgamated design, visionary fantastic architecture and real architecture into one of the most coherent and atmospherically interior design ensembles of the '80s. His versatile kitchen programme "Americana" (1993) revolutionized kitchen design more profoundly than any other design of the last several decades. His vase collection for Ritzenhoff (1993) combines classically Mediterranean with avant-garde, experimental forms.16 Imagination, verve and unmistakable erotic allusions lend them an astoundingly intense almost magical aura.

His "Città Area" or "Città Fluida" takes elements of Italian and American modernism and, with sweeping romantic curves, conjures before your very eyes a world contrasting with Bauhaus functionalism and then tosses it in the air. This justifies the hope that he, like Ettore Sottsass, his colleague of the older generation, will one day begin to practise as an architect, a profession for which he originally trained and continues to blend dream and reality.

*"I am concerned with what's true, sexual attraction.
The rest doesn't count."*[1]

Louise Bourgeois

1. Architectural Painting

A painting that has haunted me ever since my
youth is Maurice de Vlaminck's *Château*
(1928), which at the time belonged to the
famous Stuttgart art dealer Roman Norbert Ket-
terer. It shows a castle standing in a park cast in
shades of black, green and pale yellow. The
mood is one of stormy unrest, with black holes
representing doors and windows that stare the
viewer menacingly in the face. Admittedly it is a
subjective impression, but for me this picture
radiates a morbid eroticism, presumably
because from the very first moment I saw it I
associated it with Edgar Allan Poe's grim tale of
incest *The Fall of the House of Usher.* Where
Poe succeeds in capturing psychogrammes in
linguistic imagery, Vlaminck commits them to
canvas with brush and paint. Says Poe of the
ancestral seat of the Usher family, "with the first
glimpse of the building, a sense of insufferable
gloom pervaded my spirit."[2] A little later we
read:

Maurice de Vlaminck,
Château, 1928

> "I had so worked upon my imagination as really to
> believe that about the whole mansion and domain
> there hung an atmosphere peculiar to themselves
> and their immediate vicinity—an atmosphere
> which had no affinity with the air of heaven, but
> which had reeked up from the decayed trees, and
> the grey wall, and the silent tarn—a pestilent and
> mystic vapour, dull, sluggish, faintly discernible
> and leaden-hued."[3]

During the course of this story, the reader experiences a very gradual initiation into a world
of morbid, decadent eroticism in which Eros
and Thanatos melt into one. The architecture
becomes a visual expression of an eroticism of
death because the nerves and senses of the
viewer who is sensitized to it are conditioned to
observe the state of the architecture and read
into it the state of mind of its inhabitants, and
vice versa. All the ideas that the painting succeeds in simultaneously conveying are, in the
written text, subject to a chronology, becoming
a painted sequence of words. Both Poe and Vla-

Opposite page:
Medrie MacPhee,
Press, 1989

minck avoid the crudeness of being unequi-
vocal. In fact, in his representation of eroticism,
the writer very cleverly resorts to a verbal
description of an architectural painting:

> "One of the phantasmagoric conceptions of my
> friend, partaking not so rigidly of the spirit of
> abstraction, may be shadowed forth, although
> feebly, in words. A small picture presented the in-
> terior of an immensely long and rectangular vault
> or tunnel, with low wall, smooth, white, and with-
> out interruption or device. Certain accessory
> points of the design served well to convey the
> idea that this excavation lay at an exceeding depth
> below the surface of the earth. No outlet was
> observed in any portion of its vast extent, and no
> torch or other artificial source of light was discern-
> ible; yet a flood of intense rays rolled throughout,
> and bathed the whole in a ghastly and inappro-
> priate splendour."[4]

Freely interpreted according to Freudian
psychoanalysis, there is an obvious analogy with
intrauterine penetration. This room is a dreadful
place because the incestuous love between the
androgynous brother and sister is of course
laden with guilt complexes, and the "flood of
intense rays" could be interpreted as an orgas-

mic element and the "inappropriate splendour"
as the redeeming vision of light at the end of the
tunnel, a vision repeatedly described by the
mystics and which Blake often painted. At the
end of the story the House of Usher bursts asun-

Alfred Kubin, book illustration
in a German version of E. A. Poe,
*The Fall of the House of Usher, c.*1912

Bernd Zimmer,
Burning Factory (red), 1981

German Museum of Architecture in Frankfurt am Main devoted a comprehensive exhibition to it.[5] Nevertheless it was only in a few of the pictures presented there that architecture was associated with eroticism, perhaps most clearly in Bernd Zimmer's paintings of fire, in Helmut Middendorf's depictions of Berlin or—in more abstract form—in some of Markus Lüpertz's Babylonian towers.

To begin this chapter, however, we want to return to the beginning of the century, to George Grosz, a painter and caricaturist who, as a result of recent extensive exhibitions, has become the object of international attention in the '90s. Grosz is not only a social critic par excellence but also undoubtedly one of the most erotic and even pornographic painters of this century.

It is particularly in his early work, rife with the rhythms and chants from the time of World War I (1915–1918), that we find eroticism thematically paired with architecture. It is not individual examples of architecture or details that are erotically charged or have an eroticizing effect, but the overall experience of the big city: the artist's true experience of Berlin, and an imaginary experience of New York, a projection of his yearning. In the foreword to *Paß auf, hier*

George Grosz,
Nudes,
1919

kommt Grosz (*Look out, here comes Grosz*), his friend Wieland Herzfelde writes:

"The start of this artist's career was characterized by his encounter with Berlin and his dream of America, of the 'wild west', which at the same time was a nightmare to such a sensitive soul with x-ray vision and something like second sight. The nocturnal pleasures of the city and their protagonists, especially the circus and variety artists, the tough guys and loose women, but also the music and dance, the wild orgies in the séparées, dingy hotels and brothels, the different coloured bottles on the shelves in bars, all these things fascinated and repelled him simultaneously."[6]

It is the big city mixture of whores, racketeers, boozers, pimps, criminals, corrupt politicians, intellectuals, soldiers and war profiteers among the dynamic confusion of houses, towers, streets, tenement blocks, bridges, tramlines, chimneys, water towers, cranes and hoardings, buckling, plummeting, towering, and twitching, which electrifies and eroticizes Grosz:

"Eh – in the cocktail there is life –
The narrow dockside streets are alive –
There have already been some deaths;
Two sailors – – – – –
In a brothel stifling, wafting pink light –
And swaying thighs, huge and wild –
The liquor runs along red-light back streets –
What a life!!!"[7]

George Grosz is caricaturist, critic and protagonist all in one. He is caught up in this life of wild, animal eroticism:

der in a violent storm after brother and sister have sunk to the floor in an erotic paroxysm of "death agonies".

Architectural painting is a genre which dates to the Middle Ages, or at least to Ambrogio Lorenzetti's famous work *The Good Regiment in Town and Country* (1338–1339). It has been an established genre since Renaissance and Baroque times, and in the 18th and 19th centuries the relationship between architecture and painting was occasionally seen to have had erotic connotations, for example in the paintings of the Pre-Raphaelites or in Sir Lawrence Alma-Tadema's neoclassical and atmospherically antique bath scenes. In Expressionism and New Realism, as in the work of Max Beckmann and Christian Schad, architectural details often form the backdrop to overtly erotic motifs.

During the course of the 20th century, the temporary predominance of abstraction in art caused the architectural theme to fade into the background, but the narrative style of the postmodernists in the '70s and '80s reversed this trend. The architectural themes took on such prominence in the painting of the '80s that the

George Grosz,
Grosz as a Clown and a Vaudeville Girl, 1957

"There is a rose-red house coming,
A wooden leg leaning against it –
Where billiard balls jangle—
The face paints
The street pavement yellow ... – – – – – – –
Emma!! Bitch, my little swine, cheers!!!"[8]

But Grosz is also the political seismograph, foreseeing what will turn the city into a "stone corpse", with cracks in the walls of the houses foreshadowing final destruction. When nearly two decades later, in January 1933, Grosz finally emigrated to New York with vehement expectations, his view and his mood changed.[9] The critic who in Berlin was deeply empathic and well integrated became an analytical observer, recording, describing, interpreting, but for the most part without the erotically heated atmosphere of Berlin. Whereas in *"Gesang an die Welt"* ("Song to the world") Grosz comments on suitably turbulent drawings:

"Turbulence of the world!
Dear friends! – Ahoy!
Hello, boys across the Atlantic!
You I. W. Hurban, you Lewis, you Abraham,
You Theo F. More
And you Lillian Elmore.

The jungle you put in notes
With your banjo music of the New World.
Rigid, lanky tower buildings.
The eye is free.
Clean-shaven and wide."[10]

In 1933 he made note of his impressions of Broadway as though in a painting:

"Amazing street, between little old houses, red with fire escapes outside, and then suddenly skyscrapers. All façades covered with advertising, illuminated even in broad daylight. Cinemas open early. Half St. Pauli, half Friedrichstrasse, half Paris—and yet totally different because of the surprising views of tall, straight, thin tower buildings ... Everywhere there are strangely nervous-looking men standing around in groups like desperadoes, dozens of them—of every racial mixture. Half gangsters, half businessmen. What have they all got to talk about??? Cigars, big ones, between gold-filled teeth. Again and again strange lines of dissipation and tension on faces—wrinkled. A tall, ironic man with only one crutch. Soft felt-hat negroes with umbrellas. Elegant Jewish-Spanish gents with wide trousers, short jackets and loosened collars—all of them with their hands in their pockets."[11]

And the women Grosz captures with a soft or sharp pencil in his sketch books are at least as shapely and sexy as the Berlin prostitutes of earlier years. But in complete contrast to his previous expectations, even the striptease dancers seem as though stripped of their eroticism and, under the analytical eye of the emigrant, mounted on the pages like pressed flowers. As in Berlin, the architecture of New York forms the only backdrop against which specific urban forms of life can develop, but it never takes an active part in heightening the erotic effect.

The case of Richard Lindner, however, another 1933 German emigrant, is slightly different. Lindner, who had first fled to Paris, went to New York in 1941, where he made a name for himself in the late '50s and '60s as a leading light in Pop Art. A variety of topics —modern America and European memories, a visionary, pipe-dream world and the symbolically charged reality of the big city, the worm's eye perspective of the boy from the famous toy fair city of Nuremberg, adult fetishes and neurotic sexual obsessions— all of these are amalgamated into a world of painting in which the bodies of humans and the bodies of architecture merge to become one:

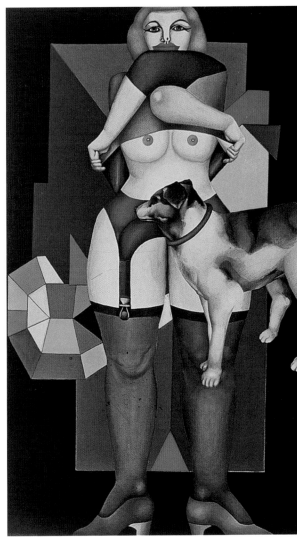

Richard Lindner,
Untitled No.1,
1962

"Here persons and their attributes are fully codified. Localities—Times Square and Coney Island—are absorbed: the bodies and the localities are fused into one epidermis of blended colour."[12]

Lindner's human bodies, particularly his female figures, are architectural, with pillar-like legs, massive breasts and thighs, squeezed into corsets to symbolize fetishism, armour and imprisonment, the signals of simultaneous attraction and repulsion. Like the skyscrapers of New York City, they represent high-tech-machines, anonymous constructions made up of moving parts. At the same time they are symbols of a terrible alienation between the sexes, the specimens of which, however, are shackled and fettered to each other by an inexplicable sexual greed:

"It is a whole universe in which sex has turned into an apparatus. It is made up of dismemberment and overlap, breasts cut off and transplanted, detached genitals, manifesting the erotic aggression of twentieth-century society and demonstrating the violence of a culture which advertising puts at the mercy of its own surplus and which fails to find a way of breaking down the solitude imprisoning its members."[13]

Richard Lindner,
Suburban,
1969

SUBURBAN, 1969, w/p/p, 39×45 in., 110×114 cm. Aberbach Fine Art, New York

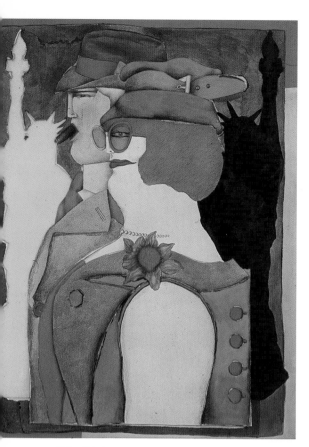

Richard Lindner,
Out of Towners, 1968

A resident of two cities, Paris and New York, Lindner is still the embodiment of the typical flaneur and city voyeur. He is fascinated by the *demimonde*, the underworld and the world of the media. In his New York of the '60s there is still a shimmer of Grosz's Berlin of the '20s.[14] The secrets of lascivious, dominating, brutal, intimidating but to him nevertheless tremendously attractive women fascinate him. They lure men into their traps with the erotically cannibalistic energy of carnivorous plants, and yet he loves and adores them, and in his art he repeatedly erects monuments to them. Lindner's New York is a depressing nightmare, a dazzlingly colourful brothel, but at the same time an extremely comical "Fun City" which stimulates all the senses: provocative, trendy, a world of fashion boutiques, urbane myths and masks. His watercolour corsage *Suburban* (1969) is a prime example of the way in which all the elements we have already mentioned concerning architecture of bodies and bodies of architecture are concentrated into an ambivalent synthesis of temptation, promise, incarceration, defence and repulsion.

In the early '90s superstar Madonna Ciccione provocatively displayed corsages and bustiers styled by Jean Paul Gaultier, garments which are positively sculptural in form and seem to have been copied directly from Lindner's pictures.

Just like Lindner, Madonna plays on the mysterious fascination of female genitals. Unlike Lindner, however, she addresses both sexes in a provocative, playful manner, favours the direct attack, and instead of repressing and sublimating she puts on an insolent show of that female power and lust that Lindner invokes in his pictures but was personally never able to live out. In an interview with John Gruen on April 14, 1978, two days before his death, he stated that he did not feel any attraction for the characters he painted, adding, however enigmatically, that everyone had to find his own way of living with his complexes.[15]

When Wilfried Dickhoff says of Francesco Clemente that "Clemente's main theme is the body as the place where the symbolic, the real and the imaginary meet,"[16] then that is precisely the common ground on which, in their affinity for eroticism and architecture, the representatives of the post-modernist Italian *transavantguardia* can be compared with Grosz and Lindner, no matter the particular characteristics the Italians claim as their own. This applies particularly to Francesco Clemente, who left Naples in 1970 at the age of eighteen to study architecture in Rome.

In the meantime Clemente has matured into one of the world's most important exponents of narrative-figurative painting, commuting between the contrasting worlds of New York, Italy and India, all of which contribute to the wealth of symbols and themes which make up his iconography. The erotically charged tales of mystery that his pictures tell are suffused with myths and with the themes of birth, sexuality, love and death. The mysterious nature of his pictures stems from the equal treatment he gives to the various elements which come together in his compositions and drift across his painted worlds. All of these aspects—in terms of association, allusion and quotation comparisons—could very well be drawn employing post-modernist narrative techniques.

As we have already seen, erotic projections, pipe dreams and sublimations have an important part to play in the work of Grosz and Lindner. Clemente commits similar themes to canvas as he paints, but unlike former generations he is uninterested in political ideologies and artistic "isms" and accepts the pluralistic coexistence of objects and topics. The erotic effect of Clemente's work is generated by such themes and the tremendously sensual warmth of colour and the techniques with which he applies it. Clemente's pictures are erotic even when they lack specifically erotic motifs:

"On the body—seen by Clemente as a film between an inner world and an outer world—erotic scenarios are acted out which no longer belong on the couch."[17]

It is also body landscapes which establish the link to architecture. Clemente's numerous interpreters and exhibition directors never tired of emphasizing that his architectural studies had not left the slightest trace in his works—that is, until Barbara Radice set them straight in 1989 by publishing, without comment, a series of eight pastel drawings in *Terrazzo* under the heading "Francesco Clemente on Architecture".[18] But even before that Clemente had stated quite plainly in an extensive interview with Rainer Crone and Georgia Marsh that he was by no means simply a lyricist dedicated to bizarre fantasies and surrealistic symbols, colours and textures, but that he was also intensely preoccupied with the relationship between bodies and rooms:

"F.C.: 'Everyone has a body and yet no one really knows what it is. You think of what is most obvious and try to keep your thoughts as banal as possible, and the result is a preoccupation with your own body. The outer limit of a room is its perimeter, the walls, and the other limit is your own skin, isn't it?'
G.M.: 'What happens between what is inside and what is outside the body?'
F.C.: 'What I mean is that the skin is the common place between what is on the inside of your body and what is going on outside, around it. It is the place that the inside and the outside of your body have in common.'
G.M.: 'When you paint self-portraits, are you saying that that is the place that you and your spirit have in common?'
F.C.: 'Here we are touching upon one of the dominant elements in art: the interest in two spaces, the space within and the space without, and the weight which the two spaces lend. There is a landscape of the outer world and a landscape within. It changes just as often as the earth has changed in the course of millennia. The landscape that we see inside ourselves, in our imagination, changes, too; it doesn't stay the same.'"[19]

Against the background of this quotation it is possible to interpret this series of Clemente's pictures, which not only have architecture as their theme but are also erotic, without in any way claiming to have the last word on these topics—for Clemente is a painter who allows for a variety of readings and tries to achieve his desired effect on levels which are non-verbal. The narrative and signal-like language of his symbolism, however, simply calls for interpretation.[20]

The first picture to show these dream-like ciphers of architecture, body and soul as landscapes bears the title *Bridge between Hands*. In the manner of the surrealists, two hands—

Francesco Clemente on architecture I,
Bridge between Hands

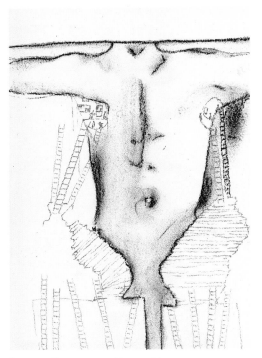

Francesco Clemente on architecture IV,
Cities under the Armpits

Francesco Clemente on architecture VI,
City in the Belly Bottom

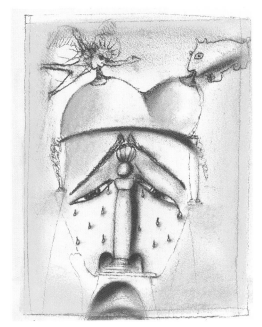

Francesco Clemente on architecture II,
House on the Head

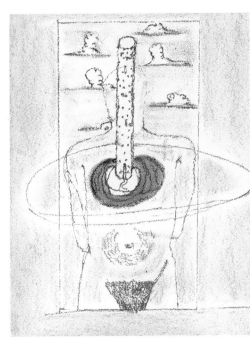

Francesco Clemente on architecture V,
Pillar on the Island

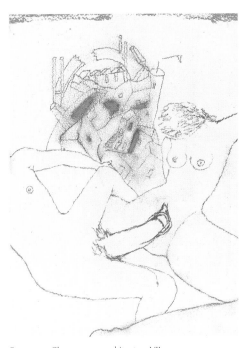

Francesco Clemente on architecture VII,
Oldest City in the World

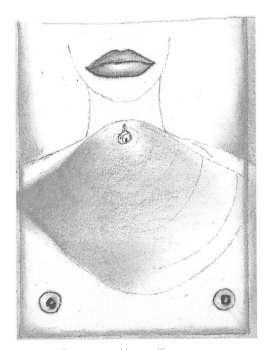

Francesco Clemente on architecture III,
House on the Throat

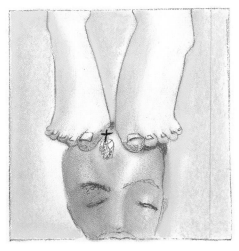

Francesco Clemente on architecture VIII,
Meaning of Sacrifice

one male and one female—emerge out of the water, the element from which all life originates. Between them, scarcely visible, is the shape of a bridge.

In the second picture, *House on the Head*, there is a particularly erotic representation of a house, the fragments of which are associated with parts of the body. A roof and pillars are arranged in the shape of Clemente's own sad face, which is, however, also projected as a house onto the body landscape of a woman, at whose breasts an angel and a fish are sucking. If the picture is inverted, the face takes on exotic, Asian features. Perspectives are superimposed onto each other and the result is a picture puzzle, in which the pillar (phallus) joins up with the eyes to form a female figure. Thus male and female essences merge in the one house.

In the third picture, *House on the Throat*, there is a tiny house located on the throat of a beautiful woman, who, although only shown as a fragment from mouth to breasts, is identifiable from the contours as Clemente's wife, Alba, a former actress of the Italian avant-garde. Thus individual associations and universal symbolism are constantly being condensed and fused into one.

Cities under the Armpits, the fourth picture in the series, shows part of a male torso undergoing one of those metamorphoses typical of Clemente's work: it transforms into the North American continent, whose native inhabitants have built *pueblo* settlements, with insignia, ladders, stairways and caves along the continent's edge. One of Clemente's theses is that American, European and Asian cultures differ in that Asians and Europeans sank the foundations of their houses and cities deep into the ground, whereas *pueblo* Indians left only faint traces scratched in the earth. For Clemente this is a sound basis for far-reaching cultural theories.

In the fifth picture, *Pillar on the Island*, male and female figures are again condensed into one unit, just as over the years Alba and Francesco had grown so similar in their outer appearances that, as a couple, they looked almost androgynous. The pillar on the island is both a phallus and a lighthouse, in which a female figure kneels, surrounded by female symbols of the uterus and mons veneris. Like so many of Clemente's pictures, this one can also be interpreted according to the viewer's own experience and knowledge, so that John Donne's famous "metaphysical" poem "Every Man is an Island" can be just as valid an association as the dream of sexual pleasures in some secluded island paradise.

City in the Belly Bottom is the title Clemente gives to his sixth picture, and here architectural and erotic symbols interact freely in a body landscape. A spiral, a labyrinth and a penis merge into one another: the spiral as a symbol of life and growth; the labyrinth as a path symbol and a symbol of seeking, of relentless determination, but also of ritual dance; the uterus as a symbol, in the centre of which lurks[21] the mysterious riddle of the world, the mystery of procreation; at the same time, the uterus symbolizes a bisexual monster, the inescapable destiny of mankind. The spiral and the uterine labyrinth, however, also mutate into a male reproductive instrument reminiscent of the endless, coiled penises of the jester-like figures in the myths of many native North American tribes. Paul Radin, Karl Kerényi and C. G. Jung jointly published a book about them[22] to which Clemente may be alluding. There the jester is both creator and destroyer. Whether giving or refusing, he is the cheat who is always cheated himself. He knows neither good nor evil, neither moral nor social values, and is at the mercy of his own lusts and passions. Such an interpretation would be consistent with Clemente's androgynous figure, depicting both bisexual humans and architecture, and with his conviction that this planet is definitely not masculine.

More obvious is the sexual symbolism in the seventh picture of the series entitled, *Oldest City in the World*. For the man copulating passionately with the woman, the interior of the female sex organs is the oldest of all cities, with zigzag walls and narrow, winding streets, with houses, a bridge and a tower—a snug shelter, promising warmth and security, life in all its manifestations.

The last of the eight pictures, *Meaning of Sacrifice*, remains mysteriously ambiguous. What is being sacrificed? Who is standing on whose head here? Alba on Francesco's, woman on man's, or vice versa? Is it the Church with its taboo buildings which stands on people's heads, forces its way into their heads and thus suppresses eroticism and the joy of living? Does the fact that the figure has its eyes closed signify dream worlds and inner worlds, which in turn determine our view of the outer world? Do head and the body represent a stage set for acting out life?

Unlike Clemente, Medrie MacPhee painted almost exclusively architectural motifs for twenty years before the fantastic element always inherent in her pictures freed itself to take on more playful shapes; architecture and machine images and fragments now only serve as background settings out of which biotic light and figure arrangements emerge.

For more than a decade MacPhee applied her magical, poetic realism to old specimens of industrial architecture, to power stations, docks, to run-down and dilapidated districts of New York and Montreal, whose "roofscapes" and enigmatic water towers endow them with a fascinating magnetism. Spellbound she examines the physical changes which the body of the city undergoes. In her work, too, the cityscape is turned into a landscape of our imagination, and that always has erotic connotations. Harsh, ugly realities are lent charm, magic, and are lyricized without ever degenerating into cotton-candy kitsch. As a result of the roughened surfaces and their many shades of colour, what is superficially ugly becomes aesthetically beautiful and, in the *chiaroscuro* mixtures of light and dark, becomes poetry and assumes the surrealistic dream qualities of imaginary cityscapes.

Since the mid-'80s, Medrie MacPhee has begun gently to anthropomorphize her industrial and urban landscapes. Her icons of lifeless technology develop a new life of fantasy. In an interview the artist said: "You see what you see, but inwardly you discover what is concealed beneath the surfaces."[23] The worlds in her painting also take on a clearly erotic quality, beginning with a picture which she named *Self-Portrait in the Mountains*. She says that with this work she suddenly became aware that the installations around a water tower in the Rocky Mountains near Banff, where she was holding a course at the famous Canadian "Banff Centre" art school, actually resembled her own female organs.

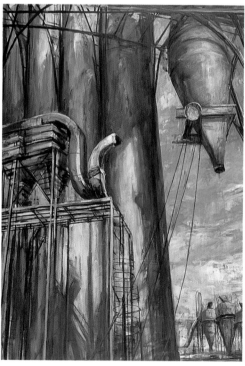

Medrie MacPhee,
Opera, 1990

Medrie MacPhee,
Timpano, 1992

fantastic. Dock cranes seem to turn into ballet dancers, steel presses have the appearance of jungle plants, cement lifts and warehouses attain a corpulent gracefulness, static things are set in motion, dramatic events take place in areas of mixed colour which have taken on an optimistic note where before dismal shades often prevailed. But there always remains a lyrical sphere of mystery, a hint of partial unveiling which constitutes the essence of eroticism that gives Medrie MacPhee's most recent works an enormous density of symbolism.

In the '90s her pictures have continued to develop under the influence of the discussion about cyberspace and cybersex, about new media, about the interest in virtual realities which one can enter with the aid of computers and within which, by manipulating symbols, one can gain access to a cosmos of information. The artist explains[24] that for her entering virtual spaces is like slipping into a realm of controlled imagination and exotic magic, and that the foreseeable implications of genetic technology in constructing bionic beings will turn science fiction into science fact, but at the same time give rise to incalculable ethical problems and open up new dimensions in eroticism. She reports that for years she has been fascinated by the idea of using techniques of painting to investigate the interaction of nature, technology, architecture and the human body.

What her latest creations—touched off by such thought processes—have to offer are spaces which combine two-dimensionality and surface radiance with a third dimension of depth

Medrie MacPhee,
Arythmia, 1992

that has a seemingly acoustic texture. The result are layered spaces, floating, flowing, with the alternation between abstraction and concretion shimmering through, spaces whose technical elements begin to dance and, illuminated by diffuse sources of light, which seem to shine out from inside the painting, metamorphose into biological, technical and botanical structures.

2. The Art of Wrapping

For a long time Christo Vladimir Javacheff bore a grudge against the Germans because they called him a packaging artist.[25] For him it is not a question of packing and tying but of wrapping or veiling. He insists that 'wrapped' is not the same as 'packed'. Christo bases his art on architecture and landscape, although it is the aesthetics of transience which give it a special quality and his art events their undoubtedly sensuous attraction. The principle behind such wrapping and the sense of secrecy which it implies are what give Christo's art an aura close to eroticism. Thus there has often been talk of the specific eroticism of such Christo projects as *Surrounded Islands* (1983), with its allusion to Claude Monet's water-lilies painting, and the wrapping of the *Pont Neuf* (1985) in Paris.

There is also an unmistakable element of hedonism in such works although it is often covered over by other layers of meaning, especially political and ecological ones. Plus, the media spectacles which Christo and Jeanne-Claude put on to accompany their projects destroy any possibility of intimate enjoyment. In *Surrounded Islands*, which Werner Spies has described as a "phantasmagorical projection of a world into the world" and as a tremendously powerful metaphor for a possible "transcendence of human life",[26] Christo takes inconspicuous islands, truly cinderella-like poetic symbols, and makes them flower like lotus blossoms. The same can be said of projects such as *Running Fence* or *Umbrella Project*, which took place in California and Japan in 1991.

The pictures of *Pont Neuf*, wrapped in lengths of polyamide, radiate an intense, sensuous fascination. In the case of architecture, veiling has a metamorphotic effect, reveals qualities which until then have been taken for granted or scarcely noticed, and causes others to disappear completely. The playful, sensual charm of the creases and folds is reminiscent of *haute couture*, and if it is possible to walk around inside the work of art, the effect is heightened by a tactile dimension. In 1980 I visited a gallery in Munich which Christo had wrapped, and it was indeed a truly synaesthetic charm which was

The process continues with old factory buildings and the machines there, which suddenly assume lives of their own. Since the end of the '80s, those lives have become more and more dancelike and bouncy, and a subtle, erotic sign language has found its way into the pictures. Medrie MacPhee believes in the aura of a work of art based on inner visions of the artist, and it is this radiance which in ever more intensive and animated colours imbues the architecture in them with eroticism.

At the same time, as the freedom of the artist increases, her architectures become purely

Christo, the wrapping of the *Pont Neuf*,
Paris, 1985

Christo / Jeanne-Claude,
the *Reichstag* wrapped, Berlin, 1995

June 1995, however, saw one of the greatest art events ever to take place on German soil: Christo's wrapping of the *Reichstag* in Berlin, the most political of all Christo projects—during the run-up to it at least—for which he had tenaciously fought for a quarter of a century.[27] Millions of visitors came from Berlin and all over the world, and art "in public" took on a completely new dimension. To even try to identify an erotic dimension in J. Paul Wallot's pompous building (1884–1896) from the time of Emperor Wilhelm II seemed absurd and frivolous in view of the fact that it is a prototypical example of the architecture of power, whose representational and repressive character has become all the more obvious thanks to the scars of war which it bears.

Deprived of the crowning glory of its cupola and the decorative features of its four corner towers, the building shows its unadorned face, without make-up, and discloses its character as a stronghold, a fortress and a palace. Far from any spirit of democracy and any forward-looking stance, it radiates an aura of restoration, a constant reminder of the dark periods of German history with which it is associated. In his prize-winning design, Norman Foster gave the building a spirit of optimism and egalitarianism, but most of his work has since fallen prey to a government pledge to thrift, which in this case can only be seen as provincial and small-minded.

Christo, however, managed to transform and enchant the building. Although beforehand he had spoken about the classical traditions in art history in which artists had been fascinated by textiles and fabrics, about the role of draperies, folds and pleats in paintings, frescoes and sculptures, and about the religious, ritual dimension of wrapping,[28] the finally wrapped work of art turned out to be an aesthetic experience which required no historical corroboration. At the sight of it the arguments of its opponents crumbled into nothing, for in its wrapping the *Reichstag* was overwhelmingly monumental yet demure in its beauty, and overnight it had lost its massiveness.

Christo had made radical changes to its three-dimensional bulk, and the result was for him, too, "the building of a building."[29] While critics struggled for words and metaphors—their impressions ranging from "gigantic diamond" and "block of ice" to "frozen waterfall" and "light mobile"—the crowds of ordinary people celebrated in festival mood, fully aware of the transitory nature of the event and united in a rare spirit of harmony and unanimity.

Emotionally everyone seems to have been touched by the cool sensuousness of the gigantic drapes. The aura of mystery which sud-

emitted visually by the outer and inner architecture and the creased lengths of packing paper, acoustically by the rustling and crackling of the paper and tactually by the unusual sensation underfoot.

This was also accompanied by a new and unforgettable sense of space. But here, too, it was the sensuous metamorphosis of architecture rather than erotic feeling which would perhaps have arisen, however, had there been a crack or a hole to look through, or a window; but all windows and doors had been covered up. So there was no possibility to go through a door or any other opening and suddenly find oneself in a hall of mirrors, for example, or in Bluebeard's chamber of horrors; instead it remained a hermetically isolated experience.

J. Paul Wallot, *Reichstag*, Berlin, 1884–96

Christo and Jeanne-Claude, the *Reichstag* wrapped, Berlin, 1995

denly engulfed the Reichstag was heightened by the tent-like character of the material, evoking a nomadic quality. It was as though through some purgatorial act the building had been provisionally given back its innocence. There was just one thing which it did not have, but which one could conceivably ascribe to the *Pont Neuf* in its wrappings, and that was eroticism. This sculpture was simply too big, too public, too cool, too much the centre of media razzmatazz to be anything more than just sensuous. There is, however, a photo by Barbara Klemm which captures the act of veiling, and just for those few moments in which the old skin makes contact with the new, as when a couturier first pins up a new creation on his model, we have a fleeting glimpse of something erotic.

Thus it became evident that events of this sort can reveal the sensuous qualities in a building which have hitherto remained hidden, or lend it qualities which it does not normally possess. But it was precisely the wrapping of the *Reichstag* in Berlin which drew a clear dividing line between the aesthetic sensuousness of such an event and the potential intensification of its erotic charge. It was a blessing that the unwrapping of the *Reichstag* afterwards also marked the beginning of the rebuilding operations which are to be carried out over the next few years. The symbolic sovereign's old clothes would have appeared so outmoded as to have been unbearable.

3. Architectural Sculptures and Installations

a) Bomarzo

Shrouded in mystery, the Sacro Bosco, the magic garden of Bomarzo, is a very different case. Its architecture, fragments and sculptures are saturated with eroticism and derive much of their charm from the fact that on the one hand they offer direct access to the Eros-Thanatos theme, even from our present-day world, and on the other hand they reveal historical, philosophical, literary, architectural or emblematic layers of meaning to be peeled off, brought to light, palimpsest-fashion, or like a décollage. Let us turn our attention back almost half a millennium, to about the year 1525, and enter Italy's valley and the garden of monsters, the *Parco dei Mostri* of Bomarzo, not far from the huge 400-room villa belonging to Duke Orsini, near Viterbo.

There is scarcely another architectural locality which has presented researchers with so many riddles over the past decades. Bomarzo is no doubt a place for fantastical feasts and dubious orgies rather than philosophical contemplation. For us, the monsters have since lost their horror but by using our imagination and historical knowledge we can relive their complex fascination. Norbert Miller writes:

"The classical garden of pleasure has become a jumble of ominous or bizarre visions, Arcadia has

been recreated as a jungle of fantasy shapes reminiscent of the Seven Wonders of the World. The mysterious path and the secret idyll become one; the bliss of awakening in Elysium, however, gives way to a derangement of the senses when confronted with the ever new monstrosities and extravagances of this riddling world. The contours of the labyrinth are just discernible beneath the masks of this Renaissance garden."[30]

Jan Pieper draws our attention to a literary analogy, if not an actual source, with important descriptions of fictitious architectures and colossal sculptures a quarter of a century before they reappear in Bomarzo. The work in question is Francesco Colonna's novel *Hypnerotomachia Poliphili*, published in Venice in 1499:

"This novel, whose importance has not been conclusively assessed, describes the dream journey of a young man on his quest for the love of a girl called Polia, a love which is left unrequited. In his dream he encounters bizarre figures and creatures, elephants with obelisks on their backs, colossal figures which are hollow so that he can climb inside them. Again and again the novel makes use of architecture, fragments and ruins to guide the dream traveller deeper and deeper into a mysterious realm of iridescent memories, longings and haunting experiences."[31]

Here is the Etrurians' old liking for monsters and chimeras, which, of course, have always symbolized mental states; here is a constructive playfulness which evokes monsters, revels in them, transfixes them and thus keeps them in check. Here is a dream world and nightmare come true. Here is delirious, carnivalesque and ultimately cannibalistic eroticism, which sweeps aside all cultural restraints and inhibition thresholds.

Here are metamorphoses of humans into animals and vice versa. Here are female figures of perfect classical beauty, too, with their sensuous but also cold, cruel smiles, "beauty in the lap of terror" being one condensed formula used to describe the manneristic aesthetics of the Gothic novel.[32] Here is passion, angst-lust and at the same time an infinitely knowing melancholy, the eternal de Sade inside every human being, intensified by the fusion with a nature run wild. The architectural highlight, however, is the *Crooked House* of which Jan Pieper remarks:

"Bewildering are the buildings, already mentioned, of an inverted world, in which the familiar laws of verticality, horizontality, gravity and equilibrium are turned upside down, and at first quite harmlessly in a bower: here a perfectly level stone settle under an arch is built into a steep slope so that one sits quite normally but finds it hard to believe. But the climax of this art is a crooked house which leans so far that one is afraid to enter. It is strange

Bomarzo, *Parco di Mostri*, c.1525

Bomarzo, *Parco di Mostri*, sphinx, c.1525

that it is not so much the sloping floors and ceilings which are disconcerting, but above all the windows, which present views of the outside world in such unusual cutout shapes that they cause a feeling of dizziness."[33]

This is deconstruction as an ancient, manneristic principle, the artistic principle per se. And the eroticism of Bomarzo is also a fragmented, dismembering eroticism of deconstruction, operating on slants and oblique perspectives, an eroticism from the depths of the abysses illuminated by Georges Bataille's poetic, analytical eye, but also possessing the knowledge of joy and suffering, life and death.

b) Kurt Schwitters' *Merzbau*

On the way from Bomarzo to the sculptures of today, inside of which it is possible to walk around, we should make a short stop, at least in passing, at a Dadaistically weird and wonderful, early constructivist-deconstructivist, uterine-erotic fantasy house-cum-cave: Kurt Schwitters' life's work, the *Merzbau*, the early stages of

Kurt Schwitters,
Merzbau,
1925–35

the visual and spatial experience of a monomaniac mixture of cathedral, uterine cave, castle, love grotto and ivory tower, the *Merzbau* is, on a deeper level, undoubtedly one of the most symbolic art structures of our century. It has eroticism engraved in it as a primal element of the constant change in surfaces and interiors. Visually and tactually, and in its depth of feeling symbolically, too, this building takes essential traits of eroticism as a life-journey and incorporates them in abstract form into a real construction.

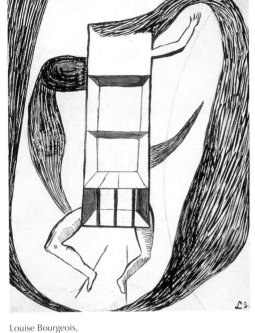

Louise Bourgeois,
Femme Maison,
1947

c) Louise Bourgeois' House-Women and Woman-Houses

Louise Bourgeois is one of those artists who strikes like a thunderbolt and churns everything up, or like a virus which spreads throughout the body, leaving its marks, which change the host and begin to lead a life of their own. She once said: "If my work provokes them [the viewers], then that is real success."[37]

Louise Bourgeois is one of those artists who, like Emil Schumacher, did not achieve any great breakthrough until in their nineties, and who mustered an energy in their late work as though

which he first named using the abbreviation *KdeE,* meaning *Kathedrale des erotischen Elends (Cathedral of Erotic Desolation).* In *Ich und meine Ziele (Myself and My Aims)* he writes:

"(...) we are living in an age of abbreviations, things left unfinished out of principle. It grows more or less according to the big city principle, whereby a house is supposed to be built somewhere and the planning authorities have to see to it that the new house doesn't mess up the overall picture of the city. I find some object or other and I know that it somehow belongs in the *KdeE,* so I take it and stick it on, paste it over and paint it in the rhythm of the overall effect."[34]

Further on he writes:

"The whole thing is symbolically inundated with cubes of the strictest geometrical shapes, to the point of complete disintegration. The name *KdeE* is only a label. It says nothing about the content, or at least very little."[35]

In the early building stages of the work there were a number of caves and grottoes with a collage-like hotchpotch of fragments and objects found, for example:

"… the brothel with a lady with three legs put together by Hannah Hoech, and the big grotto of love. The love grotto alone takes up a quarter of the lower area of the column; a broad open staircase leads up to it, and beneath it there stands the toilet lady of life in a long, narrow corridor, in which there is also camel dung on the floor. (...)"[36]

As a constantly changing monument, among other things of an erotic collage architecture which gives birth to order out of chaos, and as

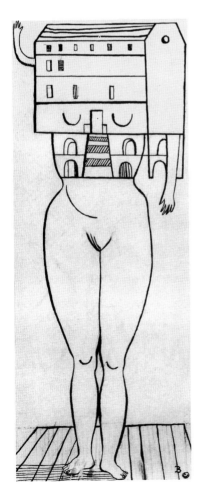

Louise Bourgeois,
Femme Maison,
1947

they were trying to unhinge the world with youthful élan. Their impetuosity, however, is tempered by an enormous depth of life experience, their directness by facetting and refraction, by unperturbable deliberation. For half a cen-

Louise Bourgeois,
Femme Maison,
1946–47

Louise Bourgeois,
Cell (You Better Grow Up), 1993

and passions which have been distilled, have evaporated, escaped, and dried up. Bedsteads evoke nights of love and nightmares, mirrors reflect multiple views, symbolic allusions and sudden recognitions. Bodies are dismembered, cut into pieces. Ears, hands, arms, legs, feet silently scream out for movement, to be used according to their original functions, directly and honestly, the way naked parts of the body are; craving, begging, imploring, wanting to be stroked, wanting to be loved, merging with spherical shapes which can roll, are round all over, are symbols of eternity, and in which space and time are suspended.

From drawings and sculptures Louise Bourgeois progresses to installations, which are midway between sculpture, stage set and live theatre, complete with flats and characters.[38] Whereas decades ago focus was on bulging, hairy, rounded, phallic, breast-shaped protuberances, like in Cheval's *Palais Ideal*, allusions to mouths, vaginas, penises, anuses, breasts, any organs through which the world may be assimilated or excreted again,[39] and through which longings, physical and emotional needs are manifested, in more recent years it has been fetishist buildings harbouring memories and fantasies, obsessions and released repressions.

Art, in the form of a mythological autobiography, turns into an imaginary museum and thus gains in terms of overindividualistic expressiveness. We are taken aback, you and I, because, in a state of waking, Louise Bourgeois captures

tury, houses and architecture have been among the central metaphors in Bourgeois' work. Whereas earlier, however, she started with the façade and worked inwards, now she begins by forming the inner rooms and then proceeds to the exterior. If one thinks about it, that is actually much more shameless and obscene, more unpretending, loving, and "truer". For Louise Bourgeois is obsessed with eroticism, with the all-embracing, creative, yet destructive power of Eros.

House, body, body, house, the house as a shelter, as a mask, as a home, as a phallus, as a total body-condom. The man goes in, forces his way in, the woman lives inside, changes into a house, is a house, a house in a woman, house-woman, the human form merges into architecture: woman-houses with rooms which are cells in the '90s. Inside is the reckoning, with the man = father = self, and with repressions, memories, obsessions, daydreams, and nightmares. Existential anxiety and mortal fear are captured in enigmatic pictures, mysteries of the blood and of sexuality are evoked: there are vials and alchemists' jars with perfumes, juices, liquids,

Louise Bourgeois,
Red Room (The Parent), 1994

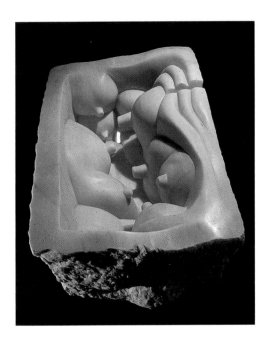

Louise Bourgeois,
Nature Study #5,
1995

what we repress, hide from our parents, partners, and ourselves in dreamlike metaphors. In her erotic bestiaries on human existence which she has compiled in the '90s, we find gathered together in "shrines steeped in reminiscence"[40] the old libidinous energies and the fetishes of her major themes: life, death, sexuality, loneliness, alienation, love and tenderness.

Here aggression and longing, violence and concern are closely associated. Here people are put away in cells and then butchered, sawn up, chopped into little pieces, life threads are cut and—together with severed limbs—drenched in blood. And yet it is "beauty in the lap of terror",[41] an incredible melancholy and poetry, occasionally coupled with the self-irony which suffuses and surrounds her late works:

> "The sculptures expose a whole life based on eroticism; it is always a question of sexuality or the lack of it. The desire to be successful and knowing how to achieve success are everything. It is important to differentiate between sexuality, which has a function, and eroticism, which includes so much more. Eroticism can be real or merely imaginary, requited or unrequited. There is desire, flirtation, fear of failure, vulnerability, jealousy and violence. I am interested in all these elements."[42]

d) Niki de Saint Phalle's *Nanas* and Fantasy Gardens

In a contemporary context, but this time not from the male's erotic perspective, which tends to break everything into fragments, but from the opposing standpoint of a cheerful, matriarchal world, Niki de Saint Phalle's *Nanas* and fantasy gardens can be seen to follow on from Bomar-

zo, above all her *Tarot Garden*, a fitting work with which to bring any "architexture" on the art of erotic building to a close.

After the self-therapy of her "shooting pictures", assemblages and all-devouring mothers with which she had freed herself from the bourgeois ties of her family, her convent education and the restraints of an upbringing and morality stifled by taboos, Niki de Saint Phalle, who from 1960 onwards lived with Jean Tinguely, gradually found her way in the mid-'60s to her *Nanas* and so to a world of high spirits, laughter and colour. But this also implies a "sexplosive" world and a profession loyal to the world of Eros. What at first she herself interpreted as symbols of an emancipated, sensuous woman, she later called in the '80s feminist models of a new matriarchal age.

This must cause considerable distress to confirmed feminists, for here again Niki de Saint Phalle conforms to no cliché and at their first exhibition in 1965, at the Galerie Iolas in Paris, these dancing *Nanas*, self-assured and high-spirited, radiated eroticism from every pore of their bodies and entered the art world with the battle-cry "Les Nanas au pouvoir" ("Power to the Nanas!"). Their intention was to spread fear among men at the unbridled power of female sexuality instead of just making promises. Niki does not subscribe to a purely intel-

lectual feminism but one in which the body enjoys priority over a world organized according to logical, scientific and technical principles. In her earlier "shooting pictures" she only ever shot at men's heads and not at their bodies. On the other hand, everything she has ever said about her work proves that she is no fool, not the sort of artist who can only emphasize bellies and bottoms, but rather a clever woman with a gift for analysis and experience in art history. Thus Niki writes of herself:

> "Niki is a special case, an outsider. Most of Niki's sculptures have something timeless about them, are reminiscences of ancient cultures and dreams. Her work and her life are like fairy tales: full of adventure, evil dragons, hidden treasures, full of people-eating mothers and witches. Birds of paradise are to be found there just as much as loving mothers, premonitions of heaven just as much as the descent to hell. (...)
> Throughout the ages and cultures, myths and symbols have constantly been reinvented and newly created. In her particularly modern fashion, Niki shows us that these myths and symbols are still alive. So although the Nanas, for example, are sculptures of our own time, in some cases they immediately remind you of the Venus of Willendorf. (...)"[43]

After this uninhibited avowal of her faith in myths, but also in art as a mode of existence and as a total experience, intellectually, emo-

Niki de Saint Phalle, *Tarot Garden*, Garavicchio, Tuscany, 1979 onwards

Niki de Saint Phalle,
The Golem, Jerusalem

Niki de Saint Phalle, *Tarot Garden*,
The Ruler's Castle

tionally, technically and practically, Niki later goes on to confess her belief in a cannibalistic eroticism in art:

"I see Niki as a devouring mother who has fed on the widest variety of influences—from Giotto, early Sienese painting or the age of Rousseau, from Mexican and Indian temples to Bosch and Picasso. All these were eaten up and digested, and the child that was born of this feast is and will remain a Niki."[44]

A visible testimony to this view is given in particular by the joint project *Hon-en Katedral* (April–June 1966), which Niki created together with Jean Tinguely and Per Olof Ultvedt for the Moderne Museet in Stockholm. In this gigantic *Nana*, woman is represented as a sculpture in which it is possible to walk around, as a temple of eroticism which one enters through the vagina in order to take part in all sorts of fun inside. Thus Niki declares her belief not only in the physical and erotic but also the emotional

and mythically narrative qualities of architecture and sculpture, whereby her irony and self-irony preclude any possibility of pathos. At the end of the event the figure destroyed itself.

With her *Nanas*, Niki begins to make use of the capabilities and opportunities they afford to exploit her brilliant gift to the full. From their very first appearance, these monumental architectural sculptures have challenged their public to a physical confrontation, to take part in the experience by climbing inside.[45]

The fantasy gardens with fantasy house sculptures like the *Bird's Dream (Le Rêve des Oiseaux)* (created in 1967–69 for the film director Rainer von Diez), the enormous Golem for a children's playground in Jerusalem (1972) or *The Dragon* (1973) in Knokke-le-Zout, Belgium, are all architecture built as sculptural art, each one embodying a scale of symbols ranging from fairy tale and the demonic, to playful and erotic and even cannibalistic connotations.

In 1979, however, with the building of her *Tarot Garden* in a disused quarry near Garavicchio in Tuscany, Niki began to sum up her life's work.[46] Secret knowledge, magic, mysticism and cabbalism are aspects of tarot cards, which presumably date back to Egyptian high priests who used such ciphers to pass on the secret knowledge which safeguarded their power. Eroticism, fantasy, a flourishing, rampant zest for life, symbols of fertility, love, life and death are all harmoniously united in Niki's conception for this garden of magic, which has among its models the garden of the Villa d'Este and Bomarzo. On this point the artist says:

"Bomarzo has a special attraction for me. One of the central figures in my garden, the high priestess with the open mouth, out of which eventually water will come flowing and spill down the steps, is a tribute to those mysterious sculptures and to the Villa d'Este. What has rubbed off on my work are the dreamlike elements of the gardens of

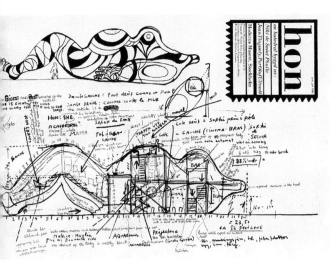

Niki de Saint Phalle / Jean Tinguely /
Per Olof Ultvedt,
Hon, draft sketch, 1966

Bomarzo, like the mermaids, the giants and monsters and the *Falling Tower*. In terms of symbolism there are also similarities between the two gardens. Alchemy is the key to Bomarzo, as archetypes are to mine."[47]

As a young woman Niki had visited the garden of Antoni Gaudí in Barcelona, and it was his work which remained influential in pointing the way throughout the whole of her career. For her *Tarot Garden* she selected twenty-two figures from a pack of tarot cards and freely adapted them for her sculptures. The magician and the high priestess (cards I and II in the tarot pack) have been fused into one central sculpture in the *Tarot Garden*, signifying a union of male and female principles. This constitutes a further development of the Ozo from the garden of Bomarzo, both philosophically and artistically.

The magician stands for primal energy in its most creative and active form, at the same time symbolizing the playful element. The high priestess, on the other hand, represents the female principle of the universe, inner wisdom in its most profound sense. She stands for the female archetype, symbolizing the passive force of nature, intuition, secret lore and the great mysteries, but also creatureliness, erotic power and knowledge. The devil is a bright, cheerful fellow with golden horns and a triple penis. Deconstructivist principles such as those found in the *Crooked House* at Bomarzo are echoed by Niki de Saint Phalle in her *Falling Tower*, which is opened up and brought tumbling down by a Tinguely machine, a divine bolt of lightning.

In the *Tarot Garden*, in the midst of a blossoming fantasy world, Niki the man-eater and

Niki de Saint Phalle / Jean Tinguely /
Per Olof Ultvedt, *Hon*, 1966

father-killer has achieved a harmonious balance between intellect and emotion, science and intuition, between Eros and Thanatos. The voluptuous sensuality of the *Nanas* is still in evidence but it has also taken on intellectual traits. Inside the body of the Empress (card III in the tarot pack), the Great Goddess, the Queen of Heaven, the Mother of Feeling, Niki has set up the studio in which she lives and works. She has fitted out the cave-like interior luxuriously to make a cosy home:

"The curvature of the one breast accommodates the kitchen, while slightly higher in the other one there is a small bedroom. The nipples have windows set into them, from which you can see the sea."[48]

And so Niki fulfilled an old dream of hers, to live inside a sculpture. This enormous sculpture is architecture in the shape of a sphinx, a monster with the body of a lion and the head of a woman which slew anyone who failed to solve its riddle. Thus it can be seen that Niki de Saint Phalle is far from considering retracting her claws completely or refraining from pointed emancipatory statements, but at the same time she has progressed in her search for identity through art, from provocation to virtually classical principles.

"But a bell rang and first, it seemed, we must all dress up. Albertina showed me to a chaste, masculine room at the front of the house with a narrow bed and a black leather armchair, many ash trays and a magazine rack containing current numbers of 'Playboy', 'The New Yorker', 'Time' and 'Newsweek'. On the dressing-table were silver-backed brushes. I opened the door of a closet and found a bathroom where I took a steaming shower, assisted by great quantities of lemon soap. When I came out, wrapped in the white, towelling robe they had provided for me, I found a dinner jacket and everything to go with it laid out ready for me on the bed, down to silk socks and white linen handkerchief. When I was dressed, I felt in the pocket and found a gold cigarette lighter and matching case filled with Balkan Sobranie Black Russian cigarettes. I looked at myself in the oval, mahogany mirror. I had been transformed again. Time and travel had changed me almost beyond my own recognition. Now I was entirely Albertina in the male aspect. That is why I know I was beautiful when I was a young man. Because I know I looked like Albertina. From my window, I could see the apple orchards, the crevasse and the road that led over the bare mountain to the military installation. Everything was perfectly calm and filled with the mushroomy, winey scents of autumn. Another bell rang and I went down the thickly carpeted staircase to the picture gallery where Albertina and her father were drinking very dry sherry. Dinner was served off an English eighteenth-century table in another of those chaste, restrained, white-walled rooms with a flower arrangement in the disappearing Japanese transcendental style on the sideboard and china, glass and cutlery so extraordinarily tasteful one was hardly aware of its presence. The meal was very simple and perfectly in tune with the season of the year—some kind of clear soup; a little trout; a saddle of hare, grilled; mushrooms; salad; fruit and cheese. The wines all matched. With the very strong black coffee there was a selection of recherché liqueurs and we all smoked probably priceless cigars. Still no servants appeared. All the courses had been sent up from subterranean kitchens in a small service elevator from which Albertina herself served us. There was no conversation during the meal but another stereo set hidden behind a white-enamelled grille was playing a Schubert song cycle, 'The Winter Journey'. 'Do you not feel,' said the doctor in his very soft but still crisp-edged voice, 'that invisible presences have more reality than visible ones? They exert more influence upon us. They make us cry more easily.'"[1]

When observed with some abstraction, exterior architecture can—and architecture criticism does this all too often—be reduced to mostly two-dimensional, sculpturally formed surfaces, that is, to façades. Interior design, however, is all about bodies, their surfaces and their enclosed

Opposite page:
Lynn Davis, *The Ministry of Sound*, discotheque, London, 1991

spaces, about staging interiors of architectural structures whose exterior often plays only a minor role.

The introductory quote from Angela Carter's novel illustrates the importance of the interplay between people, architecture and furnishings, and furthermore illustrates the erotic charging of private living spaces through accessories. It also shows the trend towards androgyny in modern times, which, as women's liberation continues to grow during the '90s, has had an increasingly formative influence on fashion, lifestyle and leisure activities. Ambience, dinner conventions, table decoration, food and eating habits, even the timbre of voices play a part in creating an erotically vibrant atmosphere.

In an age of speed and mobility such as ours, the life cycle of interior "staging" accelerates constantly. The term "staging" already points to theatre, play, drama and narration, to blending illusion and reality, as well as to imagination and reality. It also highlights a problem which is becoming more and more central to our present-day lives, one which is well known to the media as well as philosophy: that is the fact that the fiction of reality is scarcely distinguishable from the reality of fiction. The imaginary has become a part of our conception of reality, the artist or the designer puts them into material form and they become real.

The interior designer much more so than the architect of exteriors makes use of an increasingly important immaterial component, one that is closely connected to the stage character of this kind of architecture: light. With it he changes the shapes and colours of objects, gives rooms structure, creates simulated walls made of light and may in some cases even create immaterial objects composed completely of light. Lately even immaterial artwork, light and sound sculptures, computer animations and simulations, films, videos and computer graphics have been integrated into interior design.

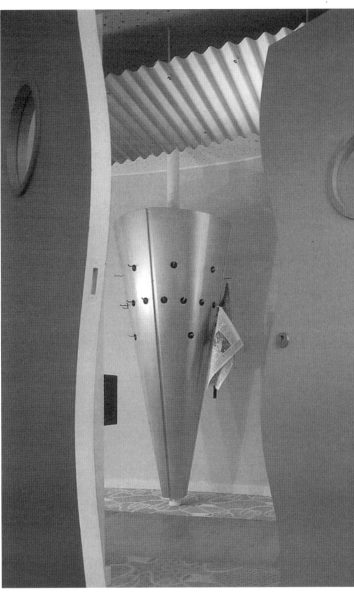

Gernot and Johanne Nalbach, *Art Hotel Sorat*, Berlin, 1990

And in interior design it is precisely the communicative functions of architecture which are highlighted, thus focusing on a high degree of interaction between user and room. Traditionally, but even more so since the introduction of *Memphis* and the post-modern design of the '80s, a host of furniture items like chairs, armchairs, cabinets, vases, pictures, all designed and selected for their erotic flair and their erotic symbolism, have had a part to play.

Even more crucial is the atmosphere, the stage managing of thoughts of lust and desire in the mind rather than sexual directness. Private living spaces increasingly display such individualism, so much so that in spite of all trends, fashions and styles, an analysis would be never ending. Therefore after a few examples of living spaces and some general remarks, we will concentrate on public spaces of a somewhat intimate nature, such as boutiques, nightclubs and bars, where erotic affinities seem to suggest themselves.

What individuals gradually build up for themselves within their own four walls is an expression of their innermost personality which is consciously or subconsciously influenced by numerous zeitgeist currents. When it comes to eroticism, a kind of underlying historical pattern plays a big role, as seen in details from different periods of one's life, in ambiguity, mixed colours vaguely suggesting romanticism, surprises, hide-and-seek games, certain objects used almost like fetishes, and the multisensory qualities of furniture and basic items. And it is not cleanliess or tidiness which creates an erotic disposition, but rather the creases, the unmade bed, the scattered clothes and accessories used for something other than their intended purpose. It is not by chance that erotic scenes in innumerable films take place in seedy locations, implying the Eros-Thanatos conception, decay and death.

In architectural photography, with which one generally has to keep in mind that reality is distorted by wide-angle lenses and special lighting, particular problems arise. This is due to the dogma that, unlike in fashion photography, interior and exterior spaces have to be presented as tidy, clinically sterile, brightly lit and without people. The reason is obvious. The building materials and the construction features should be shown off to their best advantage. But since the interaction between user and architecture is missing, the results are often misleading: beautified impressions can make critical appraisal all the more difficult.

In 1976, the architectural faun Nils-Ole Lund staged the epitome of a sultry erotic interior in the collage, *A Nude in a Decorated Setting*. Hundreds of individual pieces form the picture of a love-cave in earthy browns, the fashionable colour of the '70s' colourful pop era.[2] A mature, dark-haired beauty reclines on furs: foxy lady, cat and dog, a stuffed donkey and tiger skins for seat covers, the rotten timberwork of the old wooden house, lamps with *Art-Déco* shades and Sitting Bull hanging on the wall. And through the window a scenery in fading late summer bloom. The table is set with everything erotic and culinary imaginable, the house is awaiting the return of the hunter and gatherer who calls all of this home.

This satire is overloaded with clichés which would never be found in reality. However, Lund

Nils-Ole Lund, *A Nude in a Decorated Setting*, 1976

not only managed to capture sexual desires from a male point of view, but at the same time, this picture also contains a mood of melancholic feminine eroticism and a romanticism bordering on the burlesque.

Influenced by the youth revolts of the '60s, there was a remarkable change in interior decoration in Western Europe. Open, flowing living spaces with nooks, caves, hollows, the soft crumpled feel of easy chairs, large cushioned lounging areas, and integrated work, rest and living areas were in vogue. Even bathrooms were integrated into the living area. All this in warm, emotional oranges, reds and browns. The Danish designer Verner Panton was celebrated as the prophet of this new kind of witty, organic, emotional living culture. Styrofoam and soft foam rubber furniture took the place of traditional armchairs. But already in the '70s pluralism was taking over. New, open living concepts remained, but conventional snugness once again gained the upper hand over the shrill and happy pop worlds of a youth culture promiscuous in its desires.

In 1978, Thomas Schröder described his ideal domicile as follows:

"I would like to have a house. Of course not a house whose fourth wall I would have to share with a neighbour. (...) No, the house I dream of should be like a second skin. It should stretch with me when I am in a good mood, and crouch over me when I am not doing so well."[3]

The house of his dentist friend J. is the sort he had been looking for:

"Almost all living and utility levels are offset; there are dwelling hollows and library caves. Walking through the house you go up and down flights of stairs, small ones and larger ones. You find yourself on galleries overlooking spacious living rooms, discover sleeping caves, TV-nooks and floors with studies and guest rooms. As far as possible friend J. has banished the right angle from his house, the bane of architecture. It is a house which generally

Verner Panton, Living-room landscape of the early '60s

resembles a strange and mysterious organ rather than what you commonly call a roof over your head."[4]

A house as a living organism, a desideratum of media architecture as well as ecological architecture. As an indoor landscape to be experienced sensually, it turns out to be a constant challenge for architects who have to adapt it to changing technical knowledge and demands while keeping an eye on basic emotional needs and atavisms.

Before the '80s and the advent of pastel-coloured post-modern play-worlds, there was a turning away from the flower-power pop-culture as revealed in architectural photos found in the house-and-home magazines of the '70s: they almost all drown in moody, emotional browns. The open, hedonistic lounging areas went into decline and after the energy crises of the mid-'70s we witnessed the return of doors not to all, but to most houses and apartments.

Reviewing the rooms of conventional houses in the mind's eye and scanning them for their erotic disposition leads to surprising discoveries. Living rooms are by definition rooms with some kind of sensual aura. In keeping with the rejection of kitchenettes as communication-killers, kitchens found their way back into family and social life: their sophistication increased and their aesthetic standards rose. Cooking and eating, seen as an activity that stimulates all senses and not as fast-food consumption, are very sensual occupations, anyway. In this respect, the kitchen can become an especially erotic place in interior design.

We have already examined in detail the culture and history of the bathroom, excluding the study rooms, libraries, etc. What remains is the bedroom, which one might assume at first glance to be the most erotic place of all in the house. But far from it. Today, bedrooms have degenerated for the most part into the most boring conventional conformist rooms in middle-class houses or apartments. What could be the reason for this? Looking at the cultural history of the bed, it becomes clear very quickly that this state of affairs is neither god-given nor natural. There is no piece of furniture in which one spends more time than in one's bed—about one third of one's life.

"From its beginnings, the place of rest was a representative piece of furniture, a status symbol. It was very often placed on a pedestal and climbing into this high camp was only possible from a foot-stool. The bed was a castle, draped on all sides with heavy cloth and with a protective canopy to be safe from insects and vermin. The warmed bedpan helped to keep the insects away.
There was no special bedroom in the Middle Ages and guests were received in the same room as was

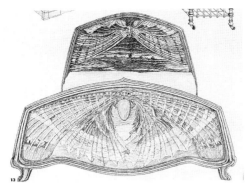

Émile Gallé,
Art Nouveau bed,
draft, 1904

used for sleeping. People did not mind spending the night with several others in one room. The lord with his servant, the lady with her maids or with visitors who stayed overnight. At this time, the bed was a showpiece, a house within the house, open to everyone. Nightclothes were almost unheard of and those who did not sleep in their clothes simply lay naked under the linen.
This uninhibitedness which was also common in the Middle Ages when taking a bath, later gave way in Rococo and Baroque times to a refined piquancy. In those times madame, sipping hot chocolate in bed, would receive her favourite cavalier for the early morning 'lever'. From his showpiece of a bed, the 'lit de parade', Louis XIV, dressed in lace, attended to France's matters of state. Beginning in the Renaissance period, fabric canopies hanging from flat baldachin roofs became common.[5]

As a house inside the house, the four-poster bed marks the centre of the world. One can also follow the history of the bed through the ages up to the present, whereby even the history of mattress stuffing, starting with straw, horsehair, kapok, springs and spring pockets, leading up to today's great variety of cleverly thought-out scientific solutions, is surprisingly revealing.

However, inquiries in a number of specialist stores show that this bedroom culture is in decline. Only a very few people buy the expensive complete program of matching bedroom furniture, either because they simply cannot afford it, or possibly because with the rising number of single households they are forced to fall back on improvisation and combinations of different elements. Or perhaps it's that the incentive of possessing a status symbol is missing, or that a pastiche of individual items serves just as well.

While living rooms, kitchens, even guest bathrooms have become showpieces, the bedroom door still fends off curious glances. Not because what lies beyond is an intimate place of erotic pleasure, but rather because most bedrooms have become junk rooms where one dumps what cannot be used anywhere else in the house.

This diagnosis might give cause for pessimistic conclusions as to the connections between contemporary lifestyles and eroticism in general. It might also serve as an occasion to give some advice to architects, for example as part of controversial proposals for cheaper building, especially concerning the extent to which American and Canadian frame constructions might be adopted. Their wall structure favors walk-in closets, which would make the obligatory wardrobe walls in European bedrooms superfluous, thereby opening a host of possibilities to make the boudoir cosier and more sensual.

In spite of generalizations like the ones above, however, there is no denying that remarkably creative individual solutions continue to exist. A particularly beautiful and at the same time erotic bedroom highlight can be found in the house of the Canadian wildlife painter Robert Bateman and his wife Birgit, who reside on Salt Spring Island in the Pacific Ocean off the northwest Canadian coast not far from Vancouver Island. The bedroom and the bathroom lead into one another. The bath opens onto the woods, the bedroom onto Fulford Harbor Bay and the ocean. Neither room is very large, but both are functionally furnished and perfectly harmonious.

The bedroom is almost completely filled with a bed covered with an orientally-colourful bedspread; on the window sills there are small sculptures from South Pacific archipelagos. The whole room breathes the stimulating synthesis of nature and civilization, of shelter and adventure all at once. At night, when falling asleep, the forest and the ocean sink into deep shades of blue, and upon waking one may be fortunate enough to see whales or watch eagles from the surrounding eyries in their merciless aerial battles against seagulls. All colours are sensually intense and completely natural, visual and tactile stimuli are strong and dominant, and man feels himself a cultural being still integrated into nature.

In spite of such positive examples it would be completely remiss to generalize about such an arrangement of intimate rooms, or to present them as the norm. Such a statement could never even be valid for one individual person. Interior design and erotic architecture can create unities in the most diverse ways, all of which can nevertheless have a strong erotic effect. This indicates that in an era of increasing immateriality, the erotic may actually be connected to attitudes and structures rather than forms and materials. Thus at the other end of the spectrum, Martin Cleffmann's glassed-in multistorey steel-girder construction in Constance may serve as an example that shows a touch of romanticism in the canopy of a tent roof in the master bedroom, an effect that creates an erotic atmosphere in the midst of a technical culture.

Researchers predict that while individualism will continue to rise in the '90s and beyond, conventional living environments will be on the decrease.[6] Living spaces that do not abide by conventions and in which material prestige does not play as great a role as it did in the '80s will take their place. According to their observations, high quality of life was the motto of the early '90s, but in the meantime the trend has shifted away from self-presentation to the less extroverted self-realization of one's own apartment as a "glove for the soul", a third skin. This attitude would ensure well-being into old age.[7]

"Ours is a ready-money society," Becky Sharp diagnosed as protagonist of William Makepeace Thackeray's social panorama novel *Vanity Fair* (1848). Thackeray derived this view from a model which was to a large extent still influenced by the Middle Ages, John Bunyan's *Pilgrim's Progress* (1674/75). Since Victorian times, and the years of rapid industrial expansion in Germany from the 1870s onwards, the role of money and commodities in society has intensified so dramatically that it would be pointless to deny the eroticism of consumption. Consequently, a number of service companies, mostly hotels, restaurants, bars, nightclubs, fashion boutiques and corporate headquarters which place great emphasis on design are predisposed to interior design based on erotic principles.

Taking as example fifteen objects from the early '90s made by ten very different designers from six countries, it is easy to understand how designers create sensual stimuli, set up and play out the erotic game of arousal, seduction and enjoyment by way of interior architecture.

Since about the middle of the '80s, interior design like many other fields has experienced a significant increase in internationalization, leading to a cross-fertilization and interpenetration of Eastern and Western cultural influences, particularly so in Japan, Western Europe and the USA. As far as eroticism is concerned, the exotic attraction of foreign elements is especially important, as, for example, in Alfredo Arriba's nightclub *Barna Crossing*, located in the basement of the hotel *Il Palazzo* in Fukuoka. Here Spanish design and Japanese high-tech meet and mix, producing a staircase which combines the tactile sensuousness of a roughed up wall with porthole-light effects, a glassed-in dance floor equipped with laser-showers, and an enthusiasm for hybrid styles in furniture.

Borrowing another example from Japan, consider the corporate symbol designed by

Philippe Starck, a huge golden flame or torch that is at once a spermatozoon and an ambiguous erotic shape on the roof of the *Asahi Brewery* in Azumabashi, a northern suburb of Tokyo. Starck, who—as everyone interested in design knows—uses an eroticized language of forms, is remarkable for the fact that for the interior of this building he reverts to body shapes, but refuses to indulge in clumsy explicitness and instead favours a transnational ambiguity of androgynous eroticism.

The Japanese have the uninhibitedness and Starck has the insolence to eroticize large architectural structures like this brewery and the adjacent spacious beer hall. Starck sets up a sometimes almost surrealistic dream-world of theatre and stage sets, one of which De Chirico could have inspired. On a subliminal level eroticism is always present, for example when Starck,[8] the bathroom fetishist, has the ladies' restrooms painted in warm iridescent reds, in front of whose high frosted-glass doors there are small mirrors, hair-dryers and cables springing up from the white marble floor which resemble objects from West Africa, the home of fetishes.[9]

Design in the early '90s is marked by new approaches to an old problem, namely how to combine aesthetics and functionality in an attractive interplay. It is mostly light and colours which are used dramatically and specifically to model rooms and produce effects. Since recessionary times cost-consciousness has been a top priority, and designers have had to employ significant doses of creative imagination to reach their goal, the stimulation of customers to buy and consume.

In achieving this, the psychological effects of colours and lighting play an important role, and new computer-based technologies have become so affordable that installing sophisticated light architecture instead of solid materials may indeed pay off. This also has the advantage of making rearranging quick and simple, and Eastern and

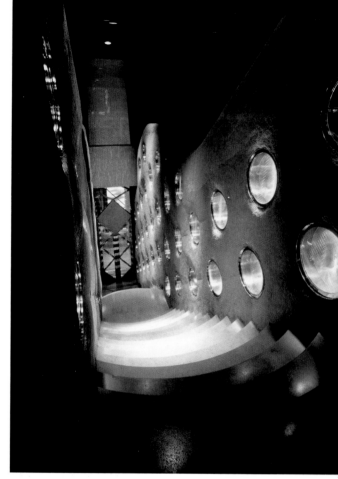

Alfredo Arribas, *Barna Crossing Nightclub,* Fukuoka, Japan, 1989

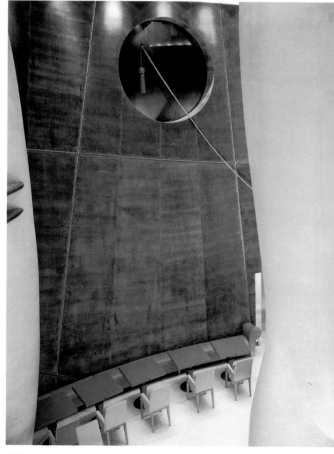

Philippe Starck, *Asahi la Flamme,* upper-floor room, Tokyo, 1989

Studio Citterio & Dwan, *Esprit Administration Building*, stairwell, Amsterdam, c.1990

Western cultural influences easily mixed. In the '90s, electronic and media effects are often paired with the smooth contours of "biodesign", in which natural elements like water, stone, metal, wood are artistically charged with light. Here colour gives identity while outstanding craftsmanship creates authenticity.

As far as our subject is concerned in the narrowest possible sense, it is the increasing interactivity between user and room which comes into play and prompts designers to fashion commercial space into rooms to be experienced, to bring out and enliven all the possible metaphors in interior design. A specifically erotic atmosphere, which is, as enquiries in architectural circles suggest, particularly attractive to women,[10] often comes into being when elegant forms are contrasted with hard materials, when high-tech elements are combined with natural ones, or when the treatment of metal surfaces becomes more and more sophisticated. The staircase and room designs which the architects of Studio Citterio & Dwan carried out for *Esprit* in Antwerp and Amsterdam create, for example, an ambivalent tingling sensation on the skin, especially as they conjure reminiscences of prisons.

Employing a large amount of punched zinc-coated sheet steel is something Terry Dwan likes to do, and in combination with spatial penetrations of enclosed and open rooms, this alludes to hard sex, evokes hidden aspects of power and violence as well as media image-worlds familiar from films. About the Amsterdam *Esprit Administration Building* with attached café and fashion boutiques we read:

> "Staircases and landings of the 'Afrikahuis' create a special kind of drama. The massive steel frame is contrasted with the perforated stairs. Ironically, the substance lies in the absence of material density."[11]

Naturally, specific groups are always being targeted, teenagers, singles, high-income middle-class people, fetishists, etc. In order for an interior design to have an effect on many levels and a larger audience, its function has to be brought into accord with complex emotional and psychological dimensions. Fashion boutiques in particular achieve an astonishing amount of theatricality and image-shaping in a limited space.

Good examples to support this thesis come from the Czech-born London architect Eva Jiricna, who has become famous for designing many shops which derive their attractiveness from the combination of high-tech, airy transparency and modern elegance. *Joseph*'s new fashion boutique on London's Sloane Street, for example, is marked by a discretely restrained architecture which gives dresses and suits the

Studio Citterio & Dwan, *Esprit Administration Building*, Amsterdam, *c.*1990

opportunity to form a sculptural focus. The central and most eye-catching feature of the shop is the dynamic, exuberant "high-tech art-deco" staircase[12] that connects the different sales floors of the shop. Its suspension construction and glass steps offer a graceful counterpart to more ponderous kinds of erotic attraction.

Eva Jiricna's trademark, however, is the synthesis of rationality and sensuality. She uses this to perfection in the Neo-Baroque setting for the

shoe boutique *Joan and David* in Los Angeles. Again, the centrepiece is a staircase constructed of black steel girders, stainless steel and glass, whose articulated female curves draw attention like a swing of the hips. It matches the long curves of the leather-covered couches whose reverse side comprises deep red, step-like ledges for displaying shoes. Like the glass display cases in a museum, there are delicate glass shelves which catch the eye, presenting shoes

Eva Jiricna, *Joseph Fashion Boutique*, London, 1989

Eva Jiricna, *Joan and David Shoe Shop*, Los Angeles, California, 1987/88

like works of art, like fetishes, which they in fact often are. Since fetishes are alternatives to rituals,[13] this practice points to the underlying connection between the eroticism of consumption and pseudo-religious proxy acts. Inertia evolves into dynamism. Although in the tradition of architectural photography the pictures show no people, one can almost feel the interaction between people and room.

If one prefers this perfect, but ritually more restrained style, one should turn to the creations of Shiro Kuramata, the most important and most influential designer in modern Japan. Kuramata is a designer who died all too young in 1991, and who was renowned as a poet of creative emptiness, an artist who knew how to add surrealistic and minimalistic elements to Western Bauhaus modernism and transpose it into Eastern thought.[14] Objects like his *Chest of Drawers* (1970), his armchair *How High the Moon* (1986) or his rose-armchair *Miss Blanche* (1988) seem almost to breathe the metaphysically condensed metaphorical language of erotic haiku. Artificial roses bloom eternally, moulded into thick glass panels as symbols of love and beauty, and each one of his furniture objects is sculpture and architecture all at once. Kuramata gives convincing proof that design can be largely dematerialized, and that at the

same time its sensual presence can be condensed.

The same applies to his interior design of bars and stores like the restaurant *Comblé* (1988) in Shizuoka or the boutique *Spiral Interior* (1990) for home furnishing accessories. It is said of Kuramata that he has taken the synaesthetical perceptions of present-day postindustrial media society and applied them to design.[15] In his work concentration and reduction lead to a floating form of condensation that only very few artists attain. Kuramata is the Shakespeare of design, whose creations resemble Ariel's songs in *The Tempest*. This implies a tragic, maybe even tragicomic outlook on the world. It is visible in *How the High Moon* as well as, for example, in his design for the Issey Miyake *Boutique* in the Shibya-Seibu Department Store in Tokyo (1987). Andrea Branzi, a renowned Italian designer, tries to capture this phenomenon in words:

"Shiro always moves between two extreme poles: on the one side he dematerializes the world, as if to

alleviate all the pain it causes, and on the other he seems suddenly to immerse himself in matter and to look at it as a metaphor of history, where flotsam and jetsam float colourfully but petrified like segments of separate and desperate stories."[16]

Branzi also touches upon the extent to which Kuramata has to be seen in the context of the architecture, the cityscape and the pulse of Tokyo, which in his view is the first metropolis born of overlapping levels of perception:

"The first level, which is not perceptible, is that of its public outer image, of its continually shattered, desultory urban scenery, crushed by a thousand glimpses and overlappings; a magma, almost a mud of fragments of scenery, unknowable, and absolutely unorganizable into an orderly perspective; an amniotic liquid of information to be absorbed through the pores of the skin and consumed through ever sharper senses. Kuramata, however, does not belong to this public level of Tokyo. Shiro works inside the other level, that of the inner space, the places, routes, stories, silences and shadows of which this vast city is full to the brim. It is this more secret and religious level that produces the indescribable quality of the Tokyo we love."[17]

Michele Saee (Building), on the other hand, is far less esoteric in his fashion boutiques for *Ecru* in L.A., indulging in a very down-to-earth, very physical interior design. Wood and metal combinations in the store on Melrose Avenue lend it a particularly masculine character, with the initiation and penetration symbolism of the entrance, the arched windows and the show-

Shiro Kuramata, *Miss Blanche*, armchair, 1988

The fascination of high-tech architecture combined with the aesthetics of a connecting element: the large staircase in Volkwin Marg's new *Leipzig Exhibition Hall*, 1996

cases. Here sophisticated lighting plays a major role. In contrast, Michele Saee's *Ecru* boutique located in a shopping centre on Marina del Rey also in Los Angeles is organically feminine. Besides visual qualities, the sculptural body shapes and tactile qualities of plywood are dominant.

> "Clothes have a direct relation to the human body. They follow its lines in a way which cannot be simulated with basic geometric principles. Inspired by a stylized little figure, the architects of *Building* use enlarged forms of organic body contours for pillars, tables and ceilings."[18]

The fashion industry has become such an important economic branch in the '80s that it seems a logical consequence that even retail businesses are restyled, employing body-architecture in order to attract and seduce customers who rarely buy out of need, but rather for the newest thrill. The game of buying and selling becomes an integral part of the erotic process. In this interior, design plays the supporting role of creating the right atmosphere, sensitizing, preparing a willingness to buy, which is often enough experienced as an erotic act. In very few other areas of consumerism is the erotic flair of the products on sale as intense as in fashion.

Nightclubs on the other hand have to do with the consumption of largely immaterial goods, namely entertainment, dance and inter-personal relationships of an erotic nature. Beverages and snacks are mostly just "appetizers" for other pleasures of the body and soul. For this reason, the interior architecture of nightclubs aims at achieving an intense multisensory sensuality.

Three very different examples serve to introduce the variety of methods employed to achieve this goal. It is certain that within limits there is a common denominator concerning the tasks and functions of such designs, maybe even as to the means by which they are applied, but that the execution is determined entirely by the personality of the individual designer. The artistic aspect of interior design is so dominant that it seems unthinkable to delegate such a task to a designer collective.

Let us begin with Alfredo Arribas' *Velvet Bar* (1987) in Barcelona. Arribas is a child of the age that declared the chaos theory as one of the mythical explanations of the world. On top of that, Arribas has internalized the continuously shifting changes of media culture. Thinking in processes, dynamism, a basic playfulness, organized chaos, making a variety of stimuli and moods visible are therefore among the constituents of his conceptual thinking. Of the *Velvet Bar* he says:

> "Velvet is a game, a reaction, amusement in an atmosphere that seems to be familiar, and which in reality is completely new. It is an amalgam of colour and light. It is a baroque scheme, purposefully variegated, in which the 'functional style' serves as an excuse for shaking off certain tics and entering onto less trodden paths."[19]

There are two different entrances, but with identical doors. One of the two leads onto a ramp obviously designed as an initiation. The doors made of dulled steel resemble human faces and convey an air of mystery, of Bluebeard and de Sade. But behind them things are quite different. In the long but narrow rooms, Arribas works with a variety of zones, moods and materials. Colours, the children of light, are atmospherically employed in shades of blue, black and red. A nostalgic atmosphere reminiscent of the '50s alternates with "new wave" impressions. All surfaces are finished with their tactile and visual qualities in mind. Slate, teak, various metals, enamelled and gilded surfaces, a variety of floor coverings in combination with round, sweeping, sensual forms underline the concept of "skin", which finally culminates in the programmatic and abudant use of velvet, from which the bar acquires its name. Again and again Arribas has surprises in store:

> "If you see the task of a designer as a lasting impression achieved through originality, then the oeuvre of the Catalan Alfredo Arribas certainly points the way forward. And you can hardly imagine an experience stranger than visiting the toilets in Arribas' nightclub *Velvet Bar*. There an infrared sensor notes the approach of every guest who enters the toilet. The sensor opens an electronically controlled valve, water flows through a thick, coloured fluid and fills a glass case. A few moments later a stroboscope is activated. The game of visual stimuli in the toilet lasts as long as the infrared sensor notes the presence of a guest. We have no idea what effect that has upon the functionality of the place. It is, at any rate, the most extreme example of interaction between visitor and interior, a principle upon which the interior design of the entire club is based."[20]

Zaha Hadid, an Iraqi architect and design star of international renown who lives in London, has her say literally and pictorially with her much-publicized *Moonsoon Club* in Sapporo (1990). The visualization of seething passions is her chosen theme, for which she invokes the full theatrical power of her fiery temperament.

Hadid's deconstructivist aesthetic comes alive in her sculpted ceilings, seats, and tables that are cunningly carried to extremes, yet balanced with a great sensitivity for shapes. Rarely has the tightrope walk of eroticism balancing tenderness and devotion on the one hand, and power, violence, fierceness, and brutality on the other, been so openly yet metaphorically converted into design. The club's ground floor is dominated by the reds, yellows and oranges of sexual passion. Moving on to the restaurant in the basement one finds the aesthetic but cold chill of glass table and walls and ceiling sculptures wedged together like pack ice. Moonsoon draws life from its contrasts and the tense vitality of its sculptural details:

> "Hadid's glass surfaces have an effect like water which expands when it freezes. Wall coverings, made of minute fragments of glass which are stuck on to etched sheets of glass mounted in steel frames, are lit from behind. (...) Above the ice chamber whirls a real firestorm of glaring red, yellow and orange, a whirl which bursts through the cupola of the restaurant beneath and flares upward to a blazing furnace on the ceiling."[21]

Sensuality in architecture has hardly ever been staged so rebelliously and with so much verve, temperament, innovation and perfection.

Michele Saee (Building), *Ecru Fashion Boutique*, Los Angeles, California, 1988

Alfredo Arribas, *Velvet Bar Nightclub*,
Barcelona, 1987

Zaha Hadid, *Moonsoon Club*,
Sapporo, Japan, 1990

For designers, youth culture is one of the most fertile soils for new ideas, and elements from subcultures stimulate the mainstream again and again, keeping it from becoming rigid and monotonous. This certainly applies to Lynn Davis' *Ministry of Sound*, one of the first rave dance clubs in London. Seen from the outside, the 1300 sq. m bunker-like building which once contained a depot and a garage is hardly visible—it ducks down between a railway and a parking lot in the Elephant and Castle area.

Architect Lynn Davis aimed to combine the rough charm of industrial aesthetics and its systems of pipes, wires, old lighting fixtures and heaters with images from the film and media worlds. Metal, textiles, graffiti and lighting effects blend into an atmospherically dense fabric of narrative, media-dominated impressions, which, as is often the case in England, also borrow heavily from amateur and student theatre:

"Grouped at the other end of the bar are a mezzanine VIP lounge, a small cinema and toilets. The lounge is sparsely furnished with white drapes hanging in tent-like swathes amongst the metallic glint of defunct heating pipes. The improvisational, almost post-apocalyptic character of the space is given a touch of low-life glamour by a huge, spidery fifties chandelier. The nearby cinema is sited in a railway arch, past an entrance showing outlines of original decorative mouldings."[22]

The *Ministry of Sound* has quickly gained cult status. In contrast to the artistically perfect, carefully styled, expensive luxury nightclubs that we have presented so far, the scene here is dominated by improvisation and imperfection. But, remembering the introductory remarks on erotic ambience in many movies, it becomes clear that the erotic charm is not so much a question of budget, but rather a matter of originality and concept elements neccessary to mobilize all the senses and evoke emotions and moods. The range is broad, from romantically soft and cuddly all the way to raucous punk, carried off

by surfaces, light, and sound, as well as the qualities of the materials, spatial structures and configurations of the rooms. Ultimately, eroticism is the result of a host of different forms of sensuous interaction between humans, materials and immaterial things.

It seems only normal that nightclubs, hotels, and boutiques should adjust their interior design to have an erotic effect since it increases sales. The fact is that industrial high-tech companies employ the principles of erotic architecture in their exhibition, training, and library facilities, like the Toulouse branch of the aluminium company *Technal*, a rather unusual design that requires explanation.

Jean-Michel Wilmotte, the French design and high-tech architect who has won a number of prizes and has worked on Norman Foster's *Carré d'Art,* the museum of contemporary art in Nîmes, the Richelieu wing of the Grand Louvre in Paris and on the new art museum in Lyon, created the rooms of the *Technal* building, an ensemble which is a perfect example in abstract form of the principles by which an architecture operates, that deserves to be called erotic.

First of all, there is the historical layering, the combination of old and new in vaults from the 17th century and state of the art technology, of elements reminiscent of Piranesi and also of industrial culture. Add to the historical dimension the spatial layering, connecting in series a variety of different effects. Add to that the appeal of contrasts, which simultaneously attract and repel. In the confrontation with the red stone arches, pillars and walls, the light, graceful qualities of aluminium are given a context which demonstrates a harmonious coupling of lightness and heaviness, warmth and coolness, emotion and intellect. The illuminated aluminium floor suggests weightlessness.

The divided up rooms offer intimacy and openness, hideouts and discoveries, working on the principle of disguising and revealing, of insights, glimpses and vistas. This in turn underscores the playful character of the setting. Areas of natural and artificial light alternate, and there are various openings and arches to let in the daylight. "The irregular brick vaulted ceilings gain a new clarity through the partially natural, partially artificial light."[23] This implies twilight and shade, but under no circumstances glaring brightness.

The large aluminium conference table in the basement takes on the shape of the floor and the vault. With its elegance it captivates like an altar—simultaneously alluding to sacred roots

Jean-Michel Wilmotte, showroom for *Technal*, aluminium manufacturer, Toulouse, *c*.1990

and to aspects of eroticism. It seems to hover above the aluminium floor illuminated from below, thus creating in the blue-green light an almost magical, mystical effect. The perfectly balanced contrasts in the design and the materials, the moods and impressions, the historical and modern dimensions and implications reveal that Wilmotte's *Technal* interior is an especially successful example of sensuous architecture, whose range of possibilities is greater in interior architecture than in the design possibilities for the exterior.

"(...) for while a description of Anastasia can only arouse wishes one after another, compelling you to repress them, for anyone who wakes up one morning to find himself in Anastasia all those wishes come alive at the same time and surround him. The city appears to you as an entity of which you are a part and where no wish is overlooked and since the city enjoys all those things which you do not possess, you have no choice but to live within this wish and be content with your lot."[1]

Italo Calvino

There can scarcely be anyone among us who is not familiar with those city reminiscences in which at first only one of our five senses dominates, then to be joined by a variety of other sensory impressions, blending and condensing into a collage of fragments which in the mind of each individual go to make up a personal image of a particular city. For me, for example, Bolzano is a city which I, ever since my childhood, have first been able to recall as a symphony of market smells, of fruit, vegetables, ham, cheese, olives, dates, before actually stepping out from under the arcade, as it were, onto the Renaissance market place.

Vancouver, my second hometown, situated in a completely different cultural environment, comes to mind first and foremost as a collage of sound: the penetrating midday siren hooting from the top of the B. C. Hydro tower, or water utility central office, with foghorns and the throbbing noise of the ships' engines entering the harbour, with the whirring of the cranes, the constant hum of traffic and the old omnibuses. Then the ubiquitous screeching of seagulls and that characteristic rumbling and honking of the Canadian Pacific Railways' passenger trains as they came rattling down from the Rocky Mountains, along the waterfront and into the beautifully restored *Art-Déco* station. Since these trains have stopped running so frequently, an essential component of the city's soundscape has been sorely missing, to my ears at least.

Similarly, when I stand on the Mönchsberg in Salzburg and take in the Renaissance and Baroque panorama of the city, with its inevitable echoes of Mozart, it pains my eyes to see, on the opposite bank of the Salzach, faceless towerblocks which cut through the soft contours of the city. In the same way, every reader will be

Opposite page:
Times Square, New York

Arthur Erickson, *Museum of Anthropology*, Vancouver, 1978–81

able to add from experience his or her own personal synaesthetic city memories.

In our context, of course, "sense appeal and city ambience" means something more: the sensuous aspect of urbanity and the role in it which architecture plays. But what is urbanity? It is business and bustle, vitality and flux, culture and commerce, education and science, art and entertainment, the harmony between past and present, the multisensory vibrancy of human communication on a variety of levels in an urban space. This gives rise to a sense of style, taste, a refinement of morals, an intellectual climate in which—in both a political and a cultural sense—public spirit can flourish, and to an ambience which combines business sense and cosmopolitanism with individual freedom and solidarity. The drawbacks of modern city life, however, constitute an opposite pole to an otherwise positive idea of urbanity: noise, stench, dirt, problems with the water supply, refuse disposal and road traffic, violence, crime, loneliness or overcrowding. All these things have elements of sensuousness, but where they pre-

dominate, urbanity quickly turns into its opposite and the city becomes a nightmare. But urban communication can only take place against a background, on top or on the inside of architecture, an architecture which forms a framework, acts as a stage, offers a setting, an architecture which itself plays a character, attracts an audience, radiates flair, offers itself as a platform on which the "comédie humaine" is acted out, an architecture which by virtue of its interior and exterior forms arouses sensuality and prepares encounters.

Which architectonic places do we actually mean, however, when we speak of city ambience and sense appeal? Old parts of places like Prague, Lisbon, Rome, residential quarters crisscrossed with canals like in Amsterdam and Venice, where it is architecture which provides stimuli pleasing to the eye, all sorts of squares, central squares, cathedral squares, market squares like the Campo Pubblico in Siena, St. Mark's Square in Venice, the central square in Linz, and the market places in Bremen, Bruges and Brussels; passages, gallerias and arcades like those

Campo Pubblico,
Siena, 14th century

impulses from designers or the zeitgeist clashes with the long-term sensory stimuli offered by the large-scale architectural forms providing the context.

City Squares and Market Squares

The bustle of markets has always had highly sensuous qualities. If it is out in the open air, architecture has only a performance role to play. The large open markets like in Brussels or the numerous street markets that lend character to various parts of London or Hamburg manage for the most part without any architectural setting. If the market is held on the traditional market square or city square, however, the stage is set by the square's architecture.

The ideal city square was described by Vitruvius as early as the first century, B.C., and the functions which he determined for both the square itself and the buildings grouped around it are—*mutatis mutandis*—still valid today:

> "The ratio of length to breadth should be three to two. The following public buildings should have their place on the town square: a hall for the courtroom, the exchange and the market, which in inclement weather assumes the function of the square. In addition, the treasury, the council hall, and the temple dedicated to the city's patron. There should also be monuments to honorable citizens."[3]

The city square is the centrepiece of the city's urge to shape and to project its own urbanity. More clearly than in any other piece of urban architecture it mirrors the history of the city and the character of its citizens alongside their regional culture. Through the centuries, the great squares have been unerring indicators of a city's vitality and cultural standing. When towns open up their main squares to trams, cars and delivery vehicles and banish the squares' characteristic features such as plants, trees, bushes, fountains, sculptures, monuments, lamps, music pavilions, and benches to the isolation of traffic islands, there is normally also a general decline in urbanity. Important squares are where central axes intersect, cleverly making use of the city's topography and gathering together architecture which is typical, outstanding, and which gives the squares their character:

> "Any business which needed to be negotiated was carried out there. Fruit and vegetables first, meat as well as fish, and then court cases, business deals, the political situation. Probably also engagement celebrations and then marriage. Funeral processions also solemnly crossed the square. Here individuals found the roles they wished to play and here everyone came together, in anger, in fear, to

in Bath, Berlin, Cleveland, Milan, Paris and London; clusters of buildings affording glimpses into or down onto enclosed yards or views out onto squares like in Barcelona and Berlin. History is always involved, however, the ageing processes of architecture and its experience of life—that in itself implies the time dimension.

From east to west, from north to south, Europe is still full of cities with historic town centres and particular districts which radiate this sort of ambience and which are steeped in history. There are even many small towns which have such an ambience to offer, and of course especially old royal seats and metropolises with organic city centres. Sensuousness should be something for all ages, however, especially for the young and the mature. Is there a difference here between architecture and people?

Disappointment sets in as soon as we start looking for this sensuous urbanity in new towns and newly built suburbs. It takes a long and laborious search before we find anything approaching it. There must be reasons for this. And they have something to do with the building materials glass, steel, concrete, the lack of colours, the larger-than-life transparency, matter-of-factness and functionality of many modern buildings, the lack of scale in common with the human figure, the tempo of modern life, the endless flow of traffic, but above all with the commercialization of time. For sensuality and eroticism require leisure, time for looking and

luring, for playing and exploring. And that applies just as much to architecture.

But what about the oft-quoted eroticism of the world of retail goods and the way in which it relates with architecture?[2] Most consumer goods are not in themselves particularly sensuous and certainly not erotic, especially not in those department stores which simply pile their wares on huge bargain counters, usually to be found in architectural monstrosities made of concrete slabs and plastic, on the edges of cities or out in the countryside.

In order to produce a sensuous or erotic effect, goods have to be put into the right setting, and that involves architecture, both interior and exterior: façades, ornamentation, arches, entrances, stairs, shop windows and lighting attract, prepare and focus attention on what is available, especially in the famous shopping streets of the Western world: the Via Condotti in Rome, Kärntner Strasse or the Graben in Vienna, Strøget in Copenhagen, the Via Monte Napoleone in Milan, the Kurfürstendamm in Berlin, the Champs-Élysées in Paris, Fifth Avenue or Madison Avenue in New York or Rodeo Drive in Beverly Hills. There boutiques and even the larger shops try to show themselves off as extravagantly as possible, usually without the slightest regard for architectural contexts. This of course is subject to rapid changes in fashion and to the prosperity of the firms in question. The consequence is that the short-lived sensuality of

reach communal decisions, to take communal action. Here people tried to win over others, here opinions were formed, in which they were either united or divided, to the point of bloody feud. Here people were always playing themselves up, each one playing himself. The city square at that time was the stage on which world history was performed."[4]

One wonders why it is so seldom the case that newly built squares are fitted out with those qualities with which historic squares seem to have been endowed by nature. After all, architects and town planners are normally no fools, and go about their work drawing on an immense wealth of historical knowledge, technical stock-in-trade and pictorial material from all over the world with which to compare their ideas. There are many reasons: the separation of traditional urban functions like commerce, trades, housing and cultural activities; the encircling of urban squares by busy roads and tramlines; the general acceleration in the pace of city life; art as an accessory, as in art in front of buildings instead of the art of building, as an integral component of the architecture of the square and the buildings surrounding it; a bureaucratic excess of planning guidelines.

But the forms of public life have also changed. Public life has found a new platform for itself in the media—in talk shows, election debates, documentaries—and that with a very doubtful claim to authenticity. Nonetheless it is also finding new forms of expression, for example on the World Wide Web, and if television should ever really become interactive, at least in part, the result will be quite new concepts of public life in the media.

Nevertheless man is an extremely resilient being, with a natural desire for company, entertainment and celebration. Topography and climate are by no means decisive factors, otherwise the squares in Copenhagen and Gothenburg (Göteborg), for example, would not be so urbane and lively. Townspeople and tourists tend to take possession of squares if these plazas offer them everything their hearts desire, but functionality and commerce alone are no more likely to capture their hearts than the mania for ostentation displayed by dictators who build gigantic squares for the sole purpose of holding parades and rallies to have themselves and their ideologies acclaimed.

But the fact is that man is also an emotional and irrational being, and accordingly he demands spaces and architecture, whether public or private, which satisfy both his lust for visual pleasure and his emotional needs. It is for this reason that the small, quiet and intimate town squares often work so well, with their mix-

Bremen market square

ture of private housing and business premises, and that not only in the mild climate of the South of France, where playing *boules* and drinking wine and coffee make urban life enjoyable.

Squares in the open beg to have life breathed into them. And yet again and again modern projects are doomed to failure no matter how intelligently they have been planned. The large square of La Défense in Paris, in front of the Grande Arche, is one such example. In effect it has everything that has made the historical squares famous, and on top of everything else it is also free of traffic. Nevertheless, La Défense refuses to come to life and radiate a really sensuous, urbane ambience. The proportional mixture of people who live in this quarter, only work there or who come as tourists simply does not function well, and the buildings around the square emit an austere coldness.

Plain glass façades are not capable of taking on the sort of patina which stone façades can boast after being exposed to the weather for only a few years. Apart from that, the proportions of the Grande Arche, with its low buildings immediately on the edge of the square and the surrounding tower blocks, are all wrong in relation to the human figure. In some respects, La Défense gives the impression of a European

Toronto, but one concocted in a laboratory, and in the process the urban chemistry is completely lost and cannot be recreated by costly works of art.

Times Square in New York, on the other hand, in all its scruffiness, its air of neglect and cheap depravity, is a highly sensual city square. But presumably it will have lost every shred of sensuality by the time the extensive renovation and redevelopment work which has since got under way really begins to have an effect. The totally media-orientated city utopia which Lise-Anne Couture and Hani Rashid envisage for the new Times Square will completely blur the line between fiction and reality and possibly create an intense virtual sensuality. But in its exclusively media-orientated architecture and the media-related entertainment and jobs to be found there, it has no chance of realization.[5]

New towns have a hard time. No matter how well planned they are and how many pseudo-historical façades they have, like in parts of the Isle of Dogs in London, a pulsating city ambience with sensual appeal simply refuses to come out of them. Here English classicism and Georgian façades, as propagated by Prince Charles and the architect Quinlan Terry, are of no help either.[6] Classicistic detail may indeed radiate infinitely more humanity than, for example, the monumental gigantism Ricardo Bofill creates, which houses just as many "down market" homes and modern offices as Terry's pseudo-historical façade mixtures. But Terry's buildings are substitutes for the real thing, artificial honey rather than art plus honey, even if they are meant as a response to the terrible wounds which an insensitive, purely functional and brutally capitalistic variety of architectural modernism inflicted on English towns in the '60s and '70s.

But architectural eyewash is no basis for sensuous flair. The much maligned architects and city planners involved in the building of a new Berlin will have to face up to being judged in ten years' time according to whether their conservative step back into the 19th century really does give the city a sense of continuity and an identity as a genuine metropolis with a specific Berlin or perhaps even Prussian charm, or whether there is more to the reintroduction of old block-style building behind modernistic façades with a pseudo-historical touch than just

Renzo Piano, *Daimler-Benz Project,*
Potsdamer Platz, Berlin

petty bourgeois delusions of grandeur or a capitalistic wolf in sheep's clothing.

Without an awareness of history it will not be
a metropolis, and without embracing the
present and its creative potential for the future it
can only be a mess. For in architecture, just as
in any other field, the truth is that tomorrow's
questions can only be partially solved with
yesterday's answers. And in this respect it is precisely the old squares in the new Berlin which
give cause for serious misgivings. Potsdamer
Platz may perhaps have the best chance of
establishing the link between the past and the
present and of thus offering a certain urban sensuality: its redevelopment involves, alongside a
number of German architects of middling quality and Hans Kollhoff's unimaginative monu-
mentalism, a few architects who have an international reputation to defend, such as Giorgio
Grassi, Renzo Piano, Arata Isozaki and Helmut
Jahn. For the Alexanderplatz and the Leipziger
Platz, on the other hand, one can only fear the
worst. And whether the *Bundesforum* (federal
forum) planned in the bend of the River Spree
as a meeting place for parliament and public,
however the latter may be defined, will ever be
more than just a rhetorical gesture remains to be
seen. The financing of the project is highly
uncertain anyway.

It is not even so important whether the elements planned into new building projects are
large or small; what matters is the mixture and
whether city neighbourhoods and the architecture of squares offer the residents a sense of
belonging and afford individual identification.
Since the end of the '80s, *Sophia Antipolis,* the

French Silicon Valley, has been under construction among the hills between Cannes and Nice.
Here scientists from France and numerous other
countries are involved in pushing the pace of
product-orientated high-tech research and

research into the future of communications
technology and bioengineering. In spite of the
fact that a variety of international star architects
have erected what are—at least in part—very
attractive and interesting office and laboratory
buildings in the Provence countryside, *Sophia
Antipolis* still has the feel of a ghost town.

Despite the topography and the climate, all
those civic anxieties aroused in Plato's *Republic*
(4th century B.C.), Bacon's *Nova Utopia* (1632)
and Jules Verne's *Une ville flottante* (1867) have
been confirmed. The fear has been—concerning
republics created and run by scholars and urban
structures inhabited almost exclusively by scientists and intellectuals—that among so many
individualists there is no chance of establishing
any sort of public spirit, especially not if they
are guests in the town for only a few years. At
the end of a working day these highly paid specialists are only interested in relaxing on the
beach or driving golf balls across the exclusive
expanses of green. And so *Sophia Antipolis* lies
like a meteorite from another planet embedded
in a circle of tiny old towns ensconced in long
tradition and cosy atmosphere.

Intensive planning does not necessarily have
to result in sterility. It is particularly the towns
built by absolutist rulers of the Renaissance and

City square of Telč, Czech Republic,
end of the 16th century

Freemen's houses,
City square of Telč, Czech Republic,
end of the 16th century

City square with St. Mary's Column,
Telč, Czech Republic,
end of the 16th century

A number of long houses on narrow plots of land were strung together like pearls, with modest interiors but splendid façades. Soft pastel colours and sensuous shades of red and ochre dominate the house fronts. The windows are richly ornamented and further stimulation is added by the diversity of gables, variously arranged in steps, curved in the shape of battlements, or decorated with scrolls or figurines. The unifying stylistic elements are the pillared arcades, which were partly rebuilt in the Baroque style but are still partly preserved in the Renaissance original. Nearly all these houses were renovated in the early '90s and since then a preservation order has safeguarded the whole of the town centre.

Like no other town, Telč radiates a sensuality, a rhythmic musicality testifying to a cultivated Renaissance zest for life even far removed from cultural centres and seats of power. It contrasts strangely with that depressingly banal poverty which socialism created and from which people at the end of the 20th century are only just recovering. Only now are they beginning to shrug off such burdens, lift their heads high and take fate into their own hands—to live instead of having their lives lived for them.

It is not always just ingenious planning or mistakes on the part of the architects which determine the success or failure of civic squares, for on top of that there are often incalculable, unforeseeable circumstances. Investors may opt out, fluctuations in the economy may thwart construction projects and necessary links with other parts of the city may not be satisfactorily realized. Between 1989 and 1991, the German-Canadian architect Eberhard Zeidler drafted the masterplan for the *Media Park* in Cologne, containing one of the most attractive civic square designs in recent German history. Zeidler was confronted with the superficial criticism that he had simply imitated the *Campo Pubblico* in Siena, but a detailed comparison shows that this accusation is false. What Zeidler did was to study the plans of all the civic squares throughout the two thousand year history of the city of Cologne, transfer them onto transparencies and lay them one on top of the other. From this blend he distilled a condensate rich in tradition, projecting a diachronic view of Cologne's city history into the future.

Although the *Media Park* is supposed to be developed with the full range of buildings which go to make up a modern city—for cultural events, education and science, high-tech companies, housing, administration, small forward-looking firms—there is no real progress to be seen because major investors have gone bankrupt, radio and TV stations have made alternative arrangements, one architect or another has considerably exceeded his own estimates, and also the road and rail links with the inner city cannot handle what is demanded of them. So instead of a genuinely sensual city flair, the result is an excruciatingly long interim phase, whereby no one actually knows whether the original intentions will ever be realized:

> "Architecture reveals the concept of culture which underlies it more strikingly than any other product of human creativity."[8]

If we take this quotation from the Canadian architect Arthur Erickson seriously and, in light of it, critically review all of the inner city construction projects which have been carried out worldwide over the past decades, the result is enough to make us shudder, especially if we happen to believe that architecture is there to serve the people and that architecture without sense appeal makes people moody, grumpy, at first emotionally unsatisfied and then physically ill.

Baroque, who were not forced to react to public opinion with democratic compromises, which show taste and a thoroughly sensualized view of life.

One of the most beautiful provincial examples of this is the civic square in the south Moravian town of Telč in the Czech Republic. "Because he did not like the miserable wooden huts of his subjects, Zacharias von Neuhaus, the ruler over South Bohemia and South Moravia in the middle of the 16th century, ordered all the houses in Telč to be torn down and a new town to be built of stone according to his strict instructions."[7] The ruler, whose prosperity was maintained by rich silver mines, wanted a town that would match the magnificent Renaissance castle into which the Italian architect Balthasar Maio da Vomio had converted the family's Gothic residence. Around the triangular civic plaza and market place rose an arrangement of two-storey middle-class houses which looks as though it could have been designed by Mozart as an opera setting on his journey to Prague, if only the main buildings had not already been completed by the end of the 16th century.

Eberhard Zeidler,
Media Park, Cologne,
masterplan, 1989–91

Arthur Erickson, *Robson Square*,
Vancouver, 1973–79

Arthur Erickson, *Robson Square Law Courts*, roof construction,
Vancouver

Arthur Erickson, *Robson Square*, roof lakes with waterfalls
and "stramps", Vancouver

Arthur Erickson, *Robson Square*, view from the roof of the
Law Courts onto the *Art Museum* (the former *Law Courts*)

With *Robson Square* in Vancouver, Erickson
has contributed one of the most convincing
examples of North American architecture achieving a symbiosis of sensuous, functional and aesthetic factors appropriate to the topography of
the country and the needs of the citizens—a
sensitive mixture of nature, culture and technology. Erickson concedes himself that his inner city
park is very different "from the beautiful, hard-
edged space of the Italian or Spanish square."[9]

A relatively sudden change of government in
1972 made it possible to replace plans for a
fifty-five-storey tower to house the courts and
parts of the provincial government of British
Columbia with a terrace-roofed structure ex-
tending over three blocks, with a total of seven
storeys above ground and three below. The site
is bounded to the north by the neoclassical law
court building from 1910, which has since been
converted into an art museum, and to the south

by the new high-tech court building. The two
buildings carry on an exciting architectural and
cultural dialogue with each other and with the
natural area between.

Here provincial government buildings are to
be found beneath a terraced, inner city roof-
park with an artificial lake, waterfalls and lux-
uriant vegetation, laid out by Cornelia Ober-
länder, another German-Canadian, to reflect the
seasons and the regions of British Columbia.
There are always flowers in bloom from the long
spring right into the autumn. During the "Indian
Summer" of early autumn the park is ablaze
with a true symphony of colour. The court
building itself is also well endowed with greenery and is more reminiscent of a Mediterranean
hotel than of typical law court architecture,
which is normally adorned with power attributes such as majestic stairways, porticos and

pillars. Even the courtrooms are light, comfortable, friendly, in fact anything but repressive.

Pyramids of "stramps" (combinations of steps and ramps) connect the individual levels of the park providing easy access for prams and somewhere to sit. In the lower, central part there are cafés, a rink for roller-skating in the summer and ice-skating in the winter, galleries and conference facilities. Here, in keeping with Canadian lifestyle, we find quite a different urbane quality from that typical of European cities. It has a nature-related, clean, bright sensuality

John Eisenmann / George H. Smith,
Cleveland Arcade, old steps,
Cleveland, Ohio, 1888–90

and an uncomplicated *joie de vivre*, which in turn derives pleasure from the aesthetic appeal of technology.

Depending on individual preferences, this can be combined with culinary delights and the enjoyment of one of the country's best art museums. Especially in summer and autumn, Vancouver's citizens and tourists alike seize possession of Robson Square, where they savour communal life and the possibility to sit and relax on the benches of a roof-park in the middle of the city. Even the wait outside courtrooms takes place in a humane, cultivated, comfortable and at the same time nature-related setting.

Jean Baptist Buron / Hippolyte Durand-Gosselin,
Passage Pommeraye, Nantes,
1840–43, lithograph by Benoist

Jean Pierre Cluysenaar, *Galeries St. Hubert*,
side passage called *Galerie de la Reine*,
Brussels, 1846–47, lithograph

Franz Ahrens, *Friedrichstrasse Arcade*,
Berlin, 1908–09

Pomeranzev, state-owned universal department store *GUM*,
Moscow, 1888–93

Market Halls — Arcades — Shopping Malls

By turning our attention to civic squares, we have temporarily lost sight of the world of consumer goods with regard to eroticism, but by way of the link between market places and market halls, it is easily brought back into focus. Market halls, which are primarily intended to give protection from the inclemency of weather, are temples of sensuous pleasures. Since my schooldays in Stuttgart I have simply never been able to go past the market hall there without stopping for a visit. I always have to go through it, and there I use all my senses and all the pores of my skin, my eyes, nose and ears, to grasp and to absorb the multicultural bustle, the mountains of skilfully arranged fruit, meats, cheeses, fish and exotic delicacies. The architecture of the building radiates solidity and the hard-working qualities of Swabian craftsmanship. From the outside it appears unfriendly, uncommunicative, but on the inside it is invitingly open. It dates from a time when there were no virtual "freewheelers" among architects to evaporate spatial relationships into total transparency.

Inside, a stage setting is created for the world of edible goods, or rather the market place creates its own stage setting. It is in market halls that we see the closest links with the organic architecture of Islamic cities, which do not have many main streets but a confusion of

Emanuele Rocco,
Galleria Umberto I,
Naples, 1887–91

Passages des Panoramas, Paris, 1800, watercolour

cul-de-sacs, which wind among houses with impenetrable outer façades and open inner yards. The *souks* and bazaars are completely organic. It is as though one has to mobilize the body's inner senses, as though one is climbing the inner organs within a body. In a mysterious semi-darkness, cave-like shops lure the passer-by with wares which glitter in the light of swinging lamps and the chanting tones of merchants' voices. The haggling and bargaining begins. If the deal is made so that neither party feels cheated, it is sealed with a conciliatory mocha or tea.

The French *passages*, Italian *gallerias* and English arcades of the 19th century introduce a dynamic element into the transitory experience of space in market halls and bazaars: they constitute the type of building whose deliberate intention it is to draw in the visitor, the *flaneur*, the customer, and to lead him through. They are passages through which one passes, and in passing something occurs. They become spaces to be experienced:

> "Seen in a historical context, a *passage* is primarily a corridor, a room with a beginning and an end. But the shell enclosing this room is a building with an independent existence and its function differs too. The user of a *passage* is a passer-through."[10]

Johann Friedrich Geist, who has gathered *passages* together and made them accessible to all who are interested, offers his German readers the following definition:

> "In German, the French word *passage* is used to denote an alley with a glass roof connecting two busy parallel streets, lined all along both sides with individual shops. The upper storeys may contain shops, offices, workshops or living quarters. The *passage* is an organizational form for retail trade. It creates a public space on a privately owned site, decongests busy streets and offers a short-cut between them, provides shelter from the weather and spaces which are strictly reserved for pedestrians. The intention was that these advantages should secure the business success of the tenants and thus of the proprietor of the *passage*."[11]

Later he adds:

> "The illusory element of the *passage* is its space: interior space conceived as exterior space— façades and exterior architecture drawn into an interior."[12]

Thus the *passage* is per se an erotic space. In his *Carceri*, Piranesi created such spaces purely as architectural fantasies, presented for the first time with all the undertones of sadism, power and violence which characterize the other side of eroticism, the one usually hidden from the public eye. Such arcades are places of erotic seduction, where passers-by are lured into looking in the windows of the little shops, drawn into the intimacy of the shop's interior, given individual service and playfully deluded into believing in the exclusiveness of a purchase. A de luxe industry for de luxe creatures. The item purchased is not so important. The most important thing is the act of buying.

Externally the passages emphasize the light-hearted side of this erotic procedure. With extravagant and intricate ornament—colourful wall paintings and flower arrangements, advertisements, sculptures and half reliefs—they present themselves frankly as places with a female connotation. And in Paris at least, painters and caricaturists have made thorough use of the opportunity to depict these passages quite plainly as places of seduction and flirting, as the hunting grounds of adventuresses and coquettish courtesans.

In the architectural style of the various arcades, regional or national characteristics are

Giuseppe Mengoni, *Galleria Vittorio Emanuele II*, Milan, 1865–67

quite clearly visible, albeit in stereotypical form. The spectrum ranges from bright and lively (Bath, *The Corridor*, 1825) and coquettishly frivolous (Paris, *Palais Royal*, 1768–1788, *Galerie Vivienne*, 1824–1825) to pompously elegant (Brussels, *Galeries St. Hubert*, 1846–1847), magnificently Piranesi-like (Berlin, *Friedrichstrassenpassage*, with a two-storey bridge, 1908–1909) and playfully technical (*Cleveland Arcade*, 1888–1889). And the *Galleria Vittorio Emanuele II* in Milan (1865–1867) is grand

opera, a romantic drama, Verdi and Puccini in architectural form, fateful, addicted to eroticism.

The market hall, the bazaar and the arcade undergo further developments, are condensed into department stores and expanded again as shopping malls, and today they again have clearly distinguishable features.

It became policy to diversify the range of stock and arrange it vertically under one roof according to the motto "attract the crowds and seduce them to stay",[13] and this applied at least

for a limited time to those splendid grands magasins in Paris like the *Louvre* (1855), the *Printemps* (1865), the *Samaritaine* (1869), the *Bon Marché* (1876), or more recently the *Trois Quartiers* or the *Galeries Lafayette* or to *Harrods* in London, *Bloomingdales* or *Macy's* in New York, the *Gum* in Moscow or the *KaDeWe* in Berlin. While such examples, including the *Gum*, actively involve architecture in their playful sensuousness and strive for a synthesis of French château and grand opera,

Rüdiger Kramm,
Zeilgalerie les Facettes,
Frankfurt am Main, 1991–92

Eberhard Zeidler,
Eaton Centre,
Toronto, 1972–79

with domed roof lights, glass-roofed squares, magnificently curved staircases, balustrades, filigreed connecting bridges, the more recent examples are more intent on the lucrative exploitation of floor space, although still revelling in a demonstration of wares in excessive supply. In the course of time, the role played by the public has been gradually edged out of the limelight as the products take centre stage, thus complying with the axioms of capitalism. It is nevertheless with sensual finesse that the food hall of the *KaDeWe*, for example, which has taken over the role of the market hall, offers 200 varieties of fish, over 800 sorts of cooked meat and 1500 cheeses—whose mouth refuses to water at such a sensuous prospect?

The overcrowding of department stores is a phenomenon of our modern society that calls out for new forms of shopping. The example of *Harrods* in London, for example, which only three decades ago was a last refuge of eccentric, British shopping culture, shows how difficult it is to preserve a veneer of refinement, luxury and exclusivity when there are several thousand local inhabitants and tourists pouring through the building every day, and when shorts and jeans now prevail where not long ago expensively perfumed and tastefully dressed ladies and gentlemen were ushered by their liveried chauffeurs into the distinguished atmosphere of deep-pile carpets, glittering chandeliers and an array of goods which spelled luxury. Since no one feels intimidated any longer by the institution *Harrods*—although this does not necessarily increase profits—it has become difficult to preserve that aura of sensuality and the display of eroticism:

> "The shopping mall has become the female temple...
> Men rule the outside, women the inside...
> Women have wombs and men have penises; ergo women protect and men project...
> It means that we all inhabit two worlds, one of projection that is artificial, abstract and male; the other of protection that is sensual, informal and female."[14]

Aaron Betzky knows himself that this centuries-old allotment of gender roles is a construction which today can no longer be maintained, and that for a long time it has been in a process of fluid and gradual change. This can be demonstrated by looking at the architecture of department stores and rediscovered arcades and at the people to be found there, as pictured in old photographs. Numerous passages, gallerias and arcades were either bombed in World War II or demolished in the '50s and '60s as being unprofitable. In the '70s, however, both the architecturally faceless shopping malls in the outer sub-

urbs of American and Canadian cities as well as the established inner city department stores suffered a serious drop in turnover.

It was Eberhard Zeidler who, with the building of his *Eaton Centre* in Toronto between 1972 and 1979, made a fresh start which was to set a new precedent worldwide.[15] He studied the architectures of old passages and gallerias in Europe and the USA, whereby he took as his models not only the *Galleria* in Milan and the *Cleveland Arcade*, but also examples of world fair architecture like the *Crystal Palace* in London of 1851. The result was a very independent solution involving the interconnection of two enormous "department stores" housing 300 individual shops and restaurants on three floors along both sides of a 300-metre-long passage. Every photo shows, and every visit makes it blatantly obvious that here the assignment of traditional gender roles, as stated in several publications, is taken to absurd lengths. Nonetheless here the architecture offers an extremely sensual experience, whereby the architect has managed to channel the stupendous streams of visitors (1 million visitors per week, 4.3 million per month, according to figures published in March 1996) so skilfully that the overcrowding effects like at *Harrods*, which largely destroy any sensual ambience, are avoided.

How was this possible? Zeidler was particularly successful in his efforts to give a megastructure human dimensions by creating inner city street scenes on three floors of a large enclosed space. Thus the dimensions here—unlike in other neighbouring buildings—never dwarf the visitor, neither objectively nor subjectively. In addition Zeidler achieved streams of pedestrian traffic which were calculated to meet and cross each other in a rhythmic pattern from both ends of the arcade, across bridges and connecting platforms, up and down stairways and glass lifts.

He integrated quieter zones into the overall structure, corners, angles, seating areas, fountains, plants, and thus created functions, impressions, views, perspectives which are constantly changing. Nautical metaphors alluding to the architect's experience in the navy—gangways, railings, and bridges—combine with high-tech and natural elements. Outside the office windows on the upper floors overlooking the arcade there are small balconies with flower boxes and hanging plants. Michael Snow's spatial fibreglass sculpture of sixty Canadian geese in flight forms a uniquely eye-catching focus offering perspectives which change with the angle of vision. The overall impression is one of solid materials, elegance and a generally buoyant atmosphere.

Commercial building projects, with the exception of certain prestigious buildings, are generally considered by architects, critics, the architecturally interested public and sometimes even by the clients themselves to be dishonourable, and so for the architects there is usually very little prestige to be earned from them. The question arises whether this is an expression of a universally bad conscience at having dealings with the devil "big business". I would say that what is called for is a diametrically opposed way of thinking. Since it is an undeniable fact that we are living in a capitalistic consumer society, the general public should interfere much more in commercial building projects. Good, interesting and exciting shopping architecture should once again become a question of prestige. That is the only way in which the sensuous qualities of experience in the city can be salvaged on a large scale and the trend towards those unspeakable architectural monstrosities which pass as shopping centres can be reversed. For when the virtual department store finally comes to prevail, cities which are drained of their own sensuality will go to rack and ruin.

In the meantime, traditional department stores have developed a very varied and flexible "shop-in-shop" system, which makes it possible to divide up large floor areas into smaller units; to adapt unprofitable spaces to changes in fashion quickly and without any great capital investment; to share out the risk by taking in independent retailers and to satisfy the customers' needs for small, intimate departments with friendly service:

> "The large department store is breaking up into a network of narrow lanes lined with little shops or trading stalls which offer the *couturiers,* the fashion designers, the furriers, including the most famous like Saint Laurent, Chanel, Fath, Lagerfeld, a high degree of autonomy—and all under one big roof."[16]

From this development and an idea of Friedrich Kiesler's, who in 1925 designed a Paris department store in the shape of a spiral, the Darmstadt architect Rüdiger Kramm derived the inspiration for his *Zeilgalerie les Facettes* in Frankfurt as a combination of arcade and vertical department store. Seldom has so much thorough and intelligent consideration gone into a commercial building project. Nevertheless the *Zeilgalerie* has had, at least from a business point of view, only moderate success; in actual fact, it has been a considerable flop. What might be the reason for this, when so much effort was invested in Germany's most lucrative but architecturally unimaginative shopping precinct to create a fresh and sensuous commercial architecture which is, an architecture meant to be experienced?

Apart from the incorrect floor area calculations which the fraudulent developer Jürgen Schneider foisted on his main investor, the Deutsche Bank, it must at least in part be due to the switching off—for financial reasons—of the arcade's unique attraction, an interactive media façade. A more important reason, however, is almost certainly the miscalculation in channelling the flow of visitors, who, having travelled up eight floors on the escalator, were indeed confronted with an exciting scene, pulsing with life and enriched with many an aesthetic element of surprise, with one main drawback: the only way down was on foot, by way of a steep spiral, which—as in the case of Frank Lloyd Wright's *Guggenheim Museum*—proved not entirely unproblematic. Also there were no connecting bridges, and because of the lack of floor space and the extremely high rents, the shops were often disappointingly small.

Since hardly anyone likes to be watched by crowds of passers-by, for example when buying jewellery or clothes, most people just stroll past without buying. There can be no doubt that the *Zeilgalerie* is an aesthetic and sensuous enrichment to city life in Frankfurt and that it is also very popular with the majority of young people. But that alone cannot guarantee financial success. As in the case of Hans Hollein's famous and widely published *Haas House* on the Stephansplatz (St. Stephen's Square) in Vienna, too much has been attempted in too small a space. A touristic attraction alone is not enough. Hollein overloaded his building

Granville Island Hotel,
1985–86

Entrance to Granville Island under
the *Granville Island Bridge*

Granville Island Arts Club Theatre,
1984–85

Granville Island Sea Village

What then is the correct approach? What solutions are there to make our cities more inhabitable, more endearing, more sensuous? How is it possible to counteract increasing abstraction, total digitalization, the virtual city? There are no doubt benefits and a great fascination in surfing the Internet and the World Wide Web, but both largely ignore people's physical and spiritual needs.

On the basis of three contemporary case studies, let us investigate these questions so that afterwards we can develop some suggestions for combatting the growing tendency of cities all over the world to develop into urban deserts, and for making use of the parallel worldwide tendency towards a civilization based on technology and media, especially as it involves or ignores the aspect of an architecture addressing the senses.

1) Granville Island, Vancouver

The first example is again from Vancouver, and it concerns an entire city district, Granville Island. A small island situated in the False Creek inlet which divides downtown Vancouver from the southern suburbs, at the beginning of the '70s Granville Island was no more than a dilapidated, rotting ghost town. Beneath the huge steel structure of Granville Bridge, scruffy little ramshackle businesses and tumbledown industrial plants eked out a meagre livelihood. What was once one of the city's original settlements had degenerated into an eyesore.

In 1971 the Canadian government decided to launch an exemplary scheme for new urban development. It bought up the land, appointed the architect Norman Hotson as head of planning and invested Can. $20 million.[17] The years which followed saw perhaps the most astounding Cinderella-like transformation known to modern urban history. In 1972 the planning began, in 1977 Granville Island was opened to the public and 1988 marked the beginning of the second phase of building, which has since been completed. Hotson was given the task of developing a masterplan and drafting a concept for the island's public spaces, such as roads, small parks, squares and parking lots. In addition it was his job to make practical suggestions for recycling the existing business structures and propose guidelines for the shapes and dimensions of buildings on the island, according to which the various architects would be able to set to work.

The plan was to build an urban area in which art and theatre would mix with small industrial plants, offices, markets and shipyards. Sea Vil-

with gimmicks, such as sensuous materials or ideas, as if to say: Look how versatile I am! Kramm, however, has not paid enough attention to sales psychology in spite of an aesthetically convincing philosophy, and perhaps without

even intending it he has found himself taking certain risks, something which would scarcely have happened to such a critical professional in commercial architecture as Eberhard Zeidler.

Sensuousness and poetry: rust on Granville Island, 1986

Corrugated iron and rust on Granville Island, detail, 1986

lage, a houseboat village directly adjoining Granville Island, was also integrated as a further residential area. For the second phase of development a ring of houses containing privately owned apartments was projected on the mainland opposite Granville Island, with buildings limited to a height of five storeys. From the very beginning the plans included multisensory elements: architectural surprises, entertainment, pleasure, sensual enjoyment for the eyes and the ears, for the nose and the palate. Precisely when such things are planned, they often end in synthetic amusement and sterility; but here in fact the opposite was the case. The Canadian mentality and ethnic mix not only accepted what was offered, but subjected it to further developments of their own choosing. In the summer Granville Island bursts with vitality, but without having turned into a tourist ghetto. For the rest of the year the local people are clearly in the majority.

For business people, to whom profit is more important than architectural flair, the bottom

line is also positive. Turnover on Granville Island has struck fear into Vancouver's traditional shopping centres, and as long as the shops retain their individual touch and do not become branches of chain stores, success should continue and even gain momentum. Where else outside Asia, for example, is it possible to find a shop with 2,000 kites?

Several factors contributed to this result. Some of them are perfectly simple architectural principles, like, for example, not turning the whole island into a pedestrian precinct. Instead all the roads were cobbled and then built without pavements so that motorists were forced to drive at walking pace. The mingling of the various road users and the increase in road safety have the effect that, like in oriental or medieval cities, the island is generally awhirl, teeming crowds and vehicles weaving this way and that.

But unity is preserved among all the variety. With the exception of a few "post and beam constructions" made of wood and glass for restaurants and market halls, all the buildings are built

in corrugated iron, however colourful, eccentric or full of post-modern quotation they may be. That reduces the building costs and lends the whole quarter a playful but rough and industrial pioneering charm, and a high-tech look which does not, however, submit to short-lived throwaway fashions. For they are either old corrugated iron buildings which have been revitalized, or new ones showing off·elements of modernist or post-modernist style, both of which still yield to the cheerful, democratic dictates of corrugated iron.

In addition, Norman Hotson designed a system of railings, handrails and tubular steel constructions which runs almost like a leitmotif throughout the island and to which the brightly coloured awnings of the shops can be fastened to give shelter from the rain or sun. Hotson copied this from Hans Hollein's play-street built for the 1972 Olympic Games in Munich, and he took the original idea—as perhaps Hollein himself—from Bernard Rudofsky's book *Streets for People* (1969).[18] There it can be seen that as

Entrance to a storage shed on
Granville Island, 1986

early as 1847 New York's Chatham Square had turned into a bustling shopping centre following the same principles.

It proved important for Granville Island that emphasis was placed on preserving existing industries and attracting new ones. Thus there are chain-making factories, forges, boatyards, and anyone is allowed access to anywhere to watch as long as it does not disturb the workers. There is a cement works in the middle of the island, which is a massive, picturesque industrial monument. There a master brewer from Bavaria, who, after analysing the Vancouver water declared that there was none better for brewing beer, founded the "Island Lager Brewery", which brews an excellent Pilsener beer. The fact that trade and industry can be directly and personally experienced everywhere, without degenerating into a tourist folklore attraction, contributes significantly to the sensuous ambience of the island.

Finally artists, gallery owners, shopkeepers and boutique owners set up on Granville Island, as well as architects and the operators of exotic travel agencies offering adventure tours to the north of Canada, to the Arctic and to the most

remote islands. In their wake came the boat outfitters and expedition specialists. On Granville Island there are two theatres, an art academy, an art school for children, several artists' studios, a post-modern high-tech hotel with bizarre works of art, and both popular and rustic restaurants. The owners of the houseboats are just as individualistic as their homes are imaginative and charmingly neat.

The gem in this ensemble is the large market hall, *Granville Island Public Market*, a symphony of flowers and fruits, meats and cheeses, wines and spices, fish, fish and yet more fish, the likes of which can be seen in very few places in Europe, enormous salmon, trout, halibut, turbot, angler fish, lobsters, prawns, shrimps...

Over 70 percent of Vancouver's population are not native born, but have poured into the city from 140 countries all over the globe. They all buy and many of them sell. This exotic mixture alone guarantees variety and imagination, important ingredients of urban sensuousness. Here the architecture plays a dominant part and is far more than just a diorama or a backdrop, for just like the homogeneous or the organically complex city architecture to be found in Europe it provides identification.

Like everywhere in Canada and the USA, and although Vancouver is only 110 years old, history has a central role to play. Here history is present in the form of corrugated iron, the poor man's building material used for sheds and small businesses from the pioneer days, robust, flexible, and cheap. Since those days it has been democratically raised to a status of nobility, and on Granville Island it is now used on trendy boutiques as well as business premises, office buildings, art academies and theatres.

In this great multicultural concert, corrugated iron architecture acts as a colourful eye-catcher, as a utility architecture, rustic and yet playful, combining high-tech with Post-modernism.

There have been many attempts to imitate Granville Island, although without any spectacular success. Norman Hotson himself tried to create a counterpart to it in North Vancouver and was commissioned to draw up similar plans for several American, Australian and Asian cities, but Granville Island has remained a one-and-only showpiece, a unique stroke of luck, thanks to its topographical location, the prevailing conditions, the population, structure and architecture. This shows that such concepts cannot be imitated, but that they can provide encouragement to summon up the daring and imagination for tackling other original and similarly local projects.

2) *Butler's Wharf* and *Shad Thames*

The dramatic structural change from an industrial society to a post-modern service-orientated society, one that is taking place with considerable vehemence in the mother country of industrialization, is scarcely discernible in the architecture of London's West End or even the City, awash in dealings in immaterial goods like information, data and money as it is. In London's Docklands, however, a district stretching for several miles and hosting businesses and industries as well as docks, the unadorned reality of this upheaval is visible in all of its job-killing brutality.

An area of 2,226 hectares has been designated for redevelopment in the heart of industrial London, where right into the '60s and early '70s hundreds of ships were loaded, unloaded and repaired, where warehouses of all kinds overflowed with goods, and where the full range of industries manufacturing marine supplies had settled. Dozens of teams of architects have been working since the early '80s to convert old industrial sites into residential areas and create new ones to attract new businesses.

In 1987 Olympia & York, which belonged to the Reichmann brothers from Toronto and at the time was the area's most firmly established and financially powerful property development company, embarked on the biggest commercial building project in the world, *Canary Wharf*. The plan was for a new "in vitro" financial quarter to match the City, with several million square metres of office space, smokeless industries, shops, hotels, restaurants, pubs and museums. The unbridled entrepreneurial capitalism of the Thatcher era granted developers a number of privileges which made it possible for the Reichmanns, with the help of numerous internationally renowned architects, to start to work on conjuring an operational city the likes of which have never been seen since Babylon out of the marshland along the Thames, and that within a space of only ten years.

The doubts voiced by the whole architectural press, both national and international, should have been a warning. This scepticism was sparked off by the deficiencies in the infrastructure which were particularly evident in the early years of the project, especially the road and underground rail links, as well as by the lack of confidence in the economic trends in Britain and the unwillingness of many executives to move out of the City into a no-man's-land down the river. If there was any truth, however, in Olympia & York's glossy prospectuses of the early years, what was to be built there was a city paradise between the river, numerous harbour basins and newly laid out areas of greenery.

The financial empire of the Reichmanns, however, whose taxable assets at the beginning of the '90s were estimated at $25 billion, started to founder in 1993, and the final collapse was due partly to the unsatisfactory utilization of development capacity and a rental income which was considerably lower than that calculated in advance, but due ultimately to the low price of oil. The Reichmanns, who were heavily engaged in the oil carrier business, had based the project's funding on a barrel price of US $18–19. When the barrel price dropped to $16, or at times even to $12–13, the Reichmanns were no longer able to pay off their interest rates.

In spite of this, *Canary Wharf* did not go under with the collapse of Olympia & York. The development has not only slowed down but also slimmed down, however, and in future it will presumably run according to a more flexible plan. Thus there is quite a good chance that the Isle of Dogs, with *Canary Wharf* as the centrepiece of Docklands, will be pulsing with sensual life in ten or twenty years and could turn out to be one of London's most attractive urban districts.

In terms of architectural revitalization, there are a number of failures on view in Docklands, but also a few extremely successful attempts. Or in the words of Stephanie Williams:

"London's Docklands contains one of the worst collections of late 20th-century buildings to be seen anywhere in the world. It is a marvel, if it were not so embarrassing, that so many very bad buildings from the same period can be found in such a comparatively small area of the city, massed so closely, and so incongruously, together.... And yet it is to Docklands that you must go to find some of the best British architecture of the 1980s..."[19]

Among the rare gems is the redevelopment of *St. Katherine's Docks* below the Tower, and *Tower Bridge* on the left bank of the Thames and directly opposite *Butler's Wharf* and *Shad Thames*. Only a few minutes' walk from the old royal cit-

Metropolitan Wharf, London

Butler's Wharf, London, under renovation since 1987

adel of the Tower of London across Tower Bridge lies Bermondsey, a district which for centuries was the capital's commercial centre and which now opens up a vista into another world.

Together with the *Anchor Brewhouse*, *Butler's Wharf* forms the biggest single complex of historical buildings in Docklands. There, all buildings were focused on the Thames or the harbour basins, while from the rear, the side

facing the street, they were rather unprepossessing, hard, even grim. On the other side of the street came the businesses and small factories with smoke-blackened chimneys, where the air was filled with chemical fumes, and beyond those there was the cheap housing of the dockworkers' families.

And so *Butler's Wharf* and the long street behind it, *Shad Thames*, together with the

Shad Thames, London

Shad Thames, London

Horselydown Lane, London

Shad Thames, inner yard with fountain, London

neighbouring streets and alleys, form a unity, an urban district which, in terms of size, is similar to Granville Island. Since the end of the '80s, after a general period of decline and decay, new forms of city life have been emerging there based on the old architectural fabric, as in a biotope. The special sensuous charm of this district derives from its working past. Every pore of these brick-built warehouses, some of them unfriendly and yet some tremendously theatrical, still exhales the perspiration from heavy manual labour and the amassing of capital.

Many of the old office buildings and warehouses, especially in *Shad Thames*, look like Sardinian mountain fortresses, with barred windows, loopholes and bizarre projections for goods lifts, with cranes whose gallows-like jibs

cast grotesque shadows on the weathered brickwork. At various heights roofed-in bridges cross the narrow streets for wheeling barrows from warehouse to warehouse. A network of wrought-iron catwalks, with or without railings and partly clad in corrugated iron, criss-crosses over the narrow alleys to link the riverside with the warehouses lying anything up to 130 metres inland.

The dismal feel of "satanic gloom" derives of course from the security measures which were necessary in the 19th century as protection against organized crime, a powerful entity which also demanded to share in the colonial wealth of the metropolis. Anyone who has read Dickens' later novels is gripped even today by a thrill of apprehension as he roams through these

narrow streets, especially in the evenings or on foggy autumn days:

> "This area of Bermondsey drew forth some of Dickens' most graphic portraits of poverty; Gustave Doré immortalized its infernal atmosphere."[20]

The tingling sensuous charm of these houses derives on the one hand from the texture of their weathered brick façades, the barred windows, the rust in all its shimmering stages of decay, the loud colours of the loading doors on various floors of the warehouses. One can easily imagine a door, a number of doors or even all of them suddenly opening in unison, singers appearing and an opera or a surrealistic film beginning. Like perhaps no one before him, the

Gerd Winner, *Clink Wharf*, silk-screen print, 1971

Gerd Winner, *London Docks—St. Katharine's Way*, silk-screen print, 1970

painter Gerd Winner, who spent years studying the old city structures of New York and the London docks, has brought out in his photographic compositions—which he projects on to silk-screens and then paints over with a brush—the erotic charm of these buildings.[21]

As if with x-ray eyes, Winner dives under their skin of stone and wood. Ambiguous symbols like the flaking layers of paint and brick are condensed to signals of mystery, temptation, decadence, sin, disappointment, and shudders of unfathomable eroticism in the spirit of Georges Bataille. Often this architecture also radiates a fair measure of brutality, violence and shackling metaphors. They express, as it were, a sadism in architectural form which reveals a sinister side of the British soul, as lived out under cover of bourgeois and aristocratic propriety in the 18th and 19th centuries by "rakes", the likes of the Earl of Rochester.

On the other hand this tingling sensation is also a result of the architectural collage of surgical operations carried out on the houses which have already been restored or rebuilt. Such operations usually involve windows, doors and staircase structures, and although often conducted very carefully, the result can occasionally come as a shock. The warehouses are converted mainly into living accommodation with apartments in the loft and a smaller area reserved for office space. Windows of various sizes, often with colourful frames, wrought iron balconies and elegantly curved, galvanized fire escapes take up the old motifs but adapt them to domestic contexts, as when the old wooden loading doors are replaced with large window units made up of smaller elements with coloured steel frames.

Openings afford intimate glimpses into backyards and enclosed courtyards which were once the scene of heavy manual labour, but where today a creative mix of travel agents, lawyers, architects, estate agents, filmmakers, fashion designers, agencies and small computer firms makes its living. This is a scene which is no less hard-working, but lacks the smell, sweat, and is certainly a lot quieter than it used to be.

That is also something which distinguishes *Butler's Wharf* from the cheery bustle of Granville Island. Both have artists' studios, small workshops, galleries and restaurants, but British understatement makes for a cooler tone, and although the Tower is not far away there are not many tourists who stray into this area. Those who do usually visit the Design Museum, which, like Saffron Wharf and Michael Hopkins' *David Mellor Building*, was designed at the end of the '80s, in this case by the firm of Conran Roche in a style perpetuating Bauhaus modern-

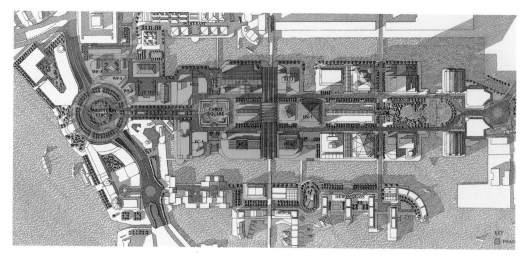

Canary Wharf, London, masterplan, 1987

Canary Wharf, London, general view, 1987

Cesar Pelli, *Canary Wharf Tower*, London, 1988–93

Canary Wharf
Station, London

ism and bringing the tension of contrast into the warehouse scenery of the 19th century.

It can happen that one pauses in front of a particularly grim façade in *Shad Thames* and sees in one's mind's eye the pale and emaciated child labourers from the early days of capitalism slaving away in vaulted cellars, just as Dickens described them. Then suddenly there is a soft, whirring sound and the electric doors of those cellars, which have now been converted into garages, open up and dispatch a de luxe limousine, a Rolls Royce, a Jaguar or a Mercedes. Often it is the extremely rich who have set up their stylish city apartments behind these façades. This too is one of the ambiguities of the district.

The reverse of British understatement has for centuries been a carefully cultivated eccentricity, which has always found one form of expression in architectural extravagance. There has to be room for this too in the *Butler's Wharf* area. The most impressive example of this is *China Wharf*, a building which was designed by the CZWG Group (Campbell, Zogolovitch, Wilkinson and Gough) and completed in 1988. The inland side of the building is only moderately elegant, wedged between two old warehouses, but the side facing the river is spectacular and, like a "flasher", it reveals everything:

"The audacity of China Wharf is only revealed from the river. The building rises from four bold black painted concrete stanchions in the water, showing a vivid orangey-red (neither proper Chinese lacquer nor red oxide, but BS 04 E51). It

looks like a stack of semi-circular windows cut and assembled using a cookie-cutter. The suspended stern of a boat disappears beneath it."[22]

The river side of the building is a bold steel-and-glass construction with generously dimensioned arch windows in each its seventeen apartments, offering a magnificent view over the Thamesside landscape. The seven-storey row of arches stretches skyward like a pale red, erect phallus.

In comparison with the shrill rave of *China Wharf, Anchor Brewhouse* and *Butler's Wharf*, the head and heart of the whole development area are like a musical with snappy melodies and popular hits. It was here that the brewer John Courage built his first small brewery in 1787, which was extended in 1870 before it was almost completely destroyed by fire in 1891. Between 1893 and 1895 it was rebuilt to include a boiler house designed by Inskip and McKenzie and given the form on which the present building is based. In 1982 Courage had to close down and the building was restored and rebuilt by the team of architects Pollard, Thomas and Edwards. It reopened in 1989 with sixty-two luxury apartments, 400 square metres of office space and a fitness club.

If there is such a thing as cheerful architecture it is to be found in this collage, which must gladden the heart of anyone who does not insist on rigid uniformity of style. With its nautical allusions, its dome-topped tower, its *Captain's Walk* with more than a dozen different window shapes along its subtly and carefully reworked riverside façade, with its squat and sturdy brewhouse, with the steel-and-glass façades which in the top three storeys of the ten-storey building take the place of the wood-panelling, the *Anchor Brewhouse* offers the most refreshing sight and affords the most diverting variety of visual impressions along the river below the City of London. With a bold high-tech flight of steps on the north end, the architects achieved a correlation between historical structural fabric and a contemporary understanding of architecture which points the way to the future.

Directly adjoining the former brewery, the central building complex of *Butler's Wharf* raises its long, massive bulk eight storeys high. It was built in 1871–73 as the largest warehouse building on the Thames and was forced to close exactly a century later. In the years which followed, it quickly fell into disrepair until it was bought in 1984 by Sir Terence Conran, divided up into five apartment blocks and restored (all in all the *Butler's Wharf* development site comprises twenty buildings). Here the Conran Roche architects have created a masterpiece of sensitive renovation and reuse.

To begin with, the buildings had to be given foundations. The arrangement of windows follows the original pattern and the loading doors have been replaced with balconies. On the ground floor there are restaurants and specialist shops, from an up-market grocery store done up in the style of the 19th century to distinguished wine merchants and artistic jewellers. Above that there are eighty-six apartments and twelve two-storey penthouses.

Butler's Wharf shows off its best side towards the promenade along the river. The rear of the building along Shad Thames is rather more rustic but has been equally carefully renovated in yellow brick, and the road cobbled in York stone,

"…except that it is the very opposite of the dangerous, dirty, greasy, wet and heavy working industry that once thrived here."[23]

If on a beautiful summer's evening, as you are dining outside one of the French restaurants along the Thames promenade of *Butler's Wharf*, long-legged models in miniskirts come parading their stylishly diet-conscious bodies in front of the guests as though on a catwalk, and if the setting sun then bathes in its golden glow the massive obelisk shape of Cesar Pelli's *Canary Wharf Tower*—which although several miles away dominates the whole of Docklands as an architectural landmark—thus imbuing this otherwise rather modest tower with the radiance of a precious gem—then this part of London acquires a down-to-earth elegance which very few other sites in Britain's capital can boast.

The realization dawns that the sensuousness of this locality is a result of the contrast between river- and cityscapes, of the various degrees of physicality which the buildings radiate and of their multi-layered symbolism and their multi-sensory appeal. Whether visible or invisible, historical reminiscences in which the buildings and the whole district are steeped, as well as the historical contrast in their utilization play a central part. The bodies of the people assume their designated places, knuckle under, play along, and are absorbed by the dominating presence of the architecture.

3. The *Kaiser Baths* in Aachen

Our third and final case study is architecturally the youngest and yet it is the one with the longest history. Since time immemorial hot springs have been welling out of the ground where the slate hills of the Rhine meet the fertile plain around Jülich, but it was the Romans who finally put them to medical and economic use, to

Ernst Kasper / Klaus Klever, *Kaiser Baths (Kaiserbad)*, Aachen, 1993–94, windows reflecting St. Foillan's Church and the cathedral

Kasper / Klever, *Kaiser Baths*, Aachen, façade on the *Büchel*

Kasper / Klever, *Kaiser Baths*, Aachen, window

ease their rheumatic aches and pains and regenerate their gout-ridden joints, here just as they did wherever they settled in the inhospitality of Germania or the desolation of Britannia.

And so it was that the city which we know today as Aachen was founded about the year 15 A.D. as a Roman spa town with its centre around the biggest concentration of thermal springs on the southeast slope of what is now the market hill, known as the *Büchel*. Extensive bathing facilities, various trades and crafts, factories, temples and hostelries grew up around the springs. According to Roman principles, the streets in the rapidly growing town intersected at right angles, a system which has been preserved to the present day. In 355 A.D. the region around Aachen was conquered by the Franconians, who in comparison with the Romans could even be called barbarians, and subsequently the hot springs fell into disuse. The spring known even at that time as the Kaiser's or Emperor's Spring (*Kaiserquelle*) is not mentioned again until King Pippinus III fought a

duel there in 765 A.D. and it is said to have been soiled with blood, fat and putrefaction:

"Under Pippinus' son Karl, Aachen regained its grandeur and importance. Karl built a palatinate, and the decisive factor for the choice of location was the existence of the hot springs. Einhard reports at length on Karl's particular liking for bathing in the hot water and that Karl visited the thermal spa to swim with his sons, with guests and even with his whole entourage. There were occasions on which Karl is said to have shared the bath with over a hundred people at one time. Other writers testify to the splendour of the baths."[24]

Throughout the centuries, the baths proved to be an important economic factor for the town. In keeping with contemporary taste and developments in bath culture, they were constantly being rebuilt, extended or supplemented with hotels. When in the 17th century doctors recognized the importance of mineral cures, a new spa centre was set up to accommodate the great influx of visitors near the lower springs, where there was enough space for the obligatory

promenading. Near the Emperor's Spring in the heart of Aachen's historical town centre, however, there were elegant spa hotels right up until World War II, during the course of which the *Kaiser Baths* were badly damaged by bombs and fire.

In 1963 a much more modest, low, flat-roofed construction, embellished with a large slate relief by the sculptor Ewald Mataré, was opened on the side facing the *Büchel*. Only two decades later, however, the building no longer satisfied the demands made on a modern thermal spa and the bath was finally closed to the public in 1984.

The question then arose of what to do about the resulting vacuum in the centre of Aachen: what should become of a site with such a remarkable cultural history, a site which in a certain respect at least played a decisive part in the very founding of the city. In 1990, after years of wrangling and alternative concepts, competition was invited for the building of a square, whereby architects were given the

Kasper / Klever, entrance to the *Kaiser Baths* from the *Coal Building*, Aachen, 1993–94

widest possible scope with regard to the public uses to which the square might be put. The rules of the competition insisted upon two stipulations, however:
– the safeguarding of a view of the cathedral from a certain vantage point on the *Büchel*;
– an architectural representation of the historical link between the site, the spring and its use over a period of almost 2,000 years.[25]

The competition ended with a joint first place being awarded to three drafts, submitted by Joachim and Margot Schürmann from Berlin, Kay Friedrichs from Aachen and the partnership of Ernst Kasper and Klaus Klever, also from Aachen. After a revision phase, the Aachen city council finally settled in 1991 for the Kasper/Klever draft and, as investors, the Ceszkowskis (husband and wife) entered into a contract giving them the hereditary right to develop the property. Starting in April 1993 the remaining buildings on the site were demolished and in October 1994 the new *Kaiser Baths* were opened.

The result is a civic square with three buildings which are uncompromisingly modern in design. In terms of three-dimensional shape, delicate sensuousness and its capacity for dialogue with the outstanding architectural monuments in Aachen's historical town centre, this draft is unequalled in recent German architectural history.

The two architects did not make life easy either for themselves or for the majority of the population in Aachen, however, since they had not designed an architecture which aims to please and is easy on the observer, but one which follows a tenet of art which says that real art—thus architecture too—involves overcoming resistances, that it forces the observer and user to do some rethinking and to see things in a fresh light, and that it does not throw itself at the observer but wants to be discovered, suffered, and experienced in a process of lively confrontation.

Here it is the deconstructivist elements which achieve this effect, the diagonals, the acute angles, the risky balancing acts, the unusual perspectives, the vortices and suction effects which arise, as well as the colours, materials and textures of the surfaces. At the same time it is precisely those elements which go to make up the playfully experimental character which is the special distinguishing feature of this architecture, with all due respect for the sound quality of the planning and construction. This is supported by the architectural confrontation with Aachen's urban history from the Middle Ages to the 1960s, in as far as this draft not only seeks a dialogue with the medieval and Renaissance

Restaurant and remains of the arcade pillars, *Kaiser Baths*, Aachen, 1993–94

Spring Square, Kaiser Baths, Aachen, 1993–94

buildings which have attained nobility by virtue of history, but also integrates into the new ensemble a much-maligned stepchild of the '60s, the *Haus der Kohle (Coal Building)*, standing on pillars on the south side of the square. And lo and behold, it plays its role with dignity and proves itself to be an honest, if not exactly outstanding example of modernism.

According to the two architects, the concept for the new *Kaiser Bath* starts with the edges of

the square and works its way inwards to the centre. It reacts to the immediate urban surroundings, supplements them, supports existing shapes and creates new ones. The architects see their buildings primarily as sculptural figures:

"Three buildings, more sculptural shapes than structured pieces of architecture, form by their very arrangement a field of tension. In the centre is the *Quellplatz (Spring Square)*—analogous to the ancient swampy headwaters and a symbol of life

Kasper / Klever, *Spring Square, Kaiser Baths*, Aachen, 1993–94

and the birth of the city. The square was not a condition but the result."[26]

These swampy headwaters are also an eminently sensual and eminently female symbol. The architectural solution of allowing the spring to well up out of a bed of green gneiss shingle cobbles and granite strips and to drain away again into the gaps between the shingle cobbles is discreetly erotic, visual and tactile. The *Spring Square* assumes the function of a mythical place of energy, of regeneration, but also of calm:

> "If we had managed to heat the running water, in cool weather the place would have been shrouded in mist. The mythicization of the place would then have been complete."[27]

The whole arrangement of the square and its buildings, however, is suffused with sensuous and profoundly erotic principles. Here the warm colours of the surfaces play their part, as well as their textural skins and wraps, for example when from a vantage point on the *Büchel* one looks down at the first building with the V-shaped indentation carved into it, allowing a view of the cathedral, or at the side of the second building which faces the square with its green trelliswork:

> "The trelliswork is like a negligée which veils and yet doesn't veil, like gossamer."[28]

The sensuous dark red of the third group of buildings on the square acts like a signal referring the viewer to the *Red House* on the *Büchel*, but it also alludes to the red of the Romans and

Charlemagne's red. Apart from that, it is a colour which triggers a surge of adrenalin with its intensity, emphasizing the sensuous tension between the groups of buildings. The buildings communicate with each other and with the whole of the surrounding architecture, but always end up orientating themselves towards the cathedral and the parish church of St. Foillan.

A further erotic principle is to be found in the specifically dynamic physicality of the buildings, which are sculptural and offer surprises, new aspects and insights from all four sides. This is supported by the mirror effects of the *Aachen Window* and the inward-facing façade of the first building on the square, and by the interaction between inside and outside, especially in the second building: striking a pose, taking up the "Mirror, mirror on the wall..." stance, emphasizing, reinforcing, and duplicating. Playful vanity is just as much part of eroticism as peeping and glimpsing, as is the play of niches and nooks, of narrow gaps and wide openings:

> "As I look along the ground level, I see stairs which appear to lead into an inner room. But that is not the case. Going up them is like the first move in a game which has not yet begun, which is no more than a project. That is the game of opposites, a game of hide-and-seek, the game of concealment and revelation."[29]

Part of this game also are the varying effects of the *Kaiser Baths* complex in the rain and in sunshine, by day and by night. *La belle de jour, la belle de nuit.* Especially the square's inner

courtyard and its adjoining façades seem to be constantly donning new apparel.

It is Kasper and Klever's great achievement that, unlike Hollein's *Haas House*, and in spite of the limited space, their *Kaiser Baths*, with its great wealth of multisensory effects, never appears overladen, but rather gives the impression that all its sensuous details have been minutely planned:

> "Plunged into a sensuous whirl, we join the old and the new, the far and the near—with the cathedral leading the way—in a magical initiation, during which the spring wells out of the ground, the roofs fly away, the walls cave in and the sky is sucked down into the square."[30]

Critics have accused the Aachen architects of having imitated Frank Gehry's sculptural building complexes. Indeed it cannot be denied that there is a certain affinity. Gehry's work can no doubt be counted among the formative architectural influences of our time, and anyone who thinks sculpturally, loves surprising effects and has a good sense of humour tends to assimilate Gehry, as if by osmosis. But Kasper and Klever possess such a powerful sense of shape of their own that there can be no question of imitation. In terms of poetic and contextual sensuousness, their *Kaiser Baths* surpasses any of the unconventional assortments of shapes that Gehry has produced so far.

After initial storms of protest and abuse, and even threats of physical violence from those people who regard the presence of modern architecture on this particular site as an affront, the great majority of the population in Aachen has since wholeheartedly accepted the new *Kaiser Baths*, partly because of the functional variety it offers, including shops, apartments, offices and public spaces for exhibitions and events organized by the city administration. And as far as the symbiosis of old and new is concerned, the *Kaiser Baths* is one of the very few examples of new architecture which not only support an aura of urban sensuousness, but actually create one, for here there is neither a busy market nor the bustle of shoppers to play a major role. The architecture sensitizes all who are prepared to open their minds and their senses to it; it gives them pleasure, establishes communicative links with its surroundings and proves that even contemporary city architecture can be sensuous and radiate an erotic flair.

Conclusion

Living within one's wishes, seeing the city as a repository in which wishes are collected, as Calvino so poetically described it, is the topic of this chapter, and justifiably so, for only those who have wishes, formulate them and strive to realize them can change anything. Like eroticism, wishes have a lot to do with imagination, and imagination has a lot to do with psychology. In the present context then, the psychology of architecture is the discipline which needs to be consulted.

How can urbanity be achieved? What role can architecture play? Those were the initial questions upon which the ideas and examples in this section were based. The conclusion reached was that architecture which aims at creating and imparting an aura of sensuousness must above all be able to fire the imagination, spark off encounters and sensitize people to sensuality. If that is achieved, city people will buy, consume and enjoy. A certain playfulness is appropriate. Eroticism is communication, the satisfying of wishes and desires, and all this is playfully culturalized. This also applies to architecture, advocates variety, eye-catching elements, the interplay of peeps, glimpses and vistas, of concealment and revelation, but not smooth façades. The use of mirror effects should be carefully calculated and never dominate. Look and discover, use the senses to empathize and test. Sensuality and eroticism imply time to spare and a relaxed state of mind.

Thus the sense appeal of a city includes setting up the architecture so that it invites people to stroll idly and to indulge their eyes and ears, even if the *flâneurs* of the likes of Richard Lindner have since become a rarity and the "19th-century *flâneur* who, in order not to lapse into an improper haste which might look like work, took his tortoise for a walk on a silver-studded lead"[31] belongs wholly in the realm of fantasy.

The implication of time extends to architecture itself. As we saw, completely new "test-tube" architecture is scarcely appropriate. Human beings obviously feel most at home when there are historical links which, at least in condensed form, are cast in new architectural shape in order to participate in a dialogue between old and new. For then in the interest of their own emotional balance they can build on things which are familiar to them. That is why Robson Square in Vancouver is so successful, and that is why reuse and revitalization are often much better than new developments. Old and new enter into a dialogue, for this older architecture already shows signs of age and has a story to tell, a biography: plus, patina is sensuous. An aura of sensuousness has more to do with emotionalism than with functionalism.

For this reason architecture has to be properly staged, like goods on sale. Here meticulous planning is important, but it must leave

Toyo Ito, *Nomad Restaurant*, ceiling, Tokyo, 1986

room for counter-movement, interspersion and spontaneity. Where everything is planned down to the last detail, sensuousness and eroticism are suffocated. Eroticism addresses partly the mind and partly the body, and so in this context the sensuousness of architectural bodies is eminently important. This is created with materials and volume, and both of these are ideally multisensory and should address both the long- and the close-range senses. The psychology of colour plays an essential part here. Architecture is not only visual, however; it should reverberate, too, both acoustically and in a metaphorical sense by means of rhythms, proportions, and accents. Architecture should also gratify the tactile senses, the feet, the hands, the skin, and should itself consist of multisensory skins.

In the urban situation, contextuality usually looks more attractive than a solitary approach. It is the latter which often makes American cities so inhospitable. Extreme individualism and developers' egotism are enemies of communication. Sensuousness and eroticism are not absolute values, but are perceived by others. Architectural auto-eroticism betrays the architect who only thinks of the realization of his own ideas. But eroticism is like a party game, or at least it involves two people. It requires intimacy, the possibility to withdraw, nooks, niches, variable lighting, but never constant glaring brightness. That, too, the architect must bear in mind. Small elements, or ones which are at least true to scale with regard to the human body, are infinitely preferable to the lack of individuality in megastructures and large-area shapes.

There is not just one form of sensuousness but many, as our case studies have shown. They are associated with individual contexts, and yet

Rüdiger Kramm, *Zeilgalerie les Facettes*, Frankfurt am Main, 1991–92

within a certain range of possibilities there are recommendations which can be made—collages and contrasts, for example, here and there a flamboyant extravagance. The skilful mixture obviously plays an important role. If the balance is lost, that is the end of that atmosphere of well-being in a city environment. For a sensuous city must offer a broad spectrum of opportunities for identification. It is not cosiness for city dens which is being propagated here, but an architecture which can adapt itself to people's needs and at the same time is able to manipulate those needs on the basis of a well-grounded knowledge of aestheticism and functionalism. Thus courses for architects should be made to include such extremely important skills as training the senses, learning to compare, and experimenting.

Society is a dynamic process, constantly changing. Since the mid-'80s, however, the rate of acceleration has increased appreciably compared with previous decades. Nevertheless it should not be overlooked that at the same time the human being is a creature of extraordinary inertia, with an emotional attachment to the bar around the corner, to the bistro which he knows like the back of his hand, to his own personal mug down at the pub, to the stain on the wall, to the creaking floorboard, etc. It is only such sensuous signals, with lifelong validity, which make it possible at all to endure change. In the long run, no one can stand up to constant acceleration.

Of course sensuousness is not only confined to rust, flaking coats of paint, walls which absorb heat and give it off again, the groaning of old plumbing, grained wood, muted tones, but also extends to gleaming technology, organic forms and new media. If we again look to artists for seismographic evidence, we can see that for a number of years a sea change has been taking place concerning the integration of new media into installations and sculptures. In the meantime this is also being reflected on the art market, where suddenly media artists like Gary Hill, Bruce Nauman, Nam June Paik

and Bill Viola are already to be found high on the ranking lists.[32]

The works of these artists are often hybrids in which media components enter into a symbiosis with traditional materials and forms of expression. But genuine media arts such as laser installations, holography and video art forms are also gaining ground, although at present they are still very expensive and have not yet reached a degree of technical development which would allow maintenance-free operation over a long period of time. There is no doubt that they have a characteristic tendency to disembodiment, and this is also particularly true of virtual realities. During the course of the coming decades, we will have to get used to the idea of living in a variety of realities, and virtual realities will be among them as a matter of course. We can fall into apocalyptic despair, like Baudrillard, at the atomization of the individual who has lost control of himself and his artificial limbs or, like Virilio, invoke the invasion of microbiotic flesh-eaters, but it will hardly be possible to hold up such development. We should be able to channel it, however, for all in all things are not as bad as they seem from the point of view of such poststructuralist philosophers.

Media forms of architecture are also gaining ground, however. Leaving aside the virtual architecture of networks and other telecommunications systems, media architecture means in principle the hybridization and substitution of traditional architectural forms of expression with media, and mostly multimedia. An example is the conversion of environmental noises into graphics which are captured on screens decorating façades, offering a variety of narrative techniques typical of the media which in animated form can give character to the face of a building in the place of formerly static elements. Thanks to high definition television and sophisticated computer animation, there is no danger that such multimedia forms of expression will not turn out to be sensuous: city scenes from Tokyo, Osaka and New York are proof enough.

But what they have had to offer so far is only a dull reflection of what will be possible in the future. What is more, in cyberspace worlds the resubstantiation of disembodied media spaces is being put to the test. In that respect there is no cause for exaggerated concern. Nevertheless, there is no doubt that with the new technologies the significance of rooms and architectural bodies in the traditional sense will diminish. On the other hand time will remain and will continue to cannibalize rooms. Space will become time, and not the other way round as Gournemanz in Richard Wagner's *Parcifal* maintains.

It will be up to the public not simply to accept everything. It would suit the business people if all department stores could be virtualized, postal services no longer had to deliver any mail order catalogues and all purchasing could be carried out online, for then they could save themselves the capital expenditure for costly buildings. But in fact it will not—and must not—come to that, for as if to spite all the media theorists the people will themselves remain as bodies, bodies which demand to experience cities with all of their senses, not just with their eyes and their ears.

In order to guarantee that this will remain so in the 21st century, too, it should be prescribed that architects study the sensuous possibilities of media technologies and at the same time recommended that they undergo intensive training in body awareness. A lesson on the directions which developments may take could be offered, for example, by the more recent drafts of Coop Himmelb(l)au, AG4 from Cologne and Toyo Ito. Against a background of Japanese aesthetic tradition which is centuries old, Toyo Ito has the special ability to build sensuousness with new means, to make it visible and, transcending the purely physical, to project it into spiritual realms which since time immemorial have vested the Japanese with their sense of ritual and ceremony and a concentration of their mental and spiritual powers—a combination of sensitivities that may ensure meaningful and sensuous architecture as we cross into the next millennium.

ARCHITECTURE AND EROTICISM IN FILM

Angela Krewani

"I like to think, if I may be so arrogant, that it's possible to compare the work of a film-maker with that of an architect."[1]

"The poetic law of eroticism is that it draws the attention away from the designated object and starts a game of symbols, a game of metaphors, of images, which then build bridges to the erotic object."[2]

The connection between film and eroticism can be found on a variety of levels. Just the particular situation of visiting a movie theatre implies a lot of sensuality in itself. The spectator sits unrecognized in the dark belly of the theatre and follows the events on the screen. He may let himself be stimulated by them and even project his secret or not-so-secret wishes onto them.[3] And these events on the screen embody the symbols, metaphors, associations and hints at eroticism of which the history of film contains such a multitude: bodies, hair, clothes, lingerie, even settings like staircases, materials like chrome, steel, glass, stone or water seduce the spectator into indulging in erotic fantasies.[4] In this regard architecture plays an important role in film, either as the setting for erotic scenes, or as an erotic metaphor or symbol.

The connection between architecture and eroticism in film has existed ever since the early days of film history. Films at the turn of the century especially took up existing patterns from painting and literature and adapted them. It is in this context, at the start of the century, that the combination of eroticism and urban experience comes to the fore. Portraits of the city as a place fostering alienation, depersonalization, sexual perversion and prostitution are a recurrent topic in modern literature that can be found in all of its principal works: prostitution in Zola's and Baudelaire's seedy and run-down Paris, Charles Dickens' foggy, industrial London, John Dos Passos' and Theodore Dreiser's mythical New York, and finally the sinful and equivocal Berlin of the 1920s as described by Alfred Döblin in his novel *Berlin, Alexanderplatz*.[5]

Indeed, films between the beginning of the century and World War II portray Berlin as the symbol of restless life, of the continuous search for new thrills, of manifold sexual and erotic desires, but at the same time as a place full of

Opposite page:
Georgy and Vladimir Stenberg,
Cheloveks Kino Apparatom,
lithograph, 1926

social misery, of unemployment, of crime and loneliness. In fine art the cubist and futuristic city portraits express uninhibited "joie de vivre", the energetic dissolution of the body, as well as widespread decadence, while Expressionism depicts prostitution, thus commenting on the processes of alienation in modern metropolitan culture.

Two films that exemplify the modern urban experience are Fritz Lang's *Metropolis* (1926) and Walter Ruttmann's *Berlin, Die Sinfonie der Großstadt* (1927). Fritz Lang's *Metropolis*, in which Manhattan symbolizes everything New York generally stands for, is valid even today as an example of the cinematographic architectural visions of a metropolis. By combining the myths of the golden city of the future and the Tower of Babel, it alludes to the myth of Babylon the whore. Here the modern city is no longer the place of political information, of general education, of rationality and modernism, the way the Bauhaus conceived it, but one catapulted out of its own history into a mythical context. It appears as the archaic and yet perpetual place of erotic consumerism.

Fritz Lang, however, sees the city as a modern whore, whose qualities lie not so much in selling her body, but rather in her mechanization and technical interchangeability.

Freder Fredersen, the son of the city's ruler, falls in love with the girl Maria, who is exchanged for an exact copy in the form of a robot. This switch symbolizes the mechanization of an eroticism which no longer stems from individual bodily qualities, like the smell and the feel of the skin, but whose appeal relies solely on the mechanical reproduction of specific bodily qualities. The correlation of mechanization and eroticism goes even so far that it is portrayed as the "more dangerous" variant.

At a dance attended by the city's influential high society, the robot woman proves to have such a bewitching effect that she is used in the political agitation of the workers. With this turn

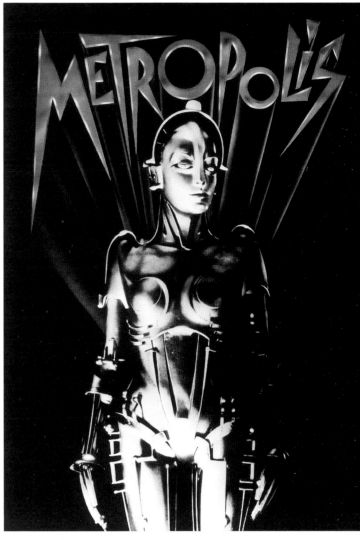

Maria, the machine woman
in *Metropolis*,
silent film by Fritz Lang, 1927

of events the film confirms the common prejudice about the subversive powers of women.

The robot woman's uncontrollable eroticism, in which the fear of female sexuality and the fear of mechanized humans are projected onto each other, is to be understood as a warning of the consequences of technology. Both "high society" as well as the workers in the futuristic megalopolis prove to be corruptible by this form of technological eroticism. Real social change cannot be realized through this kind of representation. The robot-woman has to be destroyed, the "real" Maria has to be reinstalled and her love for the ruler's son, Freder Fredersen, hints at the reconciliation of class differences. Here the film does not offer any politically motivated solution, but rather resolves the conflicts on a mythical, fairy tale

Maria's metamorphosis
in *Metropolis*,
silent film by Fritz Lang, 1927

Boris Bilinski, poster for the French premiere of *Metropolis*

level. Furthermore, the film conveys the dual image of femininity that is so common in the European cultural tradition. This city and its machine images embody the "threatening", "erotic" or "dark" aspects of femininity, aspects which are not admissible in the image of the "domesticated" middle class woman. It is only logical that these are overcome during the course of the plot through the victory over the frightening machine-woman. What is left is the demure mistress and wife well known from the 19th century.[6]

The correlation between architecture and technology on the one hand and eroticism on the other, as presented in *Metropolis* in the

character of the robot Maria, can also be found in Walter Ruttmann's documentary *Berlin, Die Sinfonie der Großstadt.* Ruttmann, however, takes his film experiment a step further than Fritz Lang in *Metropolis.* Although in *Metropolis* eroticism becomes technical, it remains con-

cerned with the female body. Ruttmann, on the other hand, transforms the city of Berlin into a very mobile urban body. This urban body that wakes up in the morning presents itself to the viewer in a machine-like rhythm. Disregarding any possible story line, Ruttmann cuts scenes in the rhythm of machine-cycles, thus destroying any contextual perception of the city in favour of its total fragmentization. A contemporary critic describes the film in terms of erotically tinged metaphors:

"The awakening of Berlin, deserted streets, idlers, a security patrol, locked windows, blinds askew, out beyond the city gates the quiet, nurturing country-side. There cows' bodies produce milk, a sign next to them—Berlin, 15 kilometres. And now Berlin awakens, quickly, in bursts, hardly takes the time to rub its eyes and open they are, bright, hasty houses spew out the blue collar workers, the office workers, streetcars catch them, buses and subway trains swallow them up and spit them into the gaping jaws of the factories. Machines clatter jubilantly, shape, destroy, are operated by people, serve humans. Berlin sends its children into the street, to school, the livestock is driven into the slaughter-houses, the state employees to the offices. Berlin now thunders, rages, booms. Advertisements, street hawkers, distinguished businessmen in automobiles, fast trains arriving, strangers pour into a city of strangers, are submerged in the whirl. On and on roars, hisses, bubbles the hell unleashed, policeman's arm goes up, goes out, somewhere a brawl, west, north, luxury."[7]

The erotic charging of the urban body of Berlin is achieved, in contrast to *Metropolis,* through the formal constituents of cut and montage.

Erich Kettelhut, film set for *Metropolis*

Poster for the film *Berlin, Die Sinfonie der Großstadt*,
Walther Ruttmann, 1924

Maria's dance
in *Metropolis*, silent film by Fritz Lang, 1927

Poster for the film
Berlin, Die Sinfonie der Großstadt

They fragmentize the city of Berlin into a twitching, rhythmically pulsating body which adapts to the movements of the machines, subordinating even the fragmented female body as the traditional symbol of eroticism. Ruttmann combines the dancing legs of the "Tiller Girls", the most famous revue troupe at the time, with images of automatic production processes. The montage picks up on the subject of the sinful city which was known since the 19th century and whose shows, vaudevilles and theatres are constantly showing scenes of prostitution. *Sinfonie der Großstadt* breaks with 19th-century clichés, however, in that it dissociates them from simple body displays and integrates machine-like rhythms and structures into the erotic presentation.

Ruttmann's montages transform the eroticism of human images into an eroticism of the modern city that has no direct relation to human bodies. This can be compared with the manifestos of the futurists, which make similarly sensuous and emotional demands on the futuristic

house when they speak of the "innate beauty of its lines and forms".[8]

In this context it is revealing that unlike Fritz Lang in *Metropolis* Ruttmann does not present the female body as a whole as an erotic symbol. Instead his analogies of body and city take up the subject of the fragmented perception of the city, which cubist and futuristic painting had already discovered. Thus all Ruttmann's city has to offer is an eroticism of fragmentation and mechanization. The neutrality of its gender, however, is striking. The rhythmically pulsating, mechanized metropolis does not have any distinctly male or female qualities. This already hints at the dissolution of gender stereotypes which stems from the gender neutrality of mechanized production processes, and has even survived into our own day, as reflected in the present gender discussion: a highly technological society that is based on the division of labour and adapts to the needs of the machines can to a certain degree do without a strict division into sexes.

Автор руководитель эксперимента
ДЗИГА ВЕРТОВ
Главный оператор М. КАУФМАН
Ассистент по монтажу Е. СВИЛОВА

ПРОИЗВОДСТВО ВУФКУ

2 СТЕНБЕРГ 2

ЧЕЛОВЕК С АППАРАТОМ

КИНО

Dziga Vertov, poster for the film
The Man with the Camera

As a formal experiment and with its analogies of mechanization and eroticism, Ruttmann's film contains numerous elements also found in the films of Russian Constructivism and which are explicitly mentioned in their manifestos. The close relationship between fine arts, architecture and film is a result of the constructivists' concern with replacing the presentation of content and image with that of form and structure as the new frame of reference for the description of reality. For the Russian constructivists, the connection between architecture and film was particularly close. According to Le Corbusier, these two are the only "true art forms of modern times". In 1929 he remarked: "I have the impression that in my line of work I think the same way as Eisenstein thinks while he is developing his type of film art."[9]

Besides this, the biographies of the most important constructivist film-makers show a certain proximity to architecture. Sergei Eisenstein's father was an architect and Eisenstein himself started as a stage designer for the Proletkult company, and took over the directorship after a short time. Lev Kulesov had started his film career as an architect with Yevgeny Bauer, the

"grandmaster of opulent melodramas".[10] Interestingly enough, the title of his first film was *Proekt inzenara Prajta (Engineer Prait's Project)* (1918).[11]

In spite of its mechanical construction fantasies, the Russian film avant-garde of the 1920s made repeated reference to the human body, making it the basis of constructivist experiments, as Kulesov states in a manifesto in 1922:

"We know that the cinematographer does not need theatre actors. We know that the ordinary human being with the perfect mechanism of his skewer-like body is unacceptable to the cinematographer. We need 'monsters'. (...) Monsters are people who have trained their bodies with exact knowledge of its mechanical construction. (...) We study the mechanisms of the human body on the basis of exact calculations and experiments. We do not do this because we love the aesthetics of machines but because the human body is really a mechanism."[12]

In the context of the Russian avant-garde it is not simply that construction is erotic, but that the human body is reconstructed according to the laws of mechanics. As a logical consequence, one of Kulesov's famous film experiments consists of the montage of a female body assembled from parts of female film characters: the lips of one woman, the legs from another, the back from a third, etc.

In his constructivist dreams, Dziga Vertov also turns to the body, whose allegedly machine-like qualities he sees as libidinous. It is interesting to note how explicitly he sees himself as an architect or "master builder":

"In the presence of machines, man's inability to control himself is disgraceful, but what can you do when the flawless functioning of electricity excites us more than the chaotic hustle and bustle of active people and the subversive listlessness of passive people. (...) Our way is from the passive citizen just lolling around to the poetry of machines and on to a perfect electric being.(...) I am the glamour of the movies (cinematic eye). I am a master builder. I have created you out of me today, placed you in this most wonderful chamber that had not existed until I created it just now. This chamber has twelve walls, which I have put on film in different parts of the world."[13]

It is in similar terms that an association between eroticism and film is shown again and again in Sergei Eisenstein's manifestos too, especially when he combines montage with the related concept of attraction and the sensuousness of its components.[14]

The erotic symbols mounted into these films tie in with the tradition of symbolism found in a great amount of 20th-century avant-garde art, which no longer depicts the human shape as a whole, usually the female body, but rather its fragmentation. The fragments, however, are unambiguously symbolic. One of the difficulties of the Russian film avant-garde was to put into visual form the erotic role of constructions, and it is at this point that I see a contradiction to the manifestos, for it relies on the conventional symbolism of the female body.

This problem becomes apparent for example in Georgy and Vladimir Stenberg's film poster for Dziga Vertov's *Man with the Camera* (1926). In the foreground are the dancing legs of a chorus girl. Falling back on traditional symbols shows the dilemma in which the constructivist film finds itself concerning the erotic role of construction. Sensualizing the otherwise "neutral" lines of construction requires symbols which are recognized and universally valid.

Like no one else, the British director Peter Greenaway takes up the discrepancy between an eroticism of construction and an eroticism of performance and makes an issue out of it, subverts it, experiments with it. Greenaway originally studied to be a painter, and most of his films deal with questions concerning the construction of spaces and images. Greenaway had begun with experimental films and later moved on to more conventional narrative films. His main focus, however, has remained the same, and that is the problem of the construction of images and their divergence between media. His films *The Draughtsman's Contract* (1982) and *The Belly of an Architect* (1986), which were both made during the renaissance of the British film in the '80s and are part of the "New British Cinema", deal explicitly with the themes of eroticism and architecture.

The Draughtsman's Contract, which is set in England at the end of the 17th century, derives a great deal of its humour from the deliberate association of architecture and sexuality. Mrs. Herbert, the wife of an estate owner, asks the famous draughtsman Mr. Neville to make twelve drawings of their house. The drawings are to be a present for Mr. Herbert, who allegedly has a closer relationship with his house and his horses than with his wife. His daughter describes the English landed gentry's hierarchical system of values as follows: "A house, a garden, a horse, a wife." Through the drawings, Mrs. Herbert hopes to direct her husband's attention away from the house and towards herself.

In spite of his objections at the start, Mr. Neville signs the contract. His fee is to be a certain sum of money, plus the freedom of having the lady of the house at his disposal—the husband is away travelling. This contract is supplemented with a further contract between the artist and Mrs. Herbert's daughter, who needs an heir in order to keep the estate in the family's possession. In the course of the plot it becomes clear that the draughtsman also includes in his drawings evidence that Mr. Herbert has been murdered. At the end, Mr. Herbert's body is found, and as the artist is suspected of having killed him, he is blinded and killed by the people of the house. The blinding of the draughtsman again takes up the discrepancy between seeing and recognizing which is postulated throughout the film. At the very moment when the artist realizes the conspiracy around him, he loses his eyesight. In Freudian terminology, blinding is equivalent to castration, which in the sense of artistic castration holds true in the particular context of this film.

In an interview, Greenaway remarked that *The Draughtsman's Contract* re-examines representational patterns and constructions of reality in both painting and film:

"This concern with the draughtsman seeking out particular characteristics of a landscape and pursuing them in an almost minimalist way. And the way the film is structured to keep going back to the same landscapes at different times of the day, to see how the light has made shapes, forms, verticals, how they've changed and what new significance they have at different times of the day. My prime interests are the landscape, the ideas involved in the sheer interplay of plot, the symmetry, and those concerns characteristic of the whole sub-text of gardening."[15]

The topics of gardening and garden design are discussed by the characters. In this discussion, the conflicting garden concepts of the draughtsman and the German son-in-law, Mr. Talman, become clear. Talman turns out to be an orthodox proponent of the Baroque garden with its geometrical forms and its clearly defined centres. In contrast, Mr. Neville advocates the dissolution of geometrical forms, an idea which was just becoming fashionable, in favour of the nature-inspired, asymmetrical, Romantic garden. These conflicting views correspond to differences on the political level. Talman, a German Protestant, is a supporter of the royal house of Hanover and its feudal political style, whereas Mr. Neville, a Scottish Catholic, opposes Eng-

Still from *The Draughtsman's Contract*,
Peter Greenaway, 1982

lish sovereignty over Scotland and Ireland, of course, and is a supporter of English liberalism.

In the course of discussions on gardening and landscape painting, the theme of ideal eroticism is touched upon. During a meeting with Mrs. Herbert, the draughtsman draws her attention to a painting by Claude Lorrain (or in his style), whose work was particularly popular with English collectors in the late 17th century. This is followed by a drawn-out sequence of shots dwelling on erotic motifs with an air of antiquity and set in an ideal garden among pseudo-ancient ruins. Here the artistically designed garden is ironically depicted as the ideal place for a variety of erotic encounters, thus forming a contrast to the sexual encounters between Mrs. Herbert and the draughtsman, which are generally characterized by hostility.

Unlike Lorrain's garden paintings, Mr. Neville makes his drawings as objective as possible, always avoiding any idealizing, "antique" style as well as any Baroque representation of the house and garden which would emphasize geometrical forms. Neville's drawings are only ever shown in full shots. The draughtsman is shown with his instruments, particularly his viewing-frame. The view through the frame underscores the perspective and construction of both the drawing and the screen image and thus reveals the artificiality of perception.[16] On top of that it is an aid to self-reflection and a means to create distance in presentation.[17] Further distance is created by the extreme stylizations in the décor, etc.: the exaggerated costumes, the rhetorical subtleties,

the mannerisms of the actors. All these features support the impression of a construction of reality. On the formal image level, the reference to construction is in the pronounced horizontal and vertical lines which characterize the film pictures.

Accordingly, the most important aspect of the film is the questioning of the constructivist claim to reality. While for the Russian avant-garde there was always a connection between the erotic symbolism in film constructions and the attempt to achieve a synthesis of the arts and with it a more valid and more universal version of reality, Greenaway bathes this preoccupation of theirs in a post-modern light by playfully quoting the issues or even parodying them.

In contrast to the Russian avant-garde films, which almost naively and thoughtlessly integrated erotic symbols into their constructions, *The Draughtsman's Contract* does not eroticize the construction itself, but rather presents each form of eroticism and erotic setting as a construction conditioned by art history, detached from bodily needs and sensations. The historical distance serves to examine the genesis of the erotic symbolism and the architecturally defined connotations. Many of the amorous meetings between the draughtsman and the two women occur in places traditionally associated with merrymaking: the women's magnificently decorated boudoirs, behind a large parasol in the pastoral idyll of the park, in the bath house, in the hay of the barn. In addition, Greenaway quotes classic 17th-century painting motifs and transposes them into his film.

Still from *The Belly of an Architect*,
Peter Greenaway, 1986

Such an examination of sensually charged places and architecture amounts to a demolition of erotic symbols. This task is fulfilled by the living statue which, like a cynical running commentary on the plot, shows up at each of the different architectural sites. A long steady take, in which the statue almost vanishes in a hedge and its stone seems transformed into green vegetation, bears testimony to the complete lack of a certain kind of eroticism, as a tactile, sensual experience of materials and surfaces, as a permutation of their specific structures.

At the same time this take parodies the struggles of an age to find a cultural access to nature. In *The Draughtsman's Contract* everything is culture, nothing is nature anymore. And in spite of its sophistication, which sometimes overtaxes the senses, this culture has not succeeded in giving people a feel for the tingling of the senses. They act like hollow, wound-up mechanical dolls in specially created, splendidly ornamental costumes and settings.

The film presents eroticism as an elaborate construction in which architecture plays a major role. Nevertheless it can never become "authentic" since it, too, is caught up in its own repertoire of symbols. The same applies to the activities of the draughtsman. He deludes himself into believing that by using the perspectives he sees through his viewing-frame he can create a true-to-life image of the country house. Equipped with the "truth-seeking" instruments of artistic investigation, he misses the fact that

his pictures record the circumstantial evidence to prove a murder that he did not commit.

Seen in this respect, the film concentrates on the discrepancy between objective depiction and subjective recognition. Since all his energy goes into the objective depiction of the house, he fails to recognize—partly due to his arrogance—that he is the victim of a conspiracy. One of the final scenes clearly shows the draughtsman as the victim: throughout the film he had been dressed in black while the other characters wore white, but now the colours are reversed. The victim, Mr. Neville, appears in symbolic white, the colour black is reserved for his killers.

Greenaway's next film, *The Belly of an Architect*, is even more closely concerned with the connection between architecture and eroticism. Stourlay Kracklite, an architect from Chicago, has the task of organizing an exhibition of the French 'ideal' architect Etienne-Louis Boullée in Rome. On the train to Rome, his wife, who had so far only ever had miscarriages, conceives a child by him. Upon arriving in Rome, Kracklite's obsession with his own belly starts, alienating him from his colleagues and from his wife. A doctor diagnoses stomach cancer, and the directorship of the exhibition is taken away from him and given to his rival Caspasian, with whom his wife has long since started an affair. As his wife opens the exhibition and unexpectedly gives birth to his son, Kracklite throws himself out of a window. The film establishes erotic-architectonic associations centring

around creativity, pregnancy, ideal shapes, bodies and death. The parallel in meaning between creativity and pregnancy is obvious. It is explicitly mentioned by Kracklite's wife Louisa at the beginning of the film with reference to her miscarriages, which always occurred when one of his architectural projects failed. During his stay in Rome, Kracklite's architectural ambitions shift to his body: as Louisa's pregnancy progresses, his obsession with his belly grows and he focusses on the artistic reproduction of bellies.

Whereas in Louisa's belly life is growing, it is death in the form of a tumour that is growing in Kracklite's belly. Both produce Boullée-like forms of body architecture. Thus doomed, Kracklite has to substitute natural reproduction with artistic reproduction. The film presents images of men in art and photography, whereby Kracklite develops a neurosis that forces him to copy pictures of bellies. Here the film parodies the familiar cliché of art as a male compensation for the inability to give birth.

The erotic and architectural witticism here is made all the more sophisticated by the reference to Boullée's work. Throughout his whole life, Boullée (1728–99), a contemporary of Piranesi, had demanded that architecture should be sublime, working with the ideal shapes of the cube, sphere and circle. The film takes up these basic shapes and makes detailed use of them in its structural principles. The Pantheon, a frequently employed setting for the action, consists of these basic shapes. Even the cakes at the stylishly set up banquets are made in the shape of spheres and cubes.

Finally even Kracklite uses them to describe a physical condition, namely his stomach pains: "It either feels like a short, sharp-cornered cube or a pyramid—I must have an old disease."[18] The analogy between the body and architecture which Kracklite addresses in his metaphor is valid for Boullée as well. His design for *Newton's Cenotaph* sees the ideal body as a sphere, again drawing parallels between human and architectural bodies:

"On the nature of bodies, their qualities, their analogy with the human organism.
In the course of my search to discover from the nature of bodies their qualities and their analogies with the organism, I began my research on bodies of indefinite form (corps bruts). (...)
Bored by the mute and sterile sight afforded by irregular bodies, I transferred my attention to regular ones. The first qualities I recognized in them were regularity, symmetry and diversity, and I saw that these qualities determined their form and appearance. (...)
By the proportions of a body I understand the effect produced by its regularity, symmetry and

Still from *The Belly of an Architect*,
Peter Greenaway, 1986

diversity. Regularity establishes the beauty of an object, symmetry produces order and the beauty of the overall impression, while diversity gives objects the variety of faces by which we can differentiate them.
Consequently the harmonious appearance of bodies is born out of the union and the mutual congruence of all these qualities. By way of an example, the sphere can be seen as the shape which combines all bodily qualities. (...)
From all these observations it can be concluded that in every respect the sphere offers an image of perfection. (...) And so we see before us all the unique virtues with which this body is endowed by nature and which exercise such an infinite power over our senses.
Thus it is proved that the proportion and harmony of bodies are bestowed by nature and that because of the analogy with our human organism the qualities which spring from the nature of bodies have power over our senses."[19]

In an interview, Greenaway mentions his interest in artistic and architectural form and its adaptation to film:

"My concerns reiterate a wish to bring the aesthetics of painting to cinema. (...) *The Belly of an Architect,* for those who want to look, has tried to explore all the different means by which art has reproduced the human form."[20]

In the course of this, Greenaway parodies Boullée's ideal types by ironically playing on the body analogies which Boullée, as can be seen from the quotation, rather naively proposes. The forms are taken from nature and there is an analogy to the human body. Green-

away takes up this idea and develops it further, debunking it at the same time. The sphere now moves into the centre of attention since it plays an important role in the exhibition, in *Newton's Cenotaph,* as well as in the bodies of Mr. and Mrs. Kracklite—namely in their bellies.

Greenaway explores the discrepancy between Boullée's ideal forms and Kracklite's abnormal obsession with his own and with other bellies. In this context, his illness becomes a symbol of his inability to create anything except ideal shapes. Paralyzed by this obsessive demand, it is logical that all his architectural projects are bound to fail, which makes him the ideal partner for Boullée, who was never able to realize any of his projects either. The view of the decaying body is extended to the figures of antiquity whose medical history and whose death are also described.

The scene in which Kracklite shows his bare and sick belly to the women eating in a street restaurant in front of the Pantheon presents in condensed form the whole theme of the film. Against a background of the geometrical forms of the surrounding architecture, he points at his belly, which is being eaten up from the inside. What is more, the act of eating implies the cynical ambiguity of eating and being eaten and the incompatibility of inside and outside.

The parallel between disease and pregnancy, which has its architectural equivalent in the contrast between the theoretically conceived ideal form and the impossibility of its practical realization, makes it possible for Greenaway to

satirically demolish idealist concepts. In this context, the last scene again summarizes cinematic reflection: the highly pregnant Louisa Kracklite is supposed to open the exhibition in front of a large model of *Newton's Cenotaph.* As she is just about to cut the ribbon, she collapses and the birth of her child commences. At this moment, the half-opened sphere is illuminated with blue light, the camera moves back and, in a full shot, permits a view of the woman giving birth to her child in front of the sphere. This is an ironic comment on Boullée's motto: "Architecture should help nature to express itself." Then the camera moves upwards and shows Kracklite throwing himself out of the window.

The images of this film also dramatize the discrepancy between architectural ideal form and a pathological focussing on the body. All rooms in the film are created in the style of monumental architectural designs: high ceilings, long passages, colonnades, and arched doorways opening up views along further corridors. The geometrical camera shots adapt the architectural ideal form to the film perspective: "If you like, the architects, by which I mean myself and Sascha, are behind the camera. Everything is seen in terms of façades, elevations, formal plans," Greenaway remarks.[21] The colours, on the other hand, symbolize the physicality of his main character, which is always prone to illness: the scenes are lit in the flesh colours of the human body, thereby negating the "sublimeness" of the architecture and giving it an archaic aspect.

The connection between eroticism and architecture can be found on a variety of levels. One requirement for this connection is that each erotic situation remains ambivalent and cannot be limited to one particular meaning, one form, one material or one particular state. In this context, the references to the use of Boullée's monumental architectures by totalitarian and fascist regimes constitute a warning against unambiguous, uncontradicted concepts of eroticism.

Seen in this light, the film's ambivalence becomes apparent. Almost all situations are accompanied by their own negation. Even Kracklite's discovery, on watching his wife's love-play with Caspasian, loses its credibility in the next scene when a young boy looks through the same keyhole into the same room and sees only a model of Boullée's lighthouse. The scene can be understood as a comment on the relationship between eroticism and architecture. As Kracklite watches the love-play between Caspasian and Louisa, Caspasian takes the lighthouse model and holds it like a phallic symbol in front of his penis. This scene, which Kracklite observes through the keyhole, demonstrates the

Anita Ekberg in *La Dolce Vita*,
Federico Fellini, 1959

lack of a self-determined sense of body in Kracklite's psyche. Boullée's architectural sense of ideal dimensions even defines his erotic jealousy fantasies.

The distance between bodies and the visual forms of eroticism and sensuality in Greenaway's movies is paralleled by the distance between the images and their content. In *The Draughtsman's Contract* the distance is created by the viewing-frame, in *The Belly of an Architect* it is the picture postcard views of Rome, the stone images of Roman icons like the Pantheon, St. Peter's Square or the Forum Romanum. The "picture postcard views" have other functions besides the aesthetically distancing effects. They point at the city's infinite cultural variety and its historical tradition, they show the foreignness of the American architect in this European setting, a foreignness which also applies to the English director in the Italian film tradition. The problem that this tradition has more than exhausted the exploration of Rome already[22] is solved by Greenaway by means of his "post-modern" postcard perspective, which no longer seems to care about any individual point of view.

Federico Fellini's film *La Dolce Vita* (1959) draws parallels between forms of erotic encounter and architecture. The eroticism of the "seedy hotel room", which has also been exhausted in other films, is the setting for Marcello's encounter with the rich girl Maddalena, who is bored in every respect. On an aimless night-time joyride through Rome they meet a prostitute,

whom they drive home. Here the film shows Rome from its shabbiest side: the cheerless, dilapidated, concrete apartment blocks on the outskirts of the city, which are not even connected by a road system anymore.

A contrasting aspect of eroticism is ironically presented in Marcello's encounters with the American film star Sylvia. They take place in front of the antiquities and tourist attractions of Rome, in churches, on open squares or in noble restaurants among ruins. During a sightseeing tour, Sylvia climbs the tower of St. Peter's Cathedral, pursued by a pack of paparazzi. The ascent up the circular staircase becomes the symbolic chase after the object of sexual desire.

Another scene with Sylvia has become one of the best known film scenes of all time. In their night-time search for a room, Marcello and Sylvia find themselves at the moonlit Fontana di Trevi. Sylvia gathers up her evening dress and steps into the fountain, throws back her head, opens her arms and calls to Marcello to come to her. Blending the symbols of woman and water produces a symbol of timeless, archaic sensuality. Fellini, however, cannot allow this interpretation without commenting on it, and so he clearly marks it as a fantasy of Marcello's. At the very moment when he wants to kiss the American film star, who, standing under the cascading water, symbolizes all that is eternally female, the fountain is turned off. The water drains away, the day starts, the dream is over.

It seems that in films the large cities are very often mysterious places of erotic tension and

erotic games, and New York is no exception. The combination of Manhattan's night-time city lights, the crowded streets and the all-pervasive signs of prostitution revives the stock cliché of the sinful city and the fragmented urban experience, the fleetingness of sexual encounters and the never-kept promises of the garish neon signs, a cliché which is as old as the film world itself.

An example of this kind of cinematic coding of eroticism and architecture is Martin Scorsese's film *Taxidriver* (1975), which superbly illustrates the theme of decadent eroticism in Manhattan's glittering sea of lights.

Another, more individualistic approach is offered by Woody Allen's films, which in the style of a tribute to New York portray its architecture and its inhabitants. The film *Manhattan* (1979) starts with a declaration of love addressed to New York: it is the extensive dolly shots along the canyons between skyscrapers, the awesome sight of façades towering into infinity, and the loving, detailed attention to *Art-Nouveau* and *Art-Déco* ornaments that make *Manhattan*'s architecture so sensually tangible. The eroticism of the buildings makes up for the lack of sensuality of the people who live in them and between them, who talk and talk, and in fact talk their relationships to death. Accordingly, *Manhattan* sees itself as an analysis of the inhabitants' inability to have satisfying, real-life erotic relationships—the city is erotic, its inhabitants are no longer.

During the last decade, Tokyo has joined Manhattan as a subject for cinematic observation. Ryu Murakami's film *Tokyo Decadence* (1992) continues the dismantling of human eroticism that Woody Allen had already started in *Manhattan*. Unlike *Manhattan*, whose inhabitants are shown to be affable egotists and romantics looking for the perfect love and always failing, this kind of relationship is unheard of in *Tokyo Decadence*.

The film centres around a young prostitute who works as an S&M whore. On the way to her various customers, the beautiful young woman moves through a chilling world of steel-and-glass high-tech architecture, which towers over people, making them appear like some strange species of insect. In this environment, in which bodies experience only hostility, it is only normal that a customer tries to "disembody" the prostitute by plastering her hair flat against her head with styling gel and then symbolically trying to remove it. "A woman's hair is her life. I can see why the Nazis liked to shave women's hair off as a punishment."

In the course of their encounter he asks her to undress in front of the window. In this scene, the camera pans to the front of the building, a high-rise tower block. It moves up the façade, shows the young woman naked and lost at the window of the hotel skyscraper, and then pans back to the inside and photographs the woman in front of an abyss, at the bottom of which the lights and the arterial roads of the city are spread. In this kind of architecture, which cruelly alienates the occupants from their own bodies, eroticism is only possible in its commercial, sadistic variety.

The city of Tokyo is also the topic of Chris Marker's documentary *Sans Soleil* (1982). This film, which was made in the same year as *Blade Runner*, again takes up the eroticizing tendencies in construction which the films of the Russian avant-garde had previously proposed, but then adapts them to media architecture. In Marker's Tokyo, the human bodies and the architectural bodies of the city are dissolved to make room for media façades, symbols, signs and ciphers. Even people's dreams take place on over-sized media screens. Unlike in *Blade Runner*, which still insists on the continuity of archaic behaviour patterns, there are no human bodies left to act out these patterns. In *Sans Soleil*, image-processing machines have taken over mythical, archaic and erotic functions. Although as a result of the city's media-orientation *Sans Soleil* holds the prospect of a return to magical thinking, the body and its eroticism have already been lost in the flood of media images.

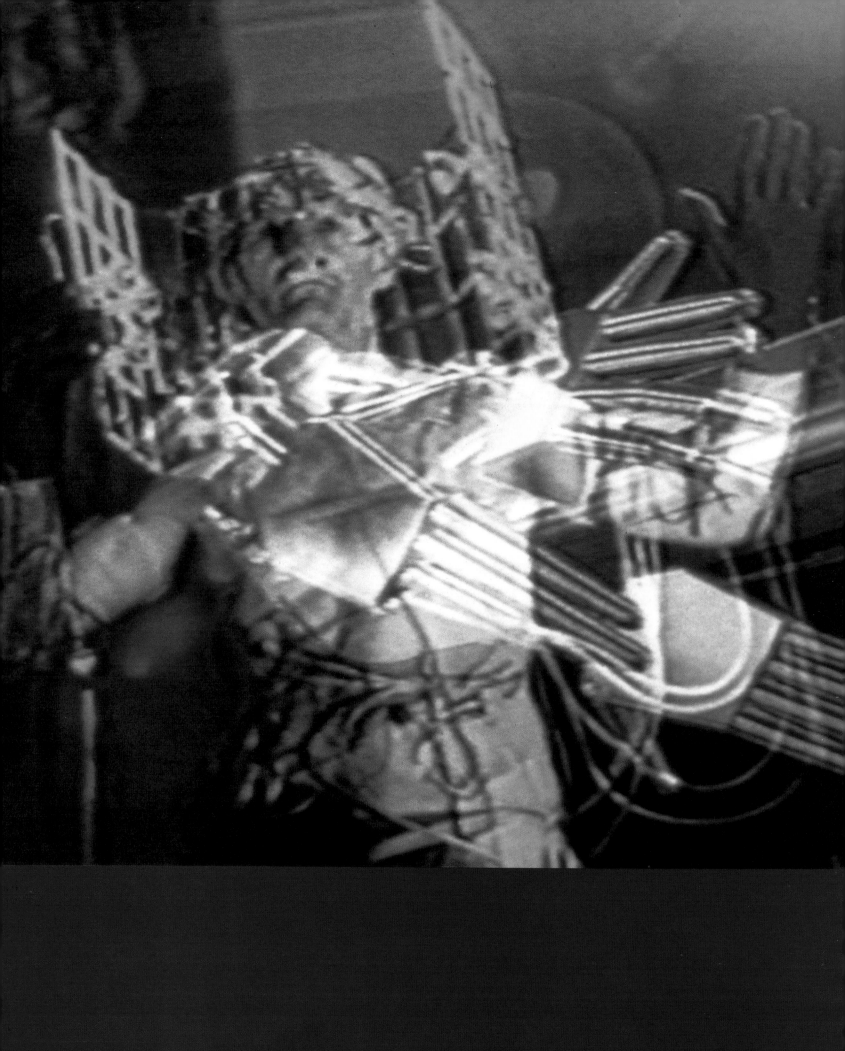

FROM MEDIA-ORIENTED AVANT-GARDE DESIGN TO VIRTUAL BODIES IN VIRTUAL ARCHITECTURE: CYBERSEX

"That is what is so schizophrenic about the conditions in which we live: telematic systems for networking virtual realities worldwide make it possible for us to be simultaneously present here and elsewhere. During the course of the coming years we will have to accustom ourselves more and more to the idea of accepting ourselves and others as virtual forms of existence in virtual space."[1]

Ray Ascott

"Mondo 2000: 'What happens to the fine arts in this world?'
Hans Moravec: 'I assume that the diversity of what humans do will be greater than ever, with tribalization. The homogenizing effects of civilization will be gone, so you're going to have tribes going off in very bizarre directions because they won't be constrained by the need to make a living. People just revert to their instinctive ways. Basically we all can be idle.'
Mondo 2000: 'And sex?'
Hans Moravec: 'I was skipping over that actually. Sure. Why not? The only thing is, it's going to get some stiff competition from things like virtual reality, which might be better because you can control more parameters. You don't have the constraints you have with an actual physical thing shaped like a person. In virtual reality you can simulate in a way that's just richer.'"[2]

Hans Moravec

"Like any other significant technical development, the 'cyber' phenomenon is going to pose ethical problems. Brainscanning, mind machines, hypermedia, synergetic relationships between humans and machines, even if today they may still be technical utopias, they are going to confront us with ethical decisions which have to be made. What possibilities are permissible?"[3]

S. J. Schmidt

All three authors address the utopia factor, an element which the architecture debate claims has been completely lost in contemporary architecture. In the wake of new technological developments and horizons, however, utopian thinking—in architecture, too—has found a considerable amount of new breeding ground since the '60s, producing revolutionary conceptions which have rocked the foundations of architectural grammar and rhetoric, such as "intelligent" architecture concepts in general, and media architecture in particular.[4]

The increase in computerization, hybridization and even virtualization in a number of

fields of day-to-day and professional life is a challenge which architecture has to face up to.[5] Architects have to accept the fact that not only have CAD programs, three-dimensional simulations and animations changed drafting operations radically, but that something as apparently nonsensical as immaterial architecture actually exists. Cyberspace is architecture, has its own architecture, contains architecture,[6] and that is the reality to which the profession has to adjust.

This development, which in the mid-'90s begins to take on more definite contours, starts out in the '60s as space age euphoria, utopias of the "affluent society" and the beginnings of pop and media culture. In the midst of a momentous craze for technology, Peter Cook and Archigram in England are the first to realize that an exploding scene in the pop and TV worlds demands architectural consequences, and so they integrate mobile elements, tubular scaffolding, cellular struc-

Peter Cook / Archigram,
Instant City, 1968

tures, pneumatic buildings and picture screens (large electronic display screens had not yet been invented) into their city designs, as in *Plug-in-City* or *Instant City*.[7] Less poppish but essentially more subversive, philosophically more provocative and more circumspect is the reaction from the avant-garde groups which formed at the end of the '60s in Vienna, particularly the Haus-Rucker-Co and Coop Himmelblau, whose impact on architectural history has long been acknowledged as irrefutable fact.

Under the influence of youth culture, the debate revolving around mind-expanding drugs, the indications of environmental disaster and a state of emergency in the cities and above all the space-mad high-tech romanticism of the late '60s, these groups developed thoroughly unusual concepts of architecture, in which traditional ideas of architectural structure underwent a radical change and sought a symbiosis with anatomical structure. The reference quantities of Euclidian geometry were thrown overboard. The architectural forms proposed instead were clearly inspired by the suits of divers and astronauts, and included pneumatic structures, spheres, balloons and amorphous shrouds. For the first time inner organs such as the heart, lungs and the amniotic sac were identified in extraordinarily metaphorical fashion as architecture and then drafted and built as models. From the very beginning there was a highly erotic dimension to such experiments, and it quickly became evident that such architecture could only be real-

Haus-Rucker-Co,
Mind-Expander I,
rear view, 1967

137

ized if they underwent a relatively complex degree of conversion into media form.[8]

Thus an early project of the Haus-Rucker-Co group, and one which was varied many times, was given the name *Mind Expander* (1967ff.). Derived from the diving and space suit idea, the *Mind Expander* was designed as an architectural skin and a specifically anatomical structure which permitted a broadening of the human's world of psychic and physical experience. With the help of such architecture, men and women were expected to have new body experiences, explore and experience in new ways the insides of their body cavities and thus develop more intense interpersonal relationships. In the group's programme we read:

"Mind Expander
Red spots before your eyes
The easy chair has a bucket seat for two people, a man and a woman, above it a PVC balloon which reaches down over the heads of the occupants of the chair. You help the girl to climb in first. Then you join her. The girl sits slightly higher and her legs lie across your right thigh. You tilt the balloon down and switch on the pulser. The heart sounds of the pulser are calm and steady. Your eyes follow the red and blue lines on the balloon. The air that you breathe flows slowly through your body, your heart begins to beat more calmly.
The girl next to you is also breathing slowly and very regularly. You have forgotten whether the girl has blonde or brown hair. The girl's legs are weightless. You sense nothing of her. You do not feel her skin, or her arm, which she has put around your shoulders. She is simply there without your having to think of her. Deep and flowing. Everything begins to flow. The girl is in your breath and in your eyes. You now only think about breathing. You have the feeling that you are being breathed. There are pink dots describing circles in front of your eyes. To the rhythm of your breath your eyes

Haus-Rucker-Co,
Mind-Expander II,
1968–69

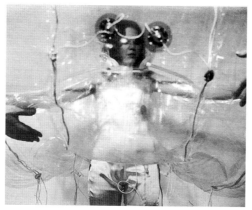

Coop Himmelblau,
Heartroom,
1969

wander across the red and blue lines. The lines become the pulse, the pulse becomes breath. The circle begins to close. You are happy about it. The journey has begun."[9]

If one ignores the relish with which the young Viennese architects adopt an attitude intended to shock, the type of autogenic training described here produces a feeling of disembodiment. With the aid of this architectural apparatus, the boundaries between architecture, sculpture and technical object are abolished, and the dividing lines between artistic, psychological, physiological and erotic experiment become fluid.

Coop Himmelblau's early architectural projects aimed in the same direction, although right from the beginning they put greater emphasis on media effects. On the one hand projects like *City with Pulsating Space Frame* (*Stadt mit pulsierendem Raumtragwerk*, 1966), *Cities that Beat like a Heart* (*Städte, die pulsieren wie das Herz*, 1967), *Heartspace* (*Herzraum*, 1969) and *Feedback Vibration City* (1971) all stress the character of organic body cavities, which, turned into architectural spaces, are formed in the shape of a human's inner organs. On the other hand they underline the intense mental and physical interaction between such architecture and the people in their media outfits, which are clearly identifiable as forerunners of cyberspace data suits.

The designs of space capsules serve as inspiration for further Haus-Rucker-Co experiments with pneumatic structures, which, shaped like amniotic sacs, caused a sensation in Vienna in 1967. But again there is particular emphasis on the erotic factor:

"Balloon for Two
(...) Our balloons help you to discover an unknown feeling of peace, security, relaxation. And love. We want to heighten your sensitivity. You are going on a journey, together with someone you love. Into inner space. Like astronauts. Except that you are travelling inwards. You will think bet-

Haus-Rucker-Co,
Yellow Heart,
1967–68

ter and love better. You will do everything better because you are calmer and more relaxed. You can set up the balloon in your own home. Next to the little flower table or over by the television set. It is not at all demanding. But you need it badly!
Haus-Rucker-Co
The Love Protector."[10]

In the balloon, in the amniotic sac, which at the same time is a model of a space capsule and an extremely rudimentarily furnished shelter, cuddly bliss is advocated as a prescription against a cold, cheerless, hostile environment.

In this respect the best known project from the early period of the Haus-Rucker-Co group was their *Yellow Heart* (*Das gelbe Herz,* 1967–68), which in a spectacular operation was installed in the excavation pit for the new Viennese police headquarters on the Schottenring. *Yellow Heart* combines ideas from body architecture, pneumatic structure, high-tech apparatus, media architecture, and the imagery of the heart and the amniotic sac, the life-sustaining cell, the love nest. Conceived as a place of relaxation and meditation, it has its own rhythm, intended to convey new kinds of tactile, visual and acoustic impressions. And on closer inspection it becomes noticeable that the Russian space station *Mir* has the same basic shape and follows the same layout principles. As architecture in the form of an inner organ, here the "heart" symbolizes in particular life, love, the energy cycle, emotion and technology.

In the years 1968–72 Coop Himmelblau was also very involved in a wide variety of experiments with models of cities based on ideas from body architecture. The contact with their colleagues may well have been the aesthetic, political, technical and environmental issues which played a part in the architectural debate of the time, but their approach was intellectually more profound and more carefully thought out. They broached subjects and had presentiments about states of being and other

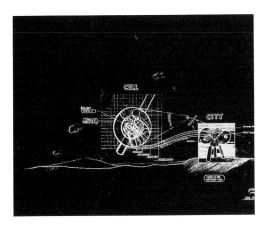

Coop Himmelblau,
Feedback Vibration City,
1971

matters which nearly thirty years later have become the object of explicit research in various technical and medical disciplines.

Among these there were visual and tactile experiments and ones employing cardiac rhythms, electroencephalograms and brainscanners, all of which can be regarded as forerunners of media architectures, of media culture, cyberspace programs and networks in our information society. The inversion of the metaphor "the heart of the city" in projects like *Cities which Pulsate like the Heart* (1967), *Heartroom* (1969) and *Heartcity* (1969) already indicates a degree of abstraction and immaterialization in architecture which can only be more closely explored using the new technologies that are available at the turn of the millennium:

> "Our architecture has no physical ground plan,
> but a mental one.
> There are no walls anymore.
> Our rooms are pulsating balloons.
> Our heartbeat becomes a room,
> our face is the building's façade." (1968)[11]

Thus rooms should be delimited and immaterialized, acoustic phenomena should be turned into living space and body fragments seen as dynamic picture screens. It certainly takes a fair

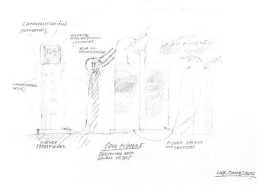

Coop Himmelblau,
Face-Space,
Soul Flipper, 1969

measure of youthfully unabashed daring to claim of a draft like *Feedback Vibration City* (1971):

> "The city is constantly changing with the heartbeats,
> the breathing, the alpha waves and the movements of the inhabitants.
> It is a city of communication thought out to the end."[12]

Nothing here is thought out to the end, but a lot of questions concerning traffic and city planning in a postindustrial, highly media-orientated society at the end of the 20th century are touched upon.[13]

In their designs, Coop Himmelblau make far more use than Haus-Rucker-Co of hybrid bodies which enter into symbiotic relationships with media elements. The elements concerned are television, radio, radiotelephony, scanners, touchscreens, electronic control systems, without there being a precise description in each case of the equipment or technology involved, apart from television, because some of them had not even been invented yet and could only have been anticipated at that time. Media-supported body architectures and architectural bodies point to the fact that in future human bodies as well as buildings will no longer be able to exist and function without media equipment, or "prostheses", to use the terminology of Baudrillard and Weibel. David Cronenberg's film *Videodrome* takes a similar direction, with its depiction of a media device developing human characteristics.

The paths indicated lead into space technology, art, medicine and above all into media architecture. One only has to read through the group's commentaries on a few of their projects in the late '60s to see what power there is in these drafts, a power which at the time was utopian but nevertheless futuristically practical:

> "The White Suit
> The cold medium of TV is getting hot.
> The audio-visual information
> that appears on and in the projection helmet
> is supported by smells. And the pneumatic
> vest presents tactile information." (1969)[14]

About *Heartspace* we read:

> "Through a transparent shell—like an enlarged
> rib-cage—the visible and audible heartbeat is
> changed into light." (1969)[15]

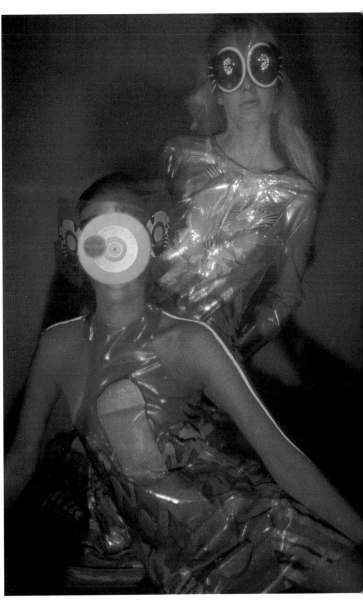

Haus-Rucker-Co,
Electric Skins and
Environment Transformer, 1968

And the project *Face-Space, Soul Flipper* has the following commentary:

> "Facial expressions, the façade of a person's moods
> are "objectivated" within the pillar. Smiles are
> translated into bright, happy colours, a sad expression
> turns the pillar blue. The sound program corresponds to the colours." (1969)[16]

In the years following, light-art, electronic sound sculptures and media art installations took up such ideas and put them into practice in a great variety of ways. One has to remember that in the late '60s and the '70s the Viennese avant-garde groups and Archigram in England belonged to an architectural subculture. And until innovations from the various subcultures have fermented sufficiently to influence mainstream trends, in architecture it is usually still a matter of at least twenty years.

It has only been since the late '80s that an explicit connection between such experiments

Coop Himmelblau,
The White Suit,
1969

Eden Bartz / Birgit Flos,
*Kraftwerk
Unplugged*

and architecture could be made visible using media façades, although even here, and yet more so in the artistic areas of cyberspace, the realization of these ideas has not progressed beyond its infancy. And there is still no sign of any far-reaching effects, except in the heads of a few theorists and futurologists working in high-tech think tanks like NASA or the research and engineering centre of BMW in Munich on visionary projects with a practical orientation. The fact, however, that in the meantime the concept of a purely structural body of architecture has generally begun to totter is definitely at least in part due to these avant-garde experimenters, a number of other less well-known groups and all those who have absorbed their ideas or who write and lecture about them.

The Body Debate in Virtual Worlds

The symbioses of human bodies and architectural bodies in the drafts of Coop Himmelblau are very early indicators of a trend towards a body debate, science fiction and cyborg creations and also proof that architecture is not only about "building" in the traditional sense. Coop Himmelblau has joined the army of image producers who draft powerful graphic symbols which from then on continue to have an effect in the minds of architects, technicians, engineers, philosophers, artists, media researchers, sociologists, doctors, etc., without ever necessarily having to exist in some tangible reality.

In contrast to the two Viennese groups, Archigram makes much greater use, in this virtualization process, of visual display screens (projection screens to begin with), which start out as independent but permanently installed room elements. In subsequent projects like *Instant City,* pictures of bodies are transported around the room on mobile, frameless screens. As a further consequence of such concepts, whole rooms become defined as picture screens, especially the case more recently with Toyo Ito and the Cologne group AG4. Ultimately whole rooms become sucked into such displays and picture walls, as shown in Jeffrey Shaw's *Virtual Museum,* and the result is a total dematerialization of the built spaces, a succession of virtual rooms within the screen or the media wall, which in turn takes the place of windows.

In the '70s a vehement body debate arose which has persisted to the present day and continues into the future, a debate conducted on several levels and in many disciplines, whereby there has hardly ever been any cross-reference between individual discourses, which have tended to run parallel or even counter to each other. To date hardly anyone has even taken a stab at demonstrating the interdisciplinary relationship between discourses and levels of discourse and establishing the cross-references between them.[17] Indeed this body debate has been partly accompanied by a grotesque hypocrisy, as though the body had first existed, then vanished, only to return and currently be faced with total extinction as it grows into a culture dominated by media and technology. The body has always been there—"naturally"—and always will be there. But its need for artificial spare parts will grow, and with these "prostheses" it will enter into a symbiotic fusion.

What has been remarkably neglected in the whole discussion, however, is the spiritual dimension, the fact that all changes to the material body involve changes to the immaterial body, the soul, and it is absurd to want to separate body and soul mechanically. This applies just as much to architecture and to building as

Jeffrey Shaw,
The Virtual Museum,
1991

to the perception of architecture and all other dealings with it.

In this context it is interesting to bear in mind the fitness trend and the ecology debate, emancipatory student movements, tendencies in holistic theory, happenings and installations in art; body-building, the body cult in the fashion industry and fashion journalism, rock, punk, New Wave, Techno and all the narcissistic implications in each case; not to mention the battle being waged by these movements against all tendencies towards a fragmentation of the body and a largely bodiless culture, as diagnosed and propagated especially by male philosophers and social and media theorists. Of central importance to this conflict is feminism, which is gradually establishing a widely acclaimed platform for itself as an academic discipline and which from the outset claimed a monopoly on the terms "body", "identity" and "gender".

The body debate in feminist theory and art was largely initiated by women addressing problems which have existed for a long time but which are nevertheless still highly topical; problems concerning power structures which have a repressive hold over the body, problems such as abortion, gynaecology, genetic engineering, political and economic discrimination. With aesthetic and journalistic means they are trying to draw attention to such problems and open up ways of tackling them. In this approach the body is seen for the most part as a bastion, as a last vestige of nature pitting itself against the unmistakable tendency of modernism and a persistently expanding culture revolving around science and technology to renounce the body and to penetrate into ever more expansive forms of cognition and existence, in which the physical body proves to be a hindrance. As a result of developments in the fields of bio-engineering and information technology, however, such positions are becoming increasingly undermined and outdated.

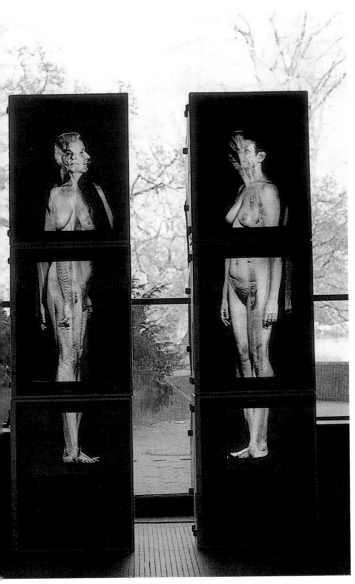

Franziska Megert,
Philemon and Baucis,
video installation, 1992/93

confront the growing cultural dominance of media and technology.

In effect it is not only "facies", the façade, the face of architecture which is changed by the new media, particularly by computers and their various display peripherals, or by the technology of sensor and control systems. This happens in fact only in the rarest of cases, as either partial or total media façades. On the contrary, the new media are conquering and cannibalizing architecture from the inside, by fundamentally restructuring and redesigning workplaces, forms of living and the technical systems with which the interiors of buildings are equipped.

And the question about the significance of physical bodies in virtual worlds: what happens when sexual identities can no longer simply be "read" from body surfaces, when biological and virtual bodies compete with each other? That is a question which even architecture can no longer shut its eyes to. It is perfectly obvious that such an eminently emotional and communicative aspect of life as eroticism is directly affected, but the direction of this development requires further illustration.

In this context it becomes more and more apparent that one pivot on which numerous developments in the virtuality debate hinge is William Gibson's *Neuromancer* trilogy (1984–1988), one of the few recent examples in which literature has effectively cut in on technological developments and, by creating images and giving impulses, has changed their direction decisively. In *Mona Lisa Overdrive*, the final volume of the trilogy, we read:

"She spread the elastic headband and settled the trodes across her temples—one of the world's characteristic human gestures, but one she seldom performed. She tapped the Ono-Sendai's battery test stud. Green for go. She touched the power stud and the bedroom vanished behind a colorless wall of sensory static. Her head filled with a torrent of white sound.
Her fingers found a random second stud and she was catapulted through the static wall, into cluttered vastness, the notional void of cyberspace, the bright grid of the matrix ranged around her like an infinite cage.

'Angela', the house said, its voice quiet but compelling, 'I have a call from Hilton Swift....'
'Executive override?' She was eating baked beans and toast at the kitchen counter.
'No,' it said, confidingly.
'Change your tone,' she said, around a mouthful of beans. 'Something with an edge of anxiety.'
'Mr. Swift is waiting,' the house said nervously.
'Better,' she said, carrying bowl and plate to the washer, 'but I want something closer to genuine hysteria....'
'Will you take the call?' The voice was choked with tension.
'No,' she said, 'but keep your voice that way, I like it.'
She walked into the living room, counting under her breath. Twelve, thirteen."[18]

In 1989, only one year after the publication of this novel, in which a house plays a character role as an emotionally controllable, interactive conversation partner, Tokyo saw the first public demonstration of the *TRON Intelligent House Concept,* under the direction of the architect Ken Sakamura, and in an exhibition park in the Netherlands Caes Dam put into operation his *House of the Future.* Both projects are essentially studies involving experiments in electronic equipment in living spaces. *TRON* is the first fully computerized single-family-unit house in the world, a conventional two-storey building for a couple with child or with integrated annex for grandparents.

The equipment consists of over 400 interconnected, computer-controlled subsystems, which

Cover of a German paperback
written by William Gibson,
Mona Lisa Overdrive, 1988

In this respect the creation of the *cyborg* as a human/machine being stands for a post-gender world, in which sexual identities can no longer be reduced to the traditional image of heterosexuality generally accepted in society, but in which the formation and definition of identities can vary within multiple options (heterosexual, homosexual, bisexual, transsexual and nonsexual).

As long as architectural discussion did not inevitably collide with theoretical positions and working models based on media and information technology, it could claim itself not to be affected, even if there were those branches of it which reached out into wider social contexts. Since the mid-'80s at the latest, however, even architecture has had to face up to these ideas, and the credit for this truly historical service to their art goes to Wolf Prix and Helmut Swiczinsky, the duo known as Coop Himmelblau, who in numerous drafts and accompanying texts at the end of the '60s and the beginning of the '70s pointed out that architecture would have to

Ken Sakamura,
TRON Intelligent House Concept,
1989

Ken Sakamura,
TRON Intelligent House Concept,
1989

cover all aspects of automation within buildings. The eighty-five windows are automatically opened and closed according to the temperature desired, wind direction, humidity of the air, the intensity of the sun's radiation and the pollution level of the air outside, as well as the heating and air conditioning are regulated via a network of sensors individualized for each living area. The transparency of some of the glazing can be adjusted according to the degree of privacy required: at the push of a button it can be darkened or made opaque. A music programme coupled up to the lighting is designed to instil equable moods in the occupants. The kitchen is equipped with a vacuum waste disposal unit and recipe files on laserdisc. The same applies in nearly all respects to Caes Dam's house project, which is a little less computerized especially concerning electronic entertainment and the personal comfort of the occupants, although

the computer-controlled cooker does have a repertoire of 500 recipes in its memory.

In the Tokyo project it was particularly the toilet which attracted attention. Apart from an automatic warm water douche, warm air drier and sensor-controlled seat-heating, it keeps the user informed about his pulse, blood pressure and the protein and sugar levels in his urine, stores all readings on a machine-readable code card and even prints out diet recommendations upon request.

In the cellar there is a computer-controlled container store for clothes and for archiving books, which here seems something of an antiquated idea. The electronics of the building also give rooms their shape and size: an acoustic generator makes it possible to simulate a variety of room volumes and sound characteristics for individual areas of the open-plan ground floor.[19]

The comparison shows that at least the direction of the experiment realized here follows the literary imagination. An immediate implementation a broader range of house technology is not to be expected; rather a more a gradual introduction of individual components.

This was also the conclusion reached at a specialist conference in Bonn on "The Intelligent House", which was jointly organized in July 1995 by the German Federal Ministry of Education, Science, Research and Technology and the Fraunhofer Institute of Systems Technology and Innovative Research (Karlsruhe). It was argued there that it was up to industry to decide when the vision of the "intelligent house" or

"smart building" should be realized, but that at present the potential market associated with it could not even be roughly estimated. At this conference, Reinhard Seyer of Daimler-Benz AG presented the intelligent house as an automation system structured as a network, and the symposium ended with a vision of future living outlined by the psychologist Carmen Lakaschus. She imagined that all functions of a really intelligent house should be controllable by the voices of its occupants, and thus the circle begins and ends with William Gibson.

During the course of the '80s, computer and sensor systems began to take more and more control over the technology with which buildings are equipped, whether factories, office towers or apartment blocks. Using PCs and media networks, they gradually but radically reorganized whole office layouts in practically every workplace, but it was not until the '90s that the real revolution actually set in. It is now in the process of thoroughly reshaping social relationships and consequently, as part of them, human eroticism too, in the way it relates to architecture and the dimension of space.

And so it is that at present the office, for example, as one of the most typical working environments of the 20th century—and for postindustrial societies this is even more the case than for industrial societies—is undergoing a radical social and economic change, but one which is also accompanied by changes in its architectural shape.[20] The office as a working environment has attracted the attention of those industries, technologies and new communica-

Gaetano Pesce, *Advertising Agency Chiat/Day*,
lobby, New York

Gaetano Pesce,
Advertising Agency Chiat/Day,
New York

tions processes which are geared to the future, for it is possible to turn the office into a specific locality which is ubiquitous: it can be anywhere, and in many cases it can be transferred into the homes of the employees. In those cases in which it remains in special office buildings, it will become largely multifunctional and media-orientated and will no longer be able to offer anyone secure, long-term employment. Thus traditional systems of order begin to feel the shock-waves and seek new structures in the form of process-orientated fields for experimentation. Under the influence of cost restraints and profitability studies this leads, for example, to levels of hierarchy being abolished, to lean management and to the downsizing of whole administration complexes, as already demonstrated worldwide in the early '90s, especially by large companies.

It is becoming more and more common for thousands of office jobs to be transferred to the outskirts of cities or into the homes of the employees and for suites of offices to be converted into living accommodation or at least redesignated as multifunctional premises. In the foreseeable future, the data highways which are rapidly being established and the forms of communication which are being routed along them will lead to a radical reduction in the floor area which firms need for their offices. The remaining office space will have to be more open, more stimulating and more communication-friendly. At the beginning of 1996, Philip Johnson, who even in ripe old age is still endowed

with an infallible nose for trends to come, diagnosed in a television interview that the skyscraper was like a dinosaur, predestined to die out. And even before that, Francis Duffy expressed the view that future office buildings must offer a wealth of information and ideas, and that every room, every wall, every conference area should promote creativity.[21]

This means that at least a part of the remaining office rooms and floor space should also become considerably more sensuous than is normally the case at present, especially for jobs and businesses with a creative, visual and communicative orientation. For the vast majority of office space, however, the exact opposite will happen: it will be depersonalized and dematerialized. A development which in the '90s has been vehemently pursued in the U.S. has been to put a stop to all forms of eroticism at the place of work, to make it a taboo and even a punishable offence. Under the cloak of emancipation, the protection of women and the prevention of sexual harassment, this is a trend which plays into the hands of the shift towards depersonalization. In the meantime men and women are required to maintain a distance of three feet from each other, male and female staff of the same firm are no longer allowed to fly in the same plane, not to mention any sort of "physical" contact between them, which can range from mere eye contact to actual body contact.

In many cultures the workplace in particular is traditionally a favourite place for getting to know people, for making contact with the

opposite sex and for meeting a partner, without this ever being synonymous with an indulgence in sexual practices. Where can one get to know someone's personal qualities better than at work? How can a team spirit ever evolve when every admiring, flirtatious glance is subject to the verdict of moral watchdogs?

This American trend towards a de-eroticization of human relationships at the workplace can in the meantime be observed in a number of European countries, too. Ultimately it can only lead to a solipsism and isolation among people who are largely incapable of making social contacts, rather than form self-determined, self-confident personalities who enjoy their individuality as well as life in the community, which is precisely the idealistic demand made by the protagonists of such developments. Architectural tendencies which run parallel to them can only be rejected by an "architecture for the senses" which supports a much more comprehensive image of humankind.

In the 21st century, however, many people working in typical office jobs will be able to establish and maintain online contact from home with their colleagues throughout the world. A lot of new firms will be built up entirely on this principle. Networks promote the creation of such online jobs, which allow a flexible arrangement concerning the time and place for work. On the other hand they will destroy more jobs than they create. The electronic, digital revolution has long been in the process of challenging and undermining the system of collective agreement between em-

Rem Koolhaas, *Centre for Art and Media Technology (ZKM),*
Karlsruhe, draft, 1988/89

Coop Himmelblau, *Campus de Jussieu*,
Paris, draft, 1992

Bibliothèque de France and the *Zentrum für Kunst und Medientechnologie (ZKM)* (1988/1989) in Karlsruhe as well as the *Campus de Jussieu* (1992) in Paris, floors and staircases as hierarchical levels are abolished in favour of large atria, variable green spaces and communication areas on the one hand, but on the other hand specific sections and components of the house, such as complete libraries, are hung into the open space like abstracted organs, and are thus reminiscent of the early projects of Haus-Rucker-Co and Coop Himmelblau.[24]

Parts of the building are connected via media, escalators and lifts; walls of monitor screens and media façades take over elements of traditional architectural rhetoric, for example from windows and walls, but turn them into something variable and dynamic. An architecture which on the outside is reduced to cubes and containers possesses façades and interiors which offer endless opportunities for creativity and playfulness. Nevertheless, the three Koolhaas drafts mentioned came to nothing because of increases in costs and the anxieties of the prospective developers, which only shows that such ideas are still far ahead of any general awareness.

The apparent contradiction between an architecture made up of boring cubes and one with traditionally modelled façades disappears as soon as one stops thinking in rigid alternatives and permits variable options, which of course include hybrid forms of all kinds. Then suddenly there is only a limited amount of truth in the statement that "the body without organs is the perfect body—forever reproducible",[25] since cybersex, for example, is precisely the attempt to take the immaterial and—in some way or other—modified satellite of a real, material body and equip it with individually controllable, organic and multisensory sensations. Thus the return of the bodies could take place in data space—cyberspace as a recorporealization of

ployers and employees which has established itself in Germany and other European countries since World War II. Jobs with precisely defined duties and areas of responsibility based on fixed contracts will become less and less common.

How will eroticism and finding a partner develop in a society in which the statement made by the American virtual reality researcher Allucquère R. Stone, that she spends more time with her computer than with any of her friends, has become the rule rather than the exception?[22] This is at least an indicator that forms of virtual sexuality, if not actually cybersex in a wider sense, will no longer be anything unusual in the foreseeable future.

It would be absolutely wrong to claim that all architecture follows the principle of dematerialization, disembodiment and Virilio's theses concerning the "disappearance of reality". Such a necessity does not even arise in the field of media architecture in its narrow sense.[23] Here it is perfectly possible to reconcile apparently opposing tendencies, as demonstrated in the oeuvre of Rem Koolhaas. In his drafts for the

Jean Nouvel,
Fondation Cartier, Paris, 1991–94

Jean Nouvel, *Media Park*,
Cologne, competition block 1,
1991

Jean Nouvel, *Galeries Lafayette*, Berlin, 1992–96

the process of abstraction and disembodiment, with a host of conceivable consequences for medicine, eroticism and architecture.

To date modern media theory has taken hardly any notice of architecture, with the exception of Paul Virilio, who is, of course, himself an architect. Architecture, on the other hand, will not be able to manage in future without approaches based on media theory. Such approaches, however, are largely characterized by a negligible degree or even a complete lack of practical orientation, and end up focusing instead on their unease concerning real or ostensible tendencies in the development of society as a whole.

By way of examples, the work of Jean Nouvel and Paul Virilio can be seen to demonstrate this creative interplay between theory and practice. Nouvel pursues a theoretical approach which corresponds fully with the practice of current media development, the trend towards

dematerialization, even immateriality and the "disappearance of reality", as Virilio calls it. But while the theorist filters a doomsday atmosphere out of his analysis, the practitioner turns it into artistically experimental, functional architecture.

Nouvel does not think much of an elaborate town planning which is constantly being outdated by the processes of reality.[26] For him the contemporary city is constantly inventing itself—with bursting vitality and in spite of the architects: the traditional visual grammar of cities, with gates, axes, and centres, has been invalidated and has become obsolete under the onslaught of a chaotic reality. It is for this reason that Nouvel, the film enthusiast, always accepts the given facts of a locality and talks of the narrative character of a city or of individual buildings as being parafilmic with videographic effects, whereby he sees his own role as that of a scenographer. Not, however, in the sense of a

theatre stage designer, but of one working with film images, who, by the use of montage and a variety of perspectives in his raw material, and with the aid of filters, rasters and textile materials, is able to produce an ingenious interplay of cultural connotations and traditions.

In keeping with the tendencies in media theory described above, Nouvel says: "*Le futur de l'architecture n'est pas architectural.*"[27] Here he can build on a wealth of additional evidence, among other things on the cost structure of modern office buildings, during the completion phase of which the share of the costs which are genuinely architectural continues to fall, so that it now accounts for only about 30 percent, while there is a corresponding rise in the share spent on technical equipment and media. Instead Nouvel talks of omnipresent media settings, of textures, hybrid surfaces, overlapping, layering, passages, monitor screens, the hyper-realism of a scanner-like eye. Here control is in

Orlan in front of her installation
Omnipresence (Entre-Deux),
1993/94

the hands of an editor who cuts his footage to offer insights, glimpses, views, which again are obstructed, filtered, partially hidden by screens.

This is where principles of eroticism come into play, but concerning the role of human bodies in Nouvel's architectural settings there is no mention to be found anywhere in the commentaries to his drafts. They obviously have to project themselves onto the scene, like animated, cut-out silhouettes. In view of so much transparency, as in the case of the *Cartier Building* in Paris, eroticism has a hard time and can only put on a two-dimensional show, a shadow play on screens of light.

Nouvel has the impudence—born of artistic sensitivity and conviction—to reintroduce to architecture what the critics had for twenty years been campaigning against: the "box", and that other related structure which in Venturi's terminology is called "the decorated shed". This time though, wherever possible, it is a media-packed high-tech box, with at least one side theatrically constructed as an enormous monitor wall. His boxes are multifunctional, they are event-boxes which play with immaterial colour and light effects, and are enveloped in half-tone screens and media façades. The tendency here is towards ever increasingly thin walls and membranes. Equipped with a number of sensors, however, they assume a variety of control functions and on top of that they are decorated with animated graphic surfaces or with moving pictures and captions. In place of the traditional

façade there is an interchangeable, cleverly layered and half-toned graphic shell, parts of it electronically high-tech, others ironically contradictory and deliberately old-fashioned in the form of printed glass or even painted canvas.

For Nouvel the architectural material which takes over the role of traditional conventions and façade symbolism is the electronic image. The façade, the dividing line between interior and exterior, becomes a skin, tempers the surface, and in so doing becomes an interface between transmitters and receivers, between sensors which register a variety of factors on the outside and convert them into impulses controlling operational sequences on the façade itself or inside the building. The dividing line between interior and exterior is erased, the entrance for example is only suggested by curtains of light or the visitor gains direct access to the interior of the building via an escalator from underground parking decks, bus bays or railway stations. In Nouvel's own words, space thus logically becomes a secondary parameter. For Virilio, however, that amounts to an apocalypse and the extinction of traditional architecture. In an interview with Andreas Ruby he stated:

"(...) for me architecture is losing its characteristic features. It is losing all its components, one by one (...) Everything by which architecture could once be defined is being replaced more and more by other technologies which so far have had nothing to do with building. (...) The image-orientated being is becoming more important than the construction-orientated being. And another example of dematerialization: architecture is threatening to drift off completely into design."[28]

For Virilio, the logical consequence of the extinction of real space is the extinction of the human body, and of human eroticism as we know it. And as is to be expected in view of the persistent faith which the French have in progress and the predominance of high-tech medicine, he derives from this basic attitude his attacks not only on the new media but also on the modern orthodox school of medicine:

"The loss, or to be more precise, the extinction of real space in any (physical or geophysical) dimension to the exclusive advantage of real-time tele-technologies with their absence of time lag inevitably leads to the fact that not just technology generally but especially micromachines will penetrate deep into the organs of living beings."[29]

In his publications in the '90s, Virilio drafts dramatic scenarios with the fervour of a religious fanatic, scenarios of human bodies pumped full of chemical stimulants, overequipped with replacement parts and other mechanical and electronic implants, invaded by biotechnological micromachines, but in each case the scenarios are utterly devoid of any reality or practical orientation. The world (and medicine) has not yet witnessed the masochist who might take pleasure in having one limb after another and one organ after another replaced with artificial spare parts. One exception, however, might be the artist Orlan, who—in live performances, well attended by media—regularly has her face altered by cosmetic surgery to vary her surface identity and to present her body as an ever new work of art. But it appears that all these opera-

Stelarc, *Amplified Body,
Laser Eyes and Third Hand*

tions have not had any effect on the inner core of her identity.

Thus it can only be intended as a deliberately theatrical, scientifically fictional warning when, for example, Virilio quotes the Australian Stelarc as a classic example of a kinetic artist addicted to technology instead of calling him a dancer:

> "Bristling with antennas and electrodes and equipped with two laser eyes, our voluntary mutant goes quite far with his analogy to teleoperator rhetoric (a form of robotics in which the operator controls the android from inside), but what he achieves is a drastic conversion, for his hopes actually go in a completely opposite direction. 'Today', he [Stelarc] says, 'technology sticks to our skin, it is becoming part of our bodies'—starting with our watches and going as far as artificial hearts. For me that means the end of the Darwinian idea of evolution, conceived as an organic development based on natural selection over a period of millions of years. Thanks to nanotechnology the human being is from now on in a position to absorb technology into its body."[30]

Cyberspace and Cybersex

Real space is extinct, the bodies are mutilated and destroyed, and so the only thing logically remaining for Virilio is virtual space, which means we have arrived in cyberspace and, in our specific context, at cybersex.

According to Donna Haraway's assessment of the situation,[31] we are in the middle of a development process towards a society of hybrid machines and organisms, which would actually agree with Virilio's theses. It seems that even the remotest prospect of a "cyborgasm" has released undreamt-of flights of creative fantasy in recent years. During the course of the '90s there has been hardly any other phenomenon concerning which so comparatively little information and experience are available, but about which there has been so much and such committed speculation as cyberspace and cybersex. Far-reaching scientific, aesthetic, ethical and sociopolitical considerations have been attached to these speculations although it is totally uncertain whether they will ever reach fulfilment.

The link between architecture and eroticism is already established in the concepts coined, although it is important to be aware that what is meant here are virtual rooms, worlds and forms of communication. In view of the large international congresses and the research and publications on the theme of "Telepolis", the discussion about virtual architecture and human behaviour conditioned by them is becoming all the more urgent, not only for the theory of architecture but also for practising architects.[32]

Definitions are as sticky as ever. Largely for commercial reasons, American exponents, researchers and commentators occasionally extend the term cyberspace so far that it embraces practically the whole field of telecommunications. But then the special kicks involved get lost. After all, in terms of speculation, the most alluring thing about cyberspace and cybersex is the prospect of being able to make use of this creative machine and its special software to plunge physically—in the form of a manipulable proxy for one's own body—into a three-dimensionally simulated, virtual world, and from there to cross boundaries to explore one's potential for adventure and enjoy the freedom to indulge with impunity in all one is denied in one's own limited reality.

High performance computers in conjunction with the corresponding software are reality machines which, according to Steinmüller, have become veritable wish-fulfilment machines even before they have been technically realized.[33] Old dreams and wishes of humanity come to life with a vengeance: the dream of ubiquity, of infinite sexual potency, of crossing the boundaries of one's own sex, one's age, looks, experience of pleasure and pain, and ultimately the dream of immortality. The body becomes a testing site for one's curiosity, for one's desires, it becomes a metaphor of one's longing for intense sensations. Hopes are pinned on the machine being able to fix what the body, bound up in its social reality, is not (any longer) capable of: cleanly, harmlessly, in mentally uncomplicated fashion, in the age of AIDS, the safe alternative to risks which could otherwise cost one's health or life. Romanticism comes alive and mingles with the prospect of pleasure and business.

It is noticeable that European cyberspace and virtual reality researchers normally consider the technical, aesthetic and ethical implications, whereas Americans always set their sights on the economic dimension as well, recognizing immediately that here there is the possibility of doing big business. Thus the only American book to date which has been published exclusively on the subject of cybersex[34] is a mixture of catalogue advertizing bulletin boards, online chat lines (for telephone sex), floppy disks and

Data suit in the magazine *Max*

interactive CD-ROMs—thinly disguised with short commentaries[35]— and a promise for the future of:

> "the ultimate cybersex experience via virtual reality (...) the experience of simulated sex (...) The marriage of that oldest and most powerful of human drives to the most sophisticated and powerful new technology is an endeavor that may soon irrevocably redefine human sexual relationships."[36]

The text gushes with sales optimism and the same up-close naivety with which top American politicians push economic interests when it is a question of opening international markets for data highway systems, and yet it is also interspersed with serious information. Ultimately the reader is left in no doubt that practically everything that has been available on the market so far is firstly in poor taste and of inferior quality and secondly has nothing whatever to do with genuine cybersex. "There's only one kind of virtual sex so far. To use it, close your eyes and fantasize."[37] So it would in fact be possible without any money at all. But how can that compare with an almost religiously euphoric prospect of bliss?

> "Just imagine yourself in the near future getting decked out in your cybersexual suit for a hot night. Out on the nets you plug your jack into your cybernetic interface device, which then enables you to receive and transmit realistic tactile sensations. Suddenly, you are in a strange new world where miraculously you can run your hands through virtual hair, touch virtual silk, (...) virtual clothing and caress virtual flesh."[38]

Seen in the sober light of day, that in fact comes much nearer to what can possibly be realized than the speculations of most of the "serious" scholars would lead us to believe. The difference in quality between the virtual and the real world is revealed. There is no attempt to delude anyone into believing in the possibility of that totally and undifferentiatedly simulated world about which writers and scholars have gone into raptures ever since Stanislav Lem's phantomatic novels *Transfer* (1961) and *The Futurological Congress* (1967), as though it could seriously be imminent. Only if such possib-

ilities were to actually take effect would S. J. Schmidt's argument become relevant:

> "The traditional differentiations into truth/falsehood, reality/appearance, reality/fiction, utopia and reality/simulation are now being supplemented with the differentiation reality/virtuality/hyperreality, so that all other differentiations will have to be newly contextualized and semantically reinterpreted accordingly."[39]

No even remotely realistic estimates have been made so far concerning the technological consequences for the fields cyberspace and cybersex. The very toying with such ideas, however, is in itself an indicator of the undoubted existence of such trends in technological and social development. It is striking that at least so far it is almost exclusively men who have been involved in these euphoric cybersex fantasies. Are they perhaps driven by the hope of being able to live out in a virtual world all those macho dreams of the complete manipulability of the female body which in their social reality ever more articulate and emancipated women are putting a stop to?

Is it escapism, inferiority complexes, delusions of omnipotence which make cybersex seem so attractive to a lot of men? Or is it in fact that intellectual and technical thirst for adventure and experimentation, the urge to discover new worlds of cognition, of sensation and experience, which makes some men more quickly prepared than women, at least in scientific experiments and in their imagination, to free themselves from their physical bodies? What losses are there to offset this possible new experience? Michael Heim's technical analysis should have rather a sobering effect:

> "Filtered through the computer matrix, all reality becomes patterns of information. When reality becomes indistinguishable from information, then even Eros fits the schemes of binary communication. Bodily sex appears to be no more than an exchange of signal blips on the genetic corporeal network. Further, the erotic-generative source of formal idealism becomes subject to the laws of information management."[40]

And the blissful prospect of crossing all sorts of erotic boundaries, without any cause for conflict, without problems, suffering, disease, interference, complications? When at last a female voice joins in the chorus of scientific experts, like that of Marilouise Kroker, then despair is surely a suitable reaction to what is being done to the human body:

> "That's why we are interested in the creation of a virus-free gender, a transgenic gender. That's why we think the only good sex today is recombinant sex. Sex without origin, localizing gender, or referential signifier."[41]

The opposing points of view seem incompatible, if only because no one has yet had the opportunity to test virtuality and cybersex intensively enough to be able find out what it is really like. Again and again, the shamans and wizards in thousands of fairy tales from various cultures have unanimously evoked what seems to be a primeval urge of humanity, to break out of the constrictions of one's own body and to go through metamorphoses. But will the morphing of one's own body really be such a wonderful experience? CAVES (Cave Automatical Virtual Environments), cyberspace test labs which for the first time really allow the total immersion into a three-dimensional virtual environment and are being established in growing numbers at enormous costs in the most advanced American and European research institutions, open totally new dimensions of virtual communication including cybersex for the years to come:

> "A floating world of sexual software that can be massaged, mirrored, uplinked and downloaded into a body that always knew that it didn't have to be content with the obsolete carcerals of nature, discourse and ideology. In the galaxy of sexual software, morphing is the only rule: the quick mutation of all the binary signs into their opposites. (...) A floating sex for the electronic body where fetishes can be transcribed into the cold language of data, and the digital libido made to send out its sex scent as part of the coded games of electronic sex."[42]

But all speculation aside, what at present are the prospects for this world of a post-male, post-female, last sex? It is certain that cyberspace will come on a considerable scale, if only because of the growing demand in various fields of application for three-dimensional animated computer graphics. But cybersex?

At the moment supply is practically non-existent, the costs are horrendous and the technical problems enormous. However, the clumsy, head-mounted visual display units of the early years, which tended to be difficult to balance, have—at least in the more advanced research institutes—since given way to lightweight, mobile displays. Monika Fleischmann's cyberspace experiments in Germany at the Society for Mathematics and Data Processing (Gesellschaft für Mathematik und Datenverarbeitung) are often attempts to reconcile the worlds of aesthetic, poetic, erotic and architectural experience.

What computers will ultimately be able to perform in substituting worlds of sensuous experience is at the moment totally uncertain. The transfer of psychological components, of emotions, of gender-specific patterns of experience,

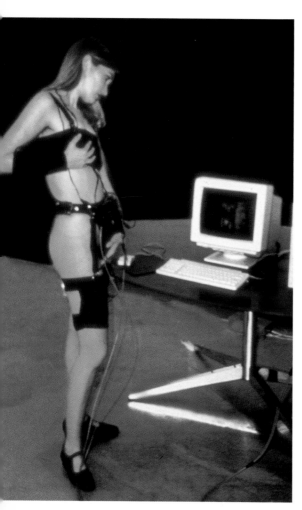

Stahl Stenslie,
Inter-Skin, 1993,
participant

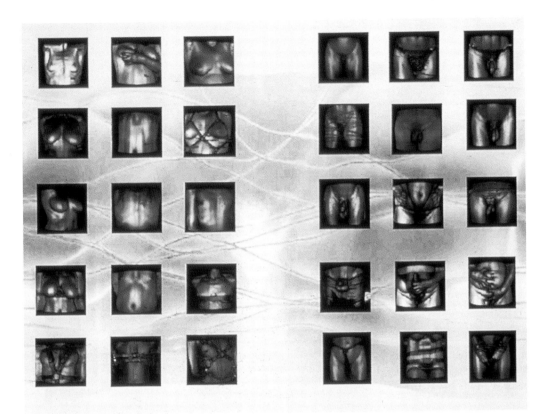

Stahl Stenslie / Kirk Woolford, *Cyber SM,*
Body Bank, 1993

Stahl Stenslie / Kirk Woolford, *Cyber SM,*
Body Bank, detail, 1993

cultural codes, metaphysics and transcendency
onto the harddisk can probably never succeed
to the extent that a perfect artificial environment
will ensue.

In 1993 the Norwegian Stahl Stenslie and the
American Kirk Woolford, two of the first gradu-
ates of the "Kunsthochschule für Medien" in
Cologne, submitted as their diploma thesis the
first genuine cybersex project, which they called
Cyber SM, "a comment on tactile technology".[43]
There they proved that over the distance
between Cologne and Paris it was in fact possible using data suits to meet another person in
three-dimensional data space and to send each
other tactile stimuli while communicating with
each other orally via the telephone.

Although not originally intended as an exercise in cybersex, it aroused so much interest in
the media that it was developed through a number of intermediate stages into a genuine cybersex project. The final result was a complex
experimental setup—far more sophisticated
than any other comparable VR installations—
which also carried implications for virtual architecture since it is just as possible to establish a
connection to a room in the same building as
it is across countries and even between continents, and using remote control it is also
possible to change virtual environments at
any distance:

"We designed the Cyber SM project to allow
people to 'touch' each other over a physical distance. The project included two suits worn by the

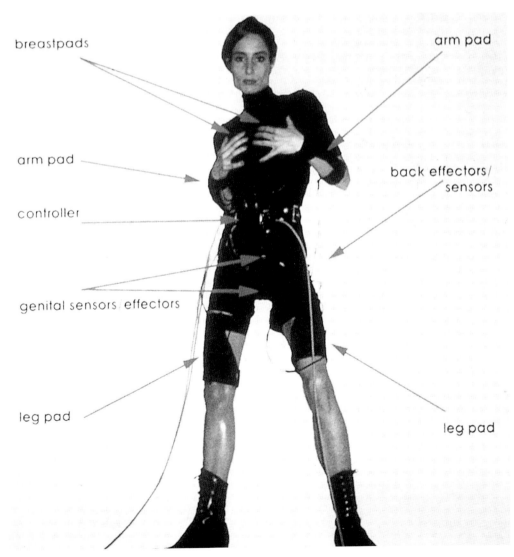

breastpads

arm pad

arm pad

controller

back effectors/
sensors

genital sensors effectors

leg pad

leg pad

Stahl Stenslie,
Inter-Skin Suit

Woody Vasulka,
Brotherhood-Table III

tion of itself in both erotic and artistic respects. Howard Rheingold points out that the ingrained ideas of a unique image of the human body will probably make way for a body concept which is far more flexible.[46]

Ingrid Stoppa-Sehlbach argues that in cyberspace the self-reference of the individual is no longer restricted to its physical existence but has access to a further level of experience,[47] and that the individual feels himself to be a participant in virtual processes incorporated into the artificial reality. Not least because of the combination of variable visual, acoustic and kinetic elements will this lead to new forms of aesthetic perception, and also of creation and experience, which, because of the overlapping of real and artificial existences, will become hybrid qualities.

Virtual, telematic architectures are invading our lives on an ever increasing scale. This will turn into an exponential increase as soon as the general access to networks via data highways has left its mark, particularly on the next generations. The nonsimultaneity of what is simultaneous, the palimpsest-like structure of post-modern reality, in which texts written on top of one another may exist simultaneously but can only be read consecutively,[48] will have an even more lasting effect on everyday life in postindustrial society than what we are seeing today.

In other words, we will have to learn to move in a constantly increasing number of "realities" and on more and more different levels of reality. The negative effects which this could have on the identity of human beings are what Baudrillard and Virilio have been propagating in their publications for several years. They project ever more apocalyptic visions of beings made up of artificial spare parts which have totally lost control of themselves and have even lost the very core of their identity, while it is precisely on the spare parts and antennas that someone like Peter Weibel pins his hopes. The prospect of a possibility to clone human beings adds an even more ambiguous turn of the screw to this discussion. And yet it is to be presumed that humanity will turn out to have a more robust nature than the prophets of doom can imagine, especially as all these processes will enter our lives only gradually and partially, and not take a sudden and complete hold on them. The undeniable aesthetic gain will have to be weighed against the losses. This network culture will presumably bring about the biggest changes in science, literature, new media arts and, of course, architecture:

"The virtual city will be global and have no territorial boundaries. It will be fractal—and thus infinite—and it will only exist in the networks of com-

participants, a database of 3-D scans used as proxies for the participants' physical bodies, and 2 computers connected with international ISDN-lines. Once the participants put on one of the suits, they would build a virtual body by picking from the database. When ready, the computers exchanged these proxies, and each participant received the other participant's body on the screen in front of them. By rotating and zooming the virtual body, participants could place the pointer over regions of the virtual body. When the participant clicked a button, the computer transmitted this 'touch' over the ISDN-lines to the owner of the virtual body. The remote computer translated this 'touch' into physical impulse (vibration or electric shock) generated by the remote participant's suit."[44]

Eight different stimulators triggered off stimuli which the participants could distribute over various parts of the body at the same time, or concentrate with accumulative effect on just one body zone. By the use of boosters amplifying stimuli to over-realistic levels, the erogenous zones could indeed be stimulated with variable intensity. From a "Synthetic Body Bank" participants could choose from twenty upper and twenty lower parts of digitalized bodies (male or female), giving a total of 400 possible combinations. The development of a Remote Environmental Control Device (RECD) showed at least

the first signs of being able to influence a remote environment, thus creating an escape route from the sterile laboratory setup and triggering off anticipatory moods such as fear and curiosity.

It is clear that this was quite a complex experiment offering grounds enough to discuss the whole spectrum of cybersex themes, from identity problems to flights of ecstasy in a world of illusion, a discussion in which all questions concerning regulations, civil law and civic duties are ultimately posed anew. This experiment also opens the way for further cybersex projects, and even for applications in medicine, sport and art.

In conclusion then let us turn to the aesthetic and architectural implications of cyberspace. There is no doubt that cyberspace possesses artistic and aesthetic dimensions,[45] but not before the equipment becomes more generally available and considerably cheaper will visual and acoustic artists be able to begin exploring and exploiting the potential of this new medium. Interactivity will be one essential feature, and it is already foreseeable that in the next century this technology—as a successor to video and other media arts—is likely to make decisive changes to humanity's percep-

Toyo Ito, *Visions of Japan*,
Installation, 1991

In architect's offices and among the animation specialists this new job type with its very own profile has already begun to emerge. Complex animations can only be created by someone who has programming skills, three-dimensional powers of imagination, the ability to write screenplays, to direct and to combine music with moving pictures. In future this will be just as important for sophisticated presentations in the context of big competitions as for the design of cyberspace settings, which can then, as hybrids, be included in exhibitions, opera and theatre performances or other artistic installations. This sector will see the emergence of special service industries.

Nevertheless in the future we will still need a roof over our heads, a partner in bed and something on the table to eat and drink because not even then will we be able to live on virtual food. And so at the end of his interview with Andreas Ruby on the extinction of real space, even Paul Virilio comes to the realistic assessment that future space will have both real and virtual characteristics:

> "Architecture will take place in both fields—in reality (materiality, for the stones will still be there) and virtuality (the transmission of electromagnetic signals). The real space of a house will no longer exist without the reality of transmission."[51]

By analogy this could also be applied to the relationship between architecture and eroticism. And as far as cyberspace is concerned, there is still truth in the old saying that things are never as bad as they seem. Or, to put it poetically: the discussion about cyberspace and cybersex has certain similarities with the debate among 17th-century metaphysical poets in England concerning reality and appearance, illusion and reality, dream and reality:

> "Dear love, for nothing lesse than thee
> Would I have broke this happy dreame,
> It was a theame
> For reason, much too strong for phantasie,
> Therefore thou wakd'st me wisely; yet
> My Dreame thou brok'st not, but continued'st it;
> Thou art so true, that thoughts of thee suffice,
> To make dreames truth; and fables histories;
> Enter these armes, for since thou thoughtst it best,
> Not to dreame all my dreame, let's do the rest."[52]

puters. Since they are not bound to any territory, hackers, cybernauts, cyberfreaks will settle in the forks of fractal space, develop their own codes, breed their own strains, and one day completely new mutations will emerge. Neuronal networks will provide the necessary supports and stimuli."[49]

If Vilèm Flusser could read these lines, they would sound to him like a confirmation of some of his main theses since they reflect a further development and the gradual realization, at least in part, of his visions of a telematic culture. The result will be a new branch of the architectural profes-

sion: the designer and architect of virtual spaces. This line of business is also something which Howard Rheingold has already described:

> "A specialist of a completely new calibre, a cyberspace architect who designs and fits out cybernetic spaces and settings. The abilities required can be compared with the talents traditionally expected from architects, film directors, novelists, generals, sports coaches, dramatists and the programmers of video games. It will be the cyberspace designer's job to ensure that the adventure appears real, and that will require both artistic and technical abilities."[50]

SENSUOUS ARCHITECTURE: THE FINAL PLEA

"One can dream of making the bodies of buildings as sensory as human bodies. Of making rooms—the spatial cavities within buildings—as intensively sensuous an experience as one's own body cavities: an architecture to see, hear, feel, 'an architecture for the sensual imagination'!"[1]

Wolfgang Meisenheimer

"Beyond architecture, our culture at large seems to drift towards a distancing, a kind of chilling, de-sensualization and de-eroticization of the human relation to reality. Painting and sculpture have also lost their sensuality, and instead of inviting sensory intimacy, contemporary works of art frequently signal a distancing rejection of sensuous curiosity."[2]

Juhani Pallasmaa

Heikkinen-Komonen, *Finnish Embassy*, Washington, D.C., 1994

It has always been appropriate to hold a pessimistic view of human civilization, and that is still so today. It opens the eyes, it may assist in becoming active, but it may also paralyse and cause all resistance to end in world-weariness. Barbara Radice, Ettore Sottsass and a number of other contributors to the unique Italian design and architecture magazine *Terrazzo* ensure that in both layout and design it breathes a sensuality from every page emulated by hardly any other publication in this century. Its staff travelled around the world in 1990 to capture in snapshot-like fashion the unvarnished reality of life in the metropolitan areas of the world. The result, presented in 1991 in the sixth issue of the magazine, can depress even the most hardened souls. The senses are continuously irritated and shocked by overbuilt, mushrooming cities, concrete deserts, masses of cars, chaotic streets, structural monstrosities, cities like festering dumps. Barbara Radice's conclusion was an admission of the failure of the modern age:

"Looking at the thousands of photographs shot at different latitudes on four continents, what hits the eye is the extraordinary compactness of the urban panorama, its disconcerting homogeneity, so that we are finally allowed to say that the "International Style" has turned into a 'Planetarian Style'."[3]

It is not that there is no room for eroticism in such chaos, but in this direct, unglossed overview most urban architecture on this globe reveals itself as ugly, repulsive, insensitive,

Opposite page:
Carlo Scarpa, *Banca Popolare*, staircase, Verona, 1973–81

depraved, arbitrary, and that is a cause for infinite sadness. What is shown here, however, is not an irreversible process at the end of which the overpopulated metropolises will simply choke to death on such problems as sinking ground water levels, air pollution, garbage, traffic jams, crime, energy crises, supply problems, etc. It is rather a question of finding control mechanisms to prevent this from happening. The experience that particularly the architecture of the big cities can make people physically and mentally ill reaches back into the 19th century, but it has been particularly intensified by the population explosion of recent decades. We have tried to show some examples of how sensuous design can turn architecture and city ambience into positive urban factors which make living and working in the city a pleasurable rather than a frustrating experience. Architecture can strengthen identification and it can even have therapeutic effects.

In this respect, architects have a special responsibility to society, especially those who train young architects. When, at the end of a book that is dedicated to sensuality and the interplay between architecture and eroticism in a great variety of fields, we plead once again for an "architecture for the senses", it is because

such an architecture is seen as a survival strategy and a factor which guarantees a self-determined life—both private and professional—of happiness and enjoyment.

What is meant by an "architecture for the senses" is not the same as the common and conventional ideal of proportional balance and aesthetic forms. It is an architecture which fulfils all its obligations in terms of functionality, but which beyond that displays to a particularly high degree multisensory qualities which turn it into an architecture that can be experienced, that keeps its occupants and users aesthetically, artistically and socially "awake", makes them critical and creative. In their various individual styles, Coop Himmelblau, Zaha Hadid and Lebbeus Woods, but also post-modern architects like Michael Graves, Hans Hollein, James Stirling and Stanley Tigerman, create architecture that meets these criteria, alludes to such sensuous qualities and gives it new shape.

A feeling for bodies, for forms and materials is as much a part of it as the emotional orientation towards certain buildings. This applies to private dwellings at least as much as to public, commercial or cultural buildings.[4] For private houses, the close cooperation between architect and builder-owner is crucial. Nowhere is indi-

Heikkinen-
Komonen,
Finnish Embassy,
Grand Canyon
Atrium,
Washington, D.C.

Jean-Claude Galibert / Alberto Gomez,
Villa Tigre del Mar, Mexico

Jean-Claude Galibert / Alberto Gomez,
Villa Tigre del Mar, Mexico, staircase

vidualism greater than in the choice of building and living styles, and it is precisely for this reason that within certain limits the builder-owner can contribute design proposals of his own. Sensual buildings increase the spiritual and physical well-being of their occupants and heighten their sense of aesthetics. Wherever possible, gardens should be part of this, as consciously shaped living environments, as extensions of the house into nature. This is not, however, an argument in favour of urban sprawl à la Los Angeles. Cities need essential structures otherwise it is not possible to achieve urbanity or to protect nature from destruction. An important task facing architects is to give a sensuous flair to the designs of tower blocks and large apartment complexes, thus raising the quality of life to be lived there.

It is an illusion to think that sensual and well thought out architecture can only go hand in hand with luxury and a fat wallet. It is precisely the clever, imaginative, economical, eccentric, sophisticated solutions and the houses that make colours, special materials or even technical processes visible which are often the ones

that offer particularly good value for money, and they are also the ones that are so joyfully and passionately shaped and experienced by their occupants. And especially in the building of private houses it is the lesser known architects, the ones who have not already made architectural history or are quoted in all the magazines, who together with the builder-owners for whom they are working often create particularly original, functional and sensuous houses.

But even famous masters of their craft excel in this field. Take for example Louis Barragan's sculptural, artistically structured, coloured walls full of sensual intensity under the light of Mexico, or take Mark Mack's astonishingly individualistic, sculptural ensembles of colourful houses that were influenced by Barragan, by the Orient and the Occident, by Mediterranean and Southern Californian regional building styles. Or, to stay on the West Coast, think of Frank Gehry's sensuously witty building complexes, which are highly unusual because they convert images, everyday objects, even fish to architectural purposes. It was after all Gehry who revived many an architect's feeling for the multisensory qual-

ities of seemingly banal materials and for the joys of improvisation.

There are very few architects with Gehry's ability to bring out the bodiliness of architecture, the interpenetration and subsequent separation of individual bodies, or with his ability to play with light and shade and, in keeping with Le Corbusier's famous definition, to see architecture as playing with bodies under the light. Or, to mention two other master-architects from Los Angeles, think of Franklin D. Israel's masculine sensuousness, or of Eric Owen Moss' witty and daring experiments with rooms and staircases. In this respect, Deconstructivism has given a previously undreamt-of freedom to architecture, new possibilities to play with ramps, platforms, acute angles, intersecting curvatures, breathing life into the increasingly sterile languages of shapes.

Modernism may be more abstract, but even Le Corbusier and Mies had an excellent feel for staging geometrical body-games. Among their many successors, Charles Gwathmey, a star architect from the American East Coast, has become a master at playing with cubes, cylin-

Paul Merrick,
private house
near Vancouver,
1973–74

Helmut Jahn's weekend house
on the Eagle River, Wisconsin

Charles Gwathmey / Robert Siegel,
De Menil Private Residence, East Hampton, New York, 1979

ders, cones, with volumes and light, a mastery which he shares with Richard Meier, combining passion with an austerity of form. Meier's residential and museum buildings are particularly marked by his enthusiasm for geometrical detail, ingenious lighting and a dialogue between architecture as an expression of civilization and the taming of nature. In Europe, too, a large number of excellent residential buildings have been produced by architects of whom similar observations could be made—although of course individually very different—such as Bela Bambek, Karla Kowalski, Carlo Scarpa, Claudio Silvestrin and Gie Wollaert, to name but a few.

The international museum boom of the '80s gave rise to some of the most beautiful, most physical buildings for a long time, perfectly integrated into the urban context. Above all James Stirling's *Neue Staatsgalerie (New State Gallery)* in Stuttgart (1983), which derives its intellectually and culturally refined sensuality from the sheer bodiliness of its individual parts,

thus—in spite of some obvious shortcomings—establishing a host of architectural references through the ages. Furthermore, its ingenious masterplan and its many multisensory details are proof that this is indeed one of the rare masterpieces of contemporary "sensuous architecture". Among museum buildings of the '90s, it is first and foremost Mario Botta's *San Francisco Museum of Modern Art* (1994) that many critics have praised as expressive evidence of erotic architecture. We can only hope that, in order to attract customers, commercial architecture will return to highlighting its buildings with much greater sensuality than has been the case under the severe pressure of competition in recent years. In this field, there has been a general degeneration in sales culture. It is indicative of this trend, for example, that for a long time Jean Nouvel's *Galeries Lafayette* in Berlin's Friedrichstrasse experienced considerable difficulties in finding tenants for the vacant shop space. When it opened in March of 1996, however, it was

often so dangerously overcrowded in the first few days that it repeatedly had to be closed, simply because the Berlin people were so eager to shop in a building (or often only to look at it!) whose interior and exterior design consciously addressed the senses.

It is just unfortunate that Nouvel's original concept, with its wealth of exciting contrasts, was trimmed down to a conventional degree of mediocrity by unimaginative shop fitters and store managers who were afraid of any sort of experiment. The media effects, too, which were supposed to give an optical quality to the game with virtuality, reality and fiction, almost all fell victim to the proposed cuts in budget. Nevertheless, the two remaining large glass cones are indicators of the finesse Nouvel had mobilized to turn the acts of buying and selling into experiences of sheer pleasure. The fact, however, that at the same time he blatantly ignored long-established and sacred consumerist ideology was just too frivolous a plan for the store-bosses.

Richard Meier, *Museum of Arts and Crafts*,
Frankfurt am Main, 1982–85

Carlos Zapata / John West, private house,
Miami Beach, Florida, 1992–94

Opposite page, bottom: Frank Gehry / Mark Mack, *John Whitney House* in Santa Monica, California. Mark Mack has taken Gehry's individual buildings and skilfully combined them into a unity reminiscent of a Mexican village

This page: *John Whitney House,* passage connecting parts of the house

Gie Wollaert, private house of a computer specialist, Antwerp, 1992

Charles Gwathmey / Robert Siegel (project architect Renny Logan), country house in Vermont, 1989

Simon Ungers / Tom Kinslow, *T-House*, Wilton, New York, 1988–94

At a symposium organized by the Berlin Senate's Department of Buildings in May 1995, where French architects introduced their projects for the redevelopment of the city—Dominique Perrault presented his two sports stadiums in the Landsberger Allee for cycling and swimming, Claude Vasconi his office building in Spandau and Jean Nouvel his Block 207 in Friedrichstrasse—it came to a typical Franco-German controversy:

Previous page:
Fernau / Hartman, private house and studio, Rutherford, California, 1987–88

"In the discussion which ensued, one of the Berlin architects stood up and tried to provoke the guests from France, saying that he maybe lacked the necessary sensuous experience, but that such an architecture could only be achieved with natural materials, using stone and forms which concealed, but not concepts involving cold, shiny glass. Jean Nouvel, dressed as usual completely in black, merely gave the corners of his mouth a brief twitch: 'Hein, Érotisme! If you penetrate a whole building with a cone made of glass, isn't that erotic?'"[5]

The demand for sensuous architecture is all about the quality of life, the culture built up around work, entertainment and homemaking, the attractiveness of cities for tourism and their emotional identification factors for each and

every citizen. It is not a noncommittal appeal of the popular kind that politicians like to launch in their Sunday speeches, but rather an urgent call to keep a keen eye (and sharpen all other senses) to recognize deficits in our cultural development, to analyse and to oppose them. Basically it involves familiar didactic concepts, which are unfortunately very rarely attended to, such as an interdisciplinary approach to all forms of education and a systematic training of the senses. Comparing, seeing, hearing, smelling, tasting, feeling, all this can be learned and much more. As someone with no formal architectural training but with a lateral access to architecture from fellow disciplines, I find again and again that many essential fields in our

Jean Nouvel, *Galeries Lafayette*, atrium, Friedrichstrasse, Berlin, 1996

architectural training are underdeveloped or entirely non-existent.

Take, for example, light as a factor of immense sensuality. No life is possible without light! But very few architects learn how to handle this dimension and this quality of building, few learn how to adapt building with light to the needs of the occupants, of those living and working in such architecture, how to adapt it to the special problems of supply, to climatic and regional conditions and finally how to create aesthetic effects.

Or, to take a brief look at another field whose importance has continuously grown since the '80s, there is the confrontation between architecture and design. It is a trend of our time that

design enjoys an ever growing importance in many new fields of our private and working lives. There is an infinite amount of bad design around, but also a lot of good design. This has to do with educating one's taste, with ergonomics, with marketing strategies, with aestheticism, with the handling of our resources and their recycling potential, with materials, with colours, with forms and the perception and shaping thereof. Unfortunately young architects are hardly ever confronted with these problems and most are helpless when they have to face the solutions which industry has to offer. Nevertheless, probably the most erotic architect of our times, Philippe Starck, is first and foremost a designer. In draft upon draft, Starck creates pan-

erotic worlds of shapes, nimbly switching back and forth across gender boundaries and reflecting the sensuous joys of living.

The do-it-yourself and home supplies superstores on the other hand, to which for financial reasons the majority of the population has to resort in order to satisfy its demand for materials for building something of its own, are filled with items of unspeakable design. Why do large numbers of people buy such architectural junk and then go on to ruin their houses with it? The turnover runs into billions. Although our increasingly specialized and increasingly alienated society has for the most part lost its natural ability to cope with a rich variety of materials, dimensions and proportions, a skill that charac-

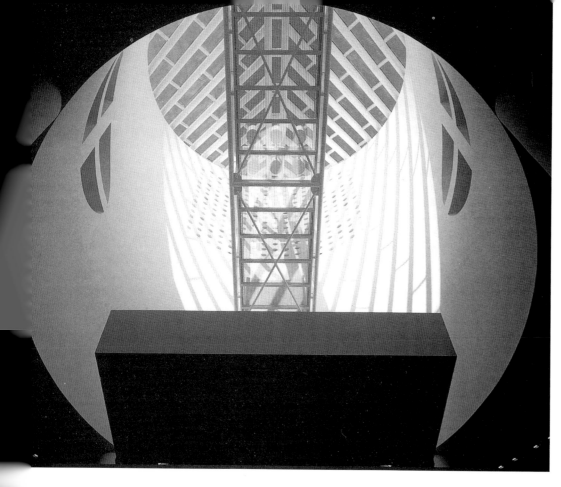

terized the culture of peasants and craftspeople up to the end of the 18th century, one still does not have to accept uncertain or overtly bad taste as God-given. It is in fact typical that in the 18th century, too, questions of taste were among the main sources of conflict in aesthetics among philosophers, writers, architects and artists.

Just as inventive people in the United States earn money by teaching people to eat with a knife and fork again, since millions of citizens have lost this ability because they stuff themselves with the products of certain hamburger and other fast food chains and only know how

Cunningham Architects, transformer station converted into a private house, Dallas, Texas, 1987–89

Matthias Eck, private house, Radolfzell, 1990–92

Brian Murphy,
house in a canyon at Santa Monica,
California

Brian Murphy,
house in a canyon at Santa Monica

Brian Murphy,
house in a canyon at Santa Monica

Brian Murphy,
house in a canyon at Santa Monica

Bela and Ingrid Bambek, private house,
bridge to the upper floor

Bela and Ingrid Bambek, private house on a tiny plot,
Stuttgart, 1988–89

to use their fingers, a training in matters of taste should be part of every school and university teacher's education. The goal would not be to instil a uniform taste, because that is nonsense, but rather to develop a responsibility in dealing with a host of phenomena and constituents of good taste. Due to market pressures, the DIY stores would automatically reorientate themselves if the demand for the bastards of architectural disfigurement declined.

Let us briefly turn to another aspect from a very different field in order to round off the range of arguments: architecture's dealings with new media. In 1993 William Gibson declared, "Cyber is out,"[6] and turned his attention as an author to other fields. And indeed one has to wonder whether a genuine cyberspace technology that goes beyond mere 3-D computer simulations (a technology that includes full body "data suits" and awkward helmets, so-called

"head mounted displays", or maybe even images directly projected onto the retina by lasers, together with all the technology and cost that this involves) will ever find widespread application in architecture. The heavy glasses and helmets, at least, are already history in the advanced research laboratories. The one thing that architecture will not be able to avoid, however, is coming to terms with the culture of media and high-tech and with dematerialized, virtual architectures. In-house technology will continue to change, just like work-place design, and interior and exterior architecture. But apart from technical media, so far very few media aspects are included in the training of architects.

But we cannot leave it up to advertising, be it of good or bad quality, to dictate the aesthetic possibilities of media architecture. Here an artistic approach is necessary to try out the new

dimensions of sensuality attainable on monitors and media walls, to make them safer, cheaper, more reliable and durable, and to develop power-saving ways of combining high-tech with nature.

But even without the media façades used for example by Jean Nouvel, Rüdiger Kramm or Toyo Ito, high-tech architecture can no longer do without computers and intelligent systems. A new generation of glass architecture, one that plays ingenious games with light, transparency and with textural motifs on a glass coated with ceramic patterns, is what is used by Helmut Jahn, for example, in the *Airport Hotel Kempinski* in Munich. The effect is a sensual, almost philosophical interplay between materiality and immateriality, a simultaneous presence of bodiliness and its dissolution, without the use of natural materials in this very masculine example of architecture.

Helmut Jahn,
*Kempinski Airport
Hotel,*
Munich,
1994

Arthur Erickson, extension to a villa in Vancouver from 1912, housing a swimming pool and combining high tech with the style of the turn of the century

Itsuko Hasegawa, on the other hand, aims at a very feminine equilibrium between artificial intelligence and nature in her *Footwork Computer Centre* in Hyogo, Japan. Depending on the time of day, the light and colours change on the glass front of the fifteen-storey entrance hall, which is located on a hill. As a completely transparent atrium, however, it almost seems to neutralize itself. In contrast to the screened-off computer workstations in the core of the building, which are fully centred on the user, the atrium and the open-plan offices open out on to nature and the urban landscape.

Odile Decq and Benoît Cornette, two architects from Paris who have only since the beginning of the '90s come to the fore on the international scene, take this experimental game of the partial disembodiment of architecture one step further in their *Banque Populaire de l'Ouest* in Rennes, giving it a very poetic, architectural-philosophical quality. In addition to the self-neutralizing effect, transparency and reflections

in the aluminium-faced walls of the covered walk which is set in front of the massive building itself create almost cinematic impressions of moving images of nature and people.

Sensuality is not exclusively connected with massive bodies, as the cybersex experiments have proved. Particularly the contrasts, the interplay of materials can create an erotic attraction between bodies of opposite type. The range here could include the loam architecture in Sanaa, Hans Hollein's ritually erotic plan for a branch of the New York *Guggenheim Museum* inside the Mönchsberg (Monk's Hill) in Salzburg, and even Bernard Tschumi's *Glass Video Gallery* (1990) in Groningen, which exploits the lighting principles of day-and-night architecture to its limits.

Philosophically speaking, this small building is the perfect example to illustrate Virilio's thesis of the "disappearance of reality". It demonstrates the growing immaterialization of art, aesthetics and human communication, thereby

commenting on the state of postindustrial humanity on the verge of the third millennium. Numerous monitors produce moving images and unstable façades, additional images are created by reflections of the outside world in the glass, while the whole installation suggests infinite space. At night, the monitors with their moving pictures create the impression of a ballet of video displays. At the same time they are windows into a telematic world devoid of stable foundations. They offer immaterial entertainment, news, art, all within an architecture whose structures have become invisible, have seemingly evaporated. This is a situation which corresponds to eroticism in virtual rooms. Wolf Prix and Helmut Swiczinsky of Coop Himmelblau demanded in 1970:

"It is not we who have to change in order to live in architecture, but architecture which has to react to our movements, our feelings, our moods, our emotions in such a way as to make us want to live in it."[7]

Although we agree with this, it does not include the aspect of social interaction. This is why we demand a multisensory architecture for the senses that takes into account the continuously changing processes of interplay between the individual, society and architecture. An architecture that is functional, open, playful, that stimulates our imagination and that gives us a built-up environment which invites us to be joyfully creative. An architecture that makes allowances for the fact that the mind cannot live without the body and the body cannot live without the mind. Such is the architecture in which we want to live, love and work.

Odile Decq / Benoît Cornette, *Banque Populaire de l'Ouest*, Rennes

Appendix

NOTES

Introduction: Architecture and Eroticism

1   Günther Feuerstein, "Eros – Architektur – Sexualität", in: *Der Architekt*, 2/1987, pp. 91–96, quotation p. 91.
2   *Questions of Perception: Phenomenology of Architecture.* Steven Holl, Juhani Pallasmaa and Alberto Pérez-Gómez. *Architecture and Urbanism (a + u)*, Special Issue, Tokyo, July 1994, p. 41.
3   In: *ad*, no. 9, *Architektur und menschlicher Körper*, Wolfgang Meisenheimer (ed.), Düsseldorf 1982, p. 88.
4   Cf. Werner Ruhnau, "Die (fehlende) Erziehung der Architekten zur Sinnlichkeit", in: *ad*, no. 9 (see note 3), pp. 54–61.
5   Cf. Wolfgang Meisenheimer, "Einführung in den Themenkreis", in: *ad*, no. 9 (see note 3), pp. 4–15.
6   Cf. Günther Kühlbacher, "Körpermaße des Menschen – ihr Einfluß auf Baugesetze", in: *ad*, no. 9 (see note 3), pp. 37–47. Among other things, Kühlbacher discovered that in contrast to earlier centuries there are very few building regulations today which are concerned with the physical nature of human beings. See also: Christian W. Thomsen, Angela Krewani, "Was ist in der Architektur Sprache, Sprechen, Dialekt?" in: *ad*, no. 17, *Architektur als Darstellung, als Zeichen, als Sprache*, Düsseldorf 1989, pp. 8–46.
7   Cf. Jacques Derrida, "Plato's Pharmacy", *Disseminations* (1972), pp. 61–172.
8   Cf. Wolfgang Meisenheimer, "Einführung in den Themenkreis", in: *ad*, no. 19, *Architektur für die Sinne*, Wolfgang Meisenheimer (ed.), Düsseldorf 1991, pp. 6–9: "The most astonishing discovery in the psychology of perception over the past decades is the realisation that sensual perception proceeds compositionally, that is to say creatively, whether as individual acts of perception or as wider, interconnected experiences: from the external stimuli data supplied by the senses and the internal comparative material available in the brain man creates his world as a 'construct of his imagination', and that never without some meaningful systematization, i.e. devoid of sense." (p. 7). The basis of this thesis is of course the philosophy of radical constructivism, as developed by Humberto R. Maturana, Francisco J. Varela and Siegfried J. Schmidt. Cf. e.g. *Der Diskurs des Radikalen Konstruktivismus*, Siegfried J. Schmidt (ed.), Frankfurt 1987; Siegfried J. Schmidt, "Liquidation oder Transformation der Moderne", in: *Besichtigung der Moderne*, Hans Holländer, Christian W. Thomsen (eds.), Cologne 1987, pp. 53–70.
9   Cf. Friedrich Christoph Wagner, "Körpererfahrung und Kreativität", in: *ad*, no. 19, (see note 8) pp. 15–24.
10   Richard Sennett, *Flesh and Stone*, New York, London 1994, p. 15–16.
11   This is dealt with in a separate book, to appear shortly with the same publisher.
12   Juhani Pallasmaa, "An Architecture of the Seven Senses", in: *Questions of Perception* (see note 2), pp. 27–38, quotation p. 29.
13   "Im Sperrgebiet", Imanuel Cuadra talking to Cora Mollay (member of a prostitutes' self-help organization in Frankfurt), in: *deutsche bauzeitung (db)*, vol. 128, 11/94, pp. 76–81, quotation pp. 78–79. Cf. also *Bauwelt*, vol. 85, no. 13, April 1994 with main feature on "Freudenhäuser – Prostitution" ("Brothels and Prostitution").
14   Walter Dmoch, "Entwicklungspsychologische Determinanten des Raum-Erlebens", in: *ad*, no. 9 (see note 3), pp. 23–33, quotation pp. 29–30. Cf. also Erik Homburger Erikson, *Identität und Lebenszyklus*, Frankfurt 1966; Thomas Verny and John Kelly, *Das Seelenleben des Ungeborenen*, Munich 1981.
15   Cf. Aaron Betsky, *Building Sex: Men, Women and the Construction of Sexuality*, New York 1995.
16   Cf. Betsky, ibid., pp. XV–XIX, 3–18.
17   Ibid., p. XIX.
18   Cf. the various contributions in: *Sexuality and Space*, Beatriz Colomina (ed.), New York 1992.
19   Heinz Peter Schwerfels, in: *Fusionen*, an essay in the catalogue of the exhibition of the same name, with works by Jean Louis Faure, Alain Fleischer, Bertrand Lavier and Georges Rousse, which took place in Building W 1 of Bayer AG, Leverkusen, Germany, Nov. 9 – Dec. 17, 1988, Leverkusen 1989, no page numbers.
20   Feuerstein (see note 1), p. 92.
21   Cf. Vera Lehndorff and Holger Trülzsch, *Oxydationen*, Altenham/Emertsham near Hamburg 1979.
22   Wolfgang Meisenheimer, "Einführung in den Themenkreis", in: *ad*, no. 9 (see note 3), p.13.
23   Cf. Bernard Tschumi, *Architecture and Disjunction*, Cambridge, Mass. 1994, especially the articles on "Disjunction", pp. 171–259.
24   Cf. Bernard Tschumi, "The Pleasure of Architecture", in: *Architecture and Disjunction* (see note 23), p. 89.

Contemporary Examples of Erotic Architecture

1   Hans Hollein, in: *Bau*, 1968, 1/2, p. 2.
2   The number of reviews of Hans Hollein's Museum Abteiberg is overwhelming. Virtually all of the world's principal journals of architecture carried detailed articles on this topic at the time. Cf. the author's, "Der Romantiker, der aus der Kälte kam. Wiener Tradition und Postmoderne auf dem Abteiberg in Mönchengladbach", in: *Parnass* III, Sept./Oct. 1983, pp. 12–19.
3   "Vision of Hans Hollein", in: *Architectural Visions for Europe*, Dirk Meyhöfer (ed.), Braunschweig/Wiesbaden 1994, pp. 76–83, quotation p. 76.
4   Alejandro Zaera, "Santiago Calatrava: The Living Structure", in: *Santiago Calatrava 1983/1993*, Richard C. Levene (ed.), *El Croquis*, vol. 38+57, Madrid 1994, p. 25.
5   *Santiago Calatrava: Ingenieur-Architektur*, Werner Blaser (ed.), with articles by Kenneth Frampton and Pierluigi Nicolin, Basel/Boston/Berlin 1989, p. 95.
6   Santiago Calatrava, "Cabaret Tabourettli Basilea", in: *domus*, Sept. 1989, pp. 52–62, quotation p. 60.
7   *Santiago Calatrava 1983/1993* (see note 4), p. 19.
8   Alejandro Zaera, in: *Santiago Calatrava 1983/1993* (see note 4), p. 23.
9   "La Ciudad de las Moreras", in: *Santiago Calatrava 1983/1993* (see note 4), p.158.
10   Cf. Dalí's illustrations on Lautréamont, *Les chants de Maldoror*, Paris 1934.
11   Coop Himmelblau, *Architektur ist jetzt. Projekte, (Un)bauten, Aktionen, Statements, Zeichnungen, Texte, 1968–1983*, Stuttgart/New York 1983, p.124.
12   Georges Bataille, *Die Tränen des Eros* (1960, 1981), Gerd Bergfleth (ed.), Munich 1981, p. 36.
13   Coop Himmelblau (see note 11), p.118.
14   In conversations with the author in October 1990 in Vienna.

Châteaux de Plaisance and an Architecture of Yearning

1   William Beckford, *Vathek*, Oxford University Press, Glasgow 1970, pp. 1–3.
2   Voltaire, cf. Frederike Wappenschmidt, *Der Traum von Arkadien: Leben, Liebe, Licht und Farbe in Europas Lustschlössern*, Munich 1990, p.115.
3   Cf. *Die Schlösser der Loire*, photos by Axel M. Mosler, text by Thorsten Droste, Munich 1994, p.115.
4   *Die Schlösser der Loire* (see note 3), p. 25.
5   Susanna Partsch, *Loire. Städte, Schlösser und Gärten von Giens bis Angers*, Munich 1993, pp.14–15.
6   Cf. the chapter "Bath Culture and Sensuality".
7   Aaron Betsky, *Building Sex: Men, Women and the Construction of Sexuality*, New York 1995, pp. 78–79.
8   Partsch (see note 5), p. 77.
9   Betsky (see note 7), p. 77.
10   Gustave Flaubert, *Tagebücher. Über Feld und Strand*, Potsdam 1919; translation by Alex Atkins.
11   Cf. Wappenschmidt (see note 2), p. 8.
12   Wappenschmidt (see note 2), p. 9: "Montplaisir, Monrepos, Solitude, Favorite, Belvedere, Amalienburg, Pagodenburg, Brimborian, Bagatelle".
13   Ibid.
14   Wappenschmidt (see note 2), p. 8.
15   Wappenschmidt (see note 2), p. 9.
16   Ibid.
17   Cf. Michael Niedermeier, *Erotik in der Gartenkunst*, Leipzig 1995, passim, especially pp.146–228.
18   George Mott and Sally Sample Aall, *Follies and Pleasure Pavilions*. Introduction by Gervase Jackson-Stops, London, 1974, p.13.
19   Mott and Sample Aall (see note 17), pp.17–18.
20   Ibid.
21   Barbara Jones, *Follies and Grottos*, revised edition, London 1974, p. 34.
22   Cf. Marlis Grüterich, "Der Orient König Ludwig II. von Bayern", in: *du*, 2/1981, pp. 26–79.
23   Cf. Susanne von Meiss, "Lady Glitters Lustpalais. Schloß Stonehaven in Texas", in: *Ambiente* 4/April 1991, pp. 64–62.

De Sade and High Tech: Body-Architecture and Fantasies of Dismemberment (Angela Krewani)

1   Nick Cave, "Slowly Goes the Night", in: Nick Cave, *Tender Prey*, Mute Records Ltd., 1988.
2   Cf. Herbert Singer, *Der galante Roman*, Stuttgart 1961.
3   Cf. Angela Carter, *The Sadeian Woman. An Exercise in Cultural History*, London 1979, p. 42.
4   Donatien Alphonse Marquis de Sade, *The 120 Days of Sodom, and Other Writings*, compiled and translated by Austrin Wainhouse and Richard Seaver, New York 1966, p. 235 ff.
5   Pier Paolo Pasolini, *Salò o le 120 Giornate*, film: Italy/France 1975.
6   Carter (see note 3), p. 42 ff.
7   de Sade (see note 4), p. 237 ff.
8   Ibid., p. 244 ff.
9   Cf. Donatien Alphonse Marquis de Sade, *Justine, Philosophy in the Bedroom, and Other Writings*, compiled and translated by Richard Seaver and Austrin Wainhouse, Grove Weidenfeld, New York 1965.
10   Carter (see note 3), p. 43.

11 Here I refer to the psychoanalysis of Jacques Lacan.

12 Gilles Deleuze and Félix Guattari, *Anti-Ödipus*, Frankfurt am Main 1977, p. 7.

13 *Architektur des 20. Jahrhunderts*, Peter Gössel and Gabriele Leuthäuser (eds.), Cologne 1990, pp. 324, 331.

14 Cf. Frederic Jameson, "Postmoderne – zur Logik der Kultur im Spätkapitalismus", in: *Postmoderne: Zeichen eines kulturellen Wandels*, Andreas Huyssen and Klaus Scherpe (eds.), Reinbek bei Hamburg 1986, p. 79.

15 Deyan Sudjic, *Norman Foster, Richard Rogers, James Stirling: New Directions in British Architecture*, London 1986, p. 23 ff.

16 Rogers and Piano, "Statement", quoted in Sudjic (see note 15), p. 24.

17 Gilles Deleuze and Félix Guattari, *Kapitalismus und Schizophrenie. Tausend Plateaus*, Berlin 1992, p. 227.

18 Sudjic (see note 15), p. 61.

19 Coop Himmelblau, "Die härtere Architektur", in: Coop Himmelblau, *Architektur ist jetzt. Projekte, (Un)bauten, Aktionen, Statements, Zeichnungen, Texte 1968–1983*, Stuttgart/New York 1983, p. 51.

20 Cf. Christian W. Thomsen, *Experimentelle Architekten der Gegenwart*, Cologne 1991, p. 67.

21 Georg C. Bertsch, *Alfredo Arribas. Architecture and Design 1986–1992*, Tübingen/Berlin, p. 8 ff.

Bath Culture and Sensuality

1 Louis Aragon, "Badelust und Wollust", in: Louis Aragon, *Pariser Landleben*, Munich 1969.

2 Ulrika Kiby "Die Badekultur ein Vergnügen der Menschheit seit der Antike", in: *Badewonnen. Gestern – Heute – Morgen*. Cologne 1993. Cf. pp. 6–90, here pp. 18–30.

3 Cf. Kiby, p. 24.

4 Cf. Kiby, p. 26.

5 Cf. Kiby, p. 31.

6 Cf. Kiby, p. 36.

7 Cf. Kiby, p. 36.

8 Cf. Ibid.

9 Cf. Ibid.

10 Cf. Kiby, p. 57.

11 Cf. Kiby, p. 86.

12 Cf. *In den Tempeln der Badelust. Architekturen der Sinnlichkeit*. Photographs: Gerhard P. Müller, essay: Joseph von Westphalen, Munich 1986.

13 Lady Mary Montague, "In einem türkischen Frauenbadehaus", in: *Briefe der Lady Mary Worthley Montague, während ihrer Reise in Europa, Asia und Africa (...) geschrieben*; which contain reports of, besides other peculiarities, the state constitution and the customs of the Turks; information from sources not accessible to other travellers, Leipzig 1764, quoted in: *In den Tempeln der Badelust* (see note 12), p. 46; re-translated by Alex Atkins.

14 Erich Küthe, "Vom 'Powder Room' zum Erlebnisbad", in: *Badewonnen* (see note 2), pp. 101–168, here the subchapter "Die Burgeoisie revolutioniert das Badewesen", pp. 101–111.

15 These slogans are taken from the Duravit advertisements for ceramic baths in their 1993 advertisement flyers and catalogues.

Erotic Symbols in Architecture

1 "Rapunzel", in: Jakob Grimm, *Märchen der Brüder Grimm*, Berlin 1937, p. 103.

2 Cf. Christian W. Thomsen, *Literatur. Wechselwirkungen zwischen Architektur, Literatur und Kunst im 20. Jahrhundert*, Cologne 1989, Chapter II: "Turmblicke", pp. 52–71.

3 Sigmund Freud, "Vorlesungen zur Einführung in die Psychoanalyse", in: *Sigmund Freud, Gesammelte Werke*, London 1940, vol. 11, pp. 157–158; re-translated by Alex Atkins.

4 *Khajurâho. Tempel der Liebe*, Louis Frédéric, text, Raghu Rai, photography, Alain Danielou, introduction, Cologne 1993, p. 91.

5 *Khajurâho* (see note 4), p. 9.

6 Salvador Dalí, *The Secret Life of Salvador Dalí*, translated by Haakon M. Chevalier, London 1973, p. 334.

7 Cf. Nils-Ole Lund, *Collage Architecture*, Christian W. Thomsen, introduction, Berlin 1990.

8 Botho Strauss, *The Young Man*, Evanston, Illinois 1995, pp. 237–238.

9 Strauss (see note 8), pp. 245–246.

10 Peter Weiss, "Der große Traum des Briefträgers Cheval", in: Peter Weiss, *Rapporte 1*, Frankfurt am Main 1968, pp. 36–50, quotations, pp. 36–37, 41.

11 Gabrielle Wittkopp-Monardeau, "Die Wärme der Sterne. Der Briefträger Cheval bleibt ein Rätsel", in: *FAZ*, January 21, 1995, no. 18, supplement *Bilder und Zeiten*, no page numbers.

Erotic Architecture Fantasies

1 Barbara Radice, *Ettore Sottsass. Leben und Werk*, Munich 1993, pp. 28–29.

2 Cf. *Stanley Tigerman, Buildings and Projects 1966–1989*, Sarah Mollman Underhill (ed.), New York 1989, pp. 58–61.

3 Cf. *Stadt und Utopie: Modelle idealer Gemeinschaften*, catalogue accompanying the exhibition of the same name by the Berliner Neuer Kunstverein, idea and conception by Lucie Schauer, Berlin 1987, p. 116.

4 The best insight into Finsterlin's works is offered by Reinhard Döhl, *Hermann Finsterlin. Eine Annäherung.* Catalogue and monograph: State Gallery of the Graphic Collection Stuttgart, Stuttgart 1988.

5 Cf. especially Finsterlin's designs from the time of his involvement with "Gläserne Kette" ("Crystal Chain") (1919–21) and Christian W. Thomsen, *Visionary Architecture: from Babylon to Virtual Reality*, Munich 1994, p. 85.

6 Hermann Finsterlin, autobiographical note, no date, no page number.

7 Cf. *Lebbeus Woods, Centricity: Architectural-Philosophical Visions*. Catalogue of the exhibition of the same name in the Aedes Gallery Berlin, Berlin 1987, and Lebbeus Woods, *Anarchitecture. Architecture is a Political Act*, London 1992, pp. 50–63.

8 Cf. Christian W. Thomsen: "Lebbeus Woods' 'Centricity'. Architecture-Philosophical Vision of the Ideal City of Universal Science" in : *Lebbeus Woods, Centricity* (see note 7), pp. 4–7, and C. W. Thomsen, "Lebbeus Woods: Visionäre Welten", in: *Experimentelle Architekten der Gegenwart*, Cologne 1991, pp. 195–215.

9 Cf. Thomsen: *Visionary Architecture*, (see note 5), p. 124–128 and Woods' *Anarchitecture* (see note 7) pp. 110–141.

10 Cf. "Italian Radical Architecture and Design 1966–1973", in: *Terrazzo*, no. 5, Fall 1990, pp. 73–144, therein: "Ettore Sottsass", pp. 102–114.

11 Ettore Sottsass: "Counterdesign" (1971), in: *Terrazzo*, no. 5 (see note 10), p. 108.

12 Ettore Sottsass, "How to Protect Beauty from Dust and Piranhas" (1967), in: *Terrazzo*, no. 5 (see note 10), pp. 103–108.

13 Radice (see note 1), p. 171.

14 Roberto Baldazzini and Lorena Canossa, "INTERIORS", in: *Terrazzo*, no. 3, Fall 1989, pp. 73–80.

15 Maurizio Castelvetro, "Flora Bolidist Manifesto. Notes for Use Inside", in: *Massimo Iosa Ghini*, N.N. Edition, Düsseldorf 1993, no page.

16 Cf. Christian W. Thomsen, *Dieter Sieger: Architect, Shipbuilder, Designer*, Tübingen 1994, pp. 294, 300–301.

Architecture—Eroticism—Art

1 Louise Bourgeois in conversation with Christiane Meyer-Thoss, in: Christiane Meyer-Thoss, *Louise Bourgeois*, Zurich 1992, p. 108.

2 Edgar Allan Poe, "The Fall of the House of Usher", in: *Tales of Mystery and Imagination*, London 1960, p. 7.

3 Ibid., p. 9.

4 Ibid., pp. 14–15.

5 Cf. Heinrich Klotz and Andrea Gleiniger, *Der Hang zur Architektur in der Malerei der Gegenwart*, a catalogue to a similarly named exhibition in the German Architecture Museum in Frankfurt am Main, September 3 until October 23, 1988, Stuttgart 1988.

6 Wieland Herzfelde "Zum Geleit", in: *George Grosz, Paß auf, hier kommt Grosz. Bilder, Rhythmen, Gesänge 1915–1918*, Wieland Herzfelde and Hans Marquardt (eds.), Leipzig 1981, p. 9.

7 George Grosz, "Gedichte und Gesänge, Berlin, Frühjahr 1917, I", in: *Grosz* (see note 6), p. 24.

8 Grosz (see note 6), p. 28. Cf. the comprehensive presentation of this theme in the accompanying catalogue to the exhibition, *George Grosz: Berlin – New York*, in Berlin's New National Gallery, Dec. 21, 1994 to April 17, 1995, and at the Kunstsammlung Nordrhein-Westphalen in Düsseldorf, May 6 to July 30, 1995, Peter-Klaus Schuster (ed.), Berlin 1994.

9 Cf. Karl Riha, "George Grosz und Amerika", in: *George Grosz, New York*, Walter Huder and Karl Riha (eds.), Siegen 1985.

10 George Grosz, "Gesang an die Welt, II", in: *Grosz* (see note 6), p. 18.

11 *George Grosz, New York* (see note 9)

12 Werner Spies, *Lindner*, a catalogue to a similarly named exhibition at the Maeght Gallery in Paris 1980, p. 23. Cf. also Hilton Kramer, *Richard Lindner*, Berlin 1975 and Judith Zilczer and Peter Selz, *Richard Lindner, Paintings and Watercolors 1948–1977*, Munich 1996.

13 Gilles Néret, *Erotik in der Kunst des 20. Jahrhunderts*, Angelika Muthesius and Burkhard Riemenschneider (eds.), Cologne 1992, pp. 44–45.

14 Richard Lindner in an interview with John Gruen for *Art News*, 14, April 1978, in: Spies (see note 12), p. 46.

15 Ibid., p. 45.

16 Wilfried Dickhoff, preface, in: *Francesco Clemente im Gespräch mit Rainer Crone und Georgia Marsh* (*Francesco Clemente in Conversation with Rainer Crone and Georgia Marsh*), Cologne 1990, p. 11.

17 Ibid.

18 "Francesco Clemente on Architecture", in: *Terrazzo*, no. 2, Spring 1989, pp. 85–93.

19 Ibid., p. 61

20 Cf. Clemente's erotic drawings inter alia, in: Ann Percy, *Franceso Clemente: Three Worlds*, with essays by Stella Kramrisch and Ettore Sottsass, Philadelphia 1990; *Francesco Clemente, Pastelle 1973–1983*, a catalogue to a similarly named exhibition at Berlin's National Gallery, March 16 to May 13, 1984, Munich 1984; Francesco Clemente, *Evening Raga & Paradiso 1992*, introduction by Francesco Clemente, Allen Ginsberg and Peter Orlovsky, Gagosian Gallery and Rizzoli, New York 1992; *Francesco Clemente. Early Morning Exercises*, a catalogue to the exhibition at the Cabinet d'Art Graphique, Centre Georges Pompidou, Paris, October 26, 1994 to January 16, 1995, Paris 1994; *Francesco Clemente. The Black Book*, a catalogue to the exhibtion at the Kunsthalle in Basle, Thomas Kelwein (ed.), Basle 1991.

21 The best survey of the typology, dissemination, history and interpretation of the labyrinth is to be found in Hermann Kern's *Labyrinthe: Erscheinungsformen und Deutungen; 5000 Jahre Gegenwart eines Urbilds*. Due to the untimely death of the author, the then planned exhibition at the Munich Haus der Kunst did not take place.

22 Cf. Paul Radin, Karl Kerény and C. G. Jung, *Der göttliche Schelm. Ein indianischer Mythenzyklus*, Hildesheim 1979.

23 Christian W. Thomsen, "Persönliche Metaphern. Medrie MacPhees magisch-phantastischer Realismus" ("Personal Metaphors. Medrie MacPhee's Magical-Fantastical Realism"), in:

Parnass, vol. 1, January/February 1990, pp. 70–76, interview p. 72.

24 Medrie MacPhee in a letter to the author, April 3, 1993.
25 Cf. Christo's workshop conversation in *art*, 12/1990, pp. 28–41.
26 Werner Spies, "Einführung", in: *Christo, Surrounded Islands*, Cologne 1984, pp. 8–27, quotation on p. 27.
27 *Christo and Jeanne Claude, Der Reichstag und urbane Projekte* (*Christo and Jeanne-Claude, The Reichstag and Urban Projects*), a catalogue to a similarly named exhibition at the KunstHaus in Vienna, June 9 to July 26, 1993 and at the Villa Stuck Museum in Munich, from May 12 to July 10, 1994, Jacob Baal-Teshuva (ed.), Munich 1993.
28 Christo und Jeanne-Claude, Press reports on "Verhüllter Reichstag: Projekt für Berlin" ("The Wrapped Reichstag: The Berlin Project"), in: *Christo, Der Reichstag* (see note 27), p. 8.
29 "Warum ist Magie so teuer, Christo und Jeanne-Claude?" ("Why is magic so expensive, Christo and Jean-Claude?"), interview with Jordan Mejias, in: *FAZ Magazin* (weekly magazine of the *Frankfurter Allgemeine Newspaper*), vol. 836, March 8, 1996, pp. 110–111.
30 Norbert Miller, "Der verwunschene Garten des Vicino Orsini" (The Bewitched Garden of Vicino Orsini), in: *Daidalos*, no. 3/March 1982, quotation on pp. 38–39.
31 Cf. Jan Pieper, "Gärten der Erinnerung. Im Sacro Bosco von Bomarzo", ("Gardens of Memories: At Bomarzo's Sacro Bosco"), in: *Kunstforum International*, vol. 69, 1984, pp. 91–97, here on p. 92.
32 Cf. Klaus Poenicke, "Schönheit im Schoße des Schreckens. Raumgefüge und Menschenbild im englischen Schauerroman", in: *Archiv*, vol. 207, 122nd issue, no. 1/June 1970, pp. 1–20.
33 Pieper (see note 31), p. 97.
34 Kurt Schwitters, "Ich und meine Ziele", in: *Kurt Schwitters: 1887–1948*, a catalogue to the 1986 retrospective in honour of the artist's 100th birthday, 1987, Sprengel Museum in Hanover, Joachim Büchner and Norbert Nobis (eds.), Berlin/Frankfurt am Main 1987, p. 200.
35 Ibid.
36 Ibid.
37 Louise Bourgeois "Twosome", in: *Louis Bourgeois: Skulpturen und Installationen* (*Sculptures and Installations*) a catalogue to a similarly named exhibition by the Kestner-Gesellschaft in Hanover, September 3 to October 30, 1994, Carl Haenlein (ed.), Hanover 1994, p. 129; the contribution first appeared in: *Dislocations*, Museum of Modern Art, Robert Storr (ed.), New York 1991.
38 Cf. Barbara Catoir, "No Exit—Der Raum im Werk von Louise Bourgeois" ("Space in the Work of Louise Bourgeois"), in: *Louise Bourgeois, Skulpturen* (see note 37).
39 Cf. Lynne Cooke, "Statement zu 'Cell II'", in: Charlotta Kodik, Terrie Sultan and Christian Leigh, *Louise Bourgeois: The Locus of Memory; Works 1982–1993*, Brooklyn Museum, New York 1994, p. 72.
40 *Louise Bourgeois: Skulpturen* (see note 37), p. 5.
41 Poenicke (see note 32), pp. 1–20.
42 Louise Bourgeois, in: Meyer-Thoss (see note 1), p. 162.
43 Niki de Saint Phalle, in: *Niki de Saint Phalle. Bilder—Figuren—phantastische Gärten*, a catalogue to a similarly named exhibition at the Kunsthalle of the Hypo-Stiftung in Munich, March 26 to June 21, 1987, Carla Schulz-Hoffmann (ed.), Munich 1987, p. 39.
44 Ibid.
45 Cf. the comprehensive catalogue by Pontus Hulten, *Niki de Saint Phalle*, prepared for the similarly named exhibition at the Federal Republic of Germany's Art and Exhibition Hall in Bonn, June 19 to November 1, 1992, Stuttgart 1992.
46 Cf. Rita Imwinkelried, "Ein magischer Garten der Mutter-Göttin", in: *art*, no. 6/June 1993, pp. 36–44.
47 Niki de Saint Phalle, in: *Niki de Saint Phalle, Bilder—Figuren—phantastische Gärten* (see note 43), p. 150.
48 Imwinkelried (see note 46), p. 44.

Staging Interiors

1 Angela Carter, *The Infernal Desire Machines of Doctor Hoffman*, Harmondsworth 1982, pp. 199–200.
2 Cf. Nils-Ole Lund, *Collage Architecture*, Christian W. Thomsen, Introduction, Berlin 1990, p. 24.
3 Thomas Schröder, "Ich hätt' so gern ein Haus", in: *Architektur & Wohnen*, 1/1978, p. 54.
4 Ibid.
5 Vera Sieveking, "Von Bett zu Bett. Aus der Kulturgeschichte des Schlafmöbels", in: *Architektur & Wohnen*, 3/1978, pp. 206–210, quote p. 206.
6 Cf. "Die Zukunft des Wohnens bestimmen Individualisten jeglicher Art", an interview with Carmen Lakaschus, in: *Architektur & Wohnen*, 1/1995, pp. 56–59.
7 Ibid.
8 On fetishism, cf. Martin Wollschläger, *Fetischismus, Transvestitismus, Transsexualität, Homosexualität*, Cologne 1983; on Starck, cf. Jörg Altwegg, "Philippe Starck", in: *FAZ-Magazin*, no. 729, February 3, 1995, pp. 6–12, and Olivier Boissière, *Philippe Starck*, Cologne 1991, and Franco Bertoni, *Philippe Starck, Architektur*, Munich 1994.
9 Cf. Michel Croce-Spinelli, *Fetisch und Fortschritt. Berichte aus dem Kongo, Dahome, Gabun und Kamerun*, Munich 1969.
10 On this subject we have conducted a survey among architecture students and young architects, which, though not representative, is very informative in many respects.
11 "Studio Citterio & Dawn. 'esprit', Modegeschäft, Café und Verwaltung in Amsterdam", in: *Internationales Interior Design 1990/91*, Lucy Bullivant (ed.), Munich 1991, pp. 136–139, quote p. 138.
12 "Eva Jiricna Architects. 'Joseph', Modeboutique in London/England", in: *Internationales Interior Design 1991/92*, Lucy Bullivant (ed.), Munich 1992, pp. 160–163, quote p. 160.
13 Cf. Wolf-Dietrich Bukow, *Ritual und Fetisch in fortgeschrittenen Industriegesellschaften: Formen kultureller Kommunikation*, Frankfurt am Main 1984, esp. chaps. V and VI, p. 64 ff.
14 Cf. *Japan-Design*. Matthias Dietz and Michael Mönninger (eds.), Cologne 1992, pp. 64–84, here p. 65.
15 Ibid.
16 Andrea Branzi, "Shiro Kuramata. Purple Shadows", in: *Terrazzo*, no. 3, Fall 1989, pp. 81–100, quote p. 81.
17 Branzi (see note 16), p. 82.
18 *Internationales Interior Design 1991/92* (see note 12), p. 147; translated by Alex Atkins.
19 *Alfredo Arribas. Architecture and Design. Arquitectura y diseno, 1986–1992*, introduction by Oscar Tusquets, text by Georg C. Bertsch, Tübingen/Berlin 1993, p. 42.
20 "Alfredo Arribas Arquitector Associados. Velvet Bar, Nachtklub in Barcelona/Spanien", in: *Internationales Interior Design 1990/91* (see note 11), pp. 122–124, quote p. 123; translated by Alex Atkins.
21 "Zaha Hadid. Moonsoon, Club in Sapporo/Japan", in: *Internationales Interior Design 1991/92* (see note 12), pp. 114–117, quote p. 116; translated by Alex Atkins.
22 Lucy Bullivant, in: *Internationales Interior Design 1993/94*, Munich 1994, pp. 114–117, quote p. 117.
23 "Jean-Michel Wilmotte. Technal, Showroom in Toulouse/Frankreich", in: *Internationales Interior Design 1991/92* (see note 12) pp. 180–181, quote p. 181.

City Ambience and Sense Appeal

1 Italo Calvino, *Die unsichtbaren Städte*, Munich 1977, pp. 15–16.
2 Cf. *Die Stadt als Gabentisch*, Hans G. Helms (ed.), Leipzig 1992; Klaus-Dieter Weiß, *Urbane Handelswelten, Zeilgalerie Les Facettes*, Berlin 1994.
3 Quoted from Heinz Coubier, *Europäische Stadt-Plätze. Genius und Geschichte*, Cologne 1985, p. 23.
4 Ibid., p. 12.

5 Lise-Anne Couture and Hani Rashid, "Film as Architecture as Film", in: *Architectural Design, Architecture and Film*, special issue, profile, no. 112, London 1994, pp. 62–67, quotation on p. 63.
6 Cf. Charles Jencks, *The Prince, the Architects and New Wave Monarchy*, London 1988; "Prince Charles and the Architectural Debate", in: *Architectural Design*, vol. 59, no. 5/6, 1989.
7 Cf. Ján Kulich, *Telč. Das Schloß und die Stadt*, Telč 1994, pp. 30–39; Vlasta Kratinová, Bohumil Samek, Milos Stehlik, *Telč. Eine historische Stadt in Südmähren*, Prague 1993, pp. 47–67.
8 Arthur Erickson in an interview with the author, July 1988.
9 Arthur Erickson, *The Architecture of Arthur Erickson*, New York 1988, p. 118.
10 Johann Friedrich Geist, *Passagen: ein Bautyp des 19. Jahrhunderts*, Munich 1978, p. 11.
11 Ibid., p. 12.
12 Ibid.
13 Weiß (see note 2), p. 36.
14 Aaron Betsky, *Building Sex: Men, Women and the Construction of Sexuality*, New York 1995, pp. XIII, XIV, XVIII.
15 Cf. the Zeidler monograph by Christian W. Thomsen, *Eberhard Zeidler. In Search of Human Space*, Berlin 1992, pp. 96–106.
16 Pierre Vago, "Urbane Verstrickungen: Paris", in: Weiß (see note 2), pp. 76–79, quotation on p. 79.
17 The author's information is based on comprehensive discussions with Norman Hotson and numerous visits to Granville Island.
18 Cf. Bernard Rudofsky, *Streets for People*, Garden City, N.Y. 1969.
19 Stephanie Williams, *Docklands*, London 1993, p. 8.
20 Ibid., p. 30.
21 Cf. *Winner. Bilder und Graphik. Paintings and Graphic, 1970–1980*, Dieter Blume (ed.), Braunschweig 1980, pp. 10–24.
22 Williams (see note 19), p. 52.
23 Ibid., p. 38.
24 Ingeborg Schild, "Zur Geschichte des Kaiserbades", in: Ernst Kasper and Klaus Klever, *Das Kaiserbad. Der Neubau und sein historischer Hintergrund*, Aachen 1995, p. 16.
25 Ernst Kasper and Klaus Klever, "Das Neue Kaiserbad", in: Kasper and Klever (see note 24), pp. 34–35.
26 Ibid., p. 38.
27 Ibid., p. 45.
28 Ibid., p. 46.
29 Carme Pinós, preface to Kasper and Klever (see note 24), p. 7.
30 Elia Zenghelis, "K.K.K. – Ein Gen urbaner Fruchtbarkeit", in: Kasper and Klever (see note 24), p. 8.
31 Gert Kähler, "Glitzerwelten. Hamburg", in: Weiß (see note 2), p. 97.
32 Cf. "Kunstkompass" ("Art Compass"), in: *Capital*, no. 11/1995, pp. 340–352 and *Focus*, no. 43/1995, p. 152.

Architecture and Eroticism in Film

1 "The Belly of an Architect. Peter Greenaway interviewed by Don Ranvaud", in: *Sight & Sound*, vol. 56, Summer 1987, p. 193.
2 Reinhard Görling, "Postmoderne Spielregeln", in: *Filmwärts*, 21/1992, p. 25.
3 Laura Mulvey, "Visuelle Lust und narratives Kino", in: Frauen in der Kunst, vol. 1, Gislind Nabakowski et. al. (eds.), Frankfurt am Main 1980.
4 Cf. Wolf Donner and Jürgen Menningen, *Signale der Sinnlichkeit. Filmerotik mit anderen Augen*. Düsseldorf/Vienna/New York 1987.
5 Cf. Christian W. Thomsen, *LiterArchitektur. Wechselwirkungen zwischen Architektur, Literatur und Kunst im 20. Jahrhundert*, Cologne 1989.
6 On femininity discourses and the city, cf. Sigrid Weigel, *Topographien der Geschlechter: kulturgeschichtliche Studien zur Literatur*, Reinbek bei Hamburg 1990.

7 *Deutsche Republik, 1927,* quoted in: Ilona Brennicke and Joe Hembus, *Klassiker des deutschen Stummfilms: 1910–1930,* Munich 1983, p. 143.

8 Antonio St. Elia, quoted in: Christian W. Thomsen, *Liter-Architektur* (see note 5), p. 158.

9 Le Corbusier, quoted in: Hans-Joachim Schlegel, "Die Utopie der universellen Synthese. Zu Konzept und Schicksal ost- und mitteleuropäischer Filmavantgarden", in: *Europa, Europa. Das Jahrhundert der Avantgarde in Mittel- und Osteuropa,* vol. 2, Ryszard Stanislawski and Christian Brockhaus (eds.), Bonn 1994, p. 153.

10 *Europa, Europa,* (see note 9); p. 76.

11 Naum Klejmann, "'Nationales', 'Internationales' und die sowjetische Filmavantgarde", in: *Europa, Europa* (see note 9), p. 16.

12 Kulesov, "Esli teper ... (If now...)", quoted in: *Europa, Europa* (see note 9), p. 162.

13 Dziga Vertov, quoted in: *Europa, Europa* (see note 9), p. 162 f.

14 Sergej Eisenstein, "Montage der Attraktion", "Montage der Filmattraktion", in: Sergej Eisenstein, *Das dynamische Quadrat. Essays on Film,* Cologne 1988, pp. 10–16 and 17–45.

15 Peter Greenaway in an interview with Peter Sainsbury-Brown, "From a View to a Death", in: *Monthly Film Bulletin,* Nov. 1982, p. 255.

16 Cf. Gabriele Jutz, Gottfried Schlemmer, "Zur Geschichtlichkeit des Blicks", in: *Sprung im Spiegel: filmisches Wahrnehmen zwischen Fiktion und Wirklichkeit,* Christa Blümlinger (ed.), Vienna 1990, pp. 15–32.

17 Cf. Yvonne Spielmann, "Framing, Fading, Fake: Peter Greenaway's Kunst der Regeln", in: *Film, Fernsehen, Video und die Künste. Strategien der Intermedialität,* Joachim Paech (ed.), Stuttgart 1994, p. 149.

18 Jeremy Clarke, "Architecture & Mortality. Director Peter Greenaway interviewed by Jeremy Clarke on the release of 'The Belly of an Architect'", in: *Films & Filming,* Oct. 1987, p. 6.

19 *Etienne Louis Boullée, Architektur, Abhandlung über die Kunst,* Beat Wyss (ed.), Adolf Max Vogt, introduction and commentary, Zurich/Munich 1987, p. 55ff.

20 "The Belly of an Architect" (see note 1), p. 196.

21 Clarke (see note 18), p. 7.

22 Cf. Peter Greenaway's response to the interview question: "And Piazza della Libertà? No Italian would dare shoot there after Fellini's Roma, and few would take their cameras into the tourist trap of the Pantheon."
PG: "You can put that down to the naive Englishman. I mean, you can imagine the reverse—a European director coming to London to set his scenes in Carnaby Street, Trafalgar Square and the Tower of London? It makes you shudder." 'The Belly of an Architect' (see note 1), p. 195.

From Media-Oriented Avant-Garde Design to Virtual Bodies in Virtual Architecture: Cybersex

1 Roy Ascott, "Zurück zur künstlichen Natur", in: *Kultur und Technik im 21. Jahrhundert,* Gert Kaiser et al. (eds.) Frankfurt/New York 1993, pp. 341–355. Quotation p. 351.

2 Hans Moravec in an interview with the magazine *Mondo 2000*: "Clever Hans and his Expert Systems Future", in: *Mondo 2000,* no. 11/1993, pp. 46–51.

3 Siegfried J. Schmidt, *Cyber als Oikos? oder: Ernste Spiele,* unpublished manuscript, Siegen 1995, p. 13.

4 Cf. Günther Feuerstein, *Visionäre Architektur,* Vienna 1958/1988, Berlin 1988; Christian W. Thomsen, *Experimentelle Architekten der Gegenwart,* Cologne 1994.

5 *Hybridkultur,* Christian W. Thomsen (ed.), Siegen 1994.

6 Cf. Marcos Novak, "Liquid Architectures in Cyberspace", in: *Cyberspace,* Michael Benedikt (ed.), Cambridge, Mass. 1992, pp. 225–254, here p. 226.

7 Cf. *Peter Cook 1961–1989, Architecture and Urbanism (a + u),* Extra Edition, Tokyo, December 1989; *Archigram,* Peter Cook (ed.), London 1972.

8 Cf. Christian W. Thomsen, "The Viennese Avantgarde of the '60s and Beyond", in: *Architecture and Urbanism (a + u),* No. 289, October 1994, pp. 74–95.

9 Reproduced in: *Haus-Rucker-Co: Denkräume – Stadträume 1967–1992,* Dieter Bogner (ed.), Klagenfurt 1992, p. 13.

10 *Haus-Rucker-Co,* (see note 9), p. 17.

11 Coop Himmelblau, *Architektur ist jetzt. Projekte, (Un)bauten, Statements, Zeichnungen, Texte, 1968–1983,* Stuttgart 1983, p. 182.

12 Coop Himmelblau, (see note 11), p. 174.

13 Cf. *Multimediale Stadt. Entwicklungen, Trends, Visionen auf dem Weg ins nächste Jahrhundert,* Ingrid Stoppa-Sehlbach (ed.), Sekretariat für Zukunftsforschung, Gelsenkirchen 1993.

14 Coop Himmelblau, (see note 11), p. 178.

15 Coop Himmelblau, (see note 11), p. 176.

16 Ibid.

17 Marie-Luise Angerer (Vienna) plans to gather together the various theories and discourses in her projected habilitation thesis (working title: "Body/Options. Kommunikationstechnologische Rahmenbedingungen für Körper/Repräsentationen/Geschlechts/Identitäten" ["General Conditions Provided by Communications Technologies for Body/Representations/Gender/Identities"]). Derrick de Kerckhove, the director of the McLuhan Institute in Toronto, is also one of those scholars who attempt to establish connections between various interdisciplinary approaches. Cf. Derrick de Kerckhove, *Brainframes. Technology, Mind and Business,* Utrecht 1991.

18 William Gibson, *Mona Lisa Overdrive,* New York/Toronto/London/Sydney/Auckland 1988, p. 49.

19 Cf. *ARCH+,* no. 108, Berlin 1991, p. 90.

20 Otto Riewoldt, "Büro-Nomaden auf der Info-Autobahn", in: *mobil. Das Magazin der Deutschen Bahn,* no. 2, March/April 1995, pp. 16–25, quotation p. 18.

21 Francis Duffy, director of the office design company DEGW, quoted in Riewoldt, (see note 20), p. 18.

22 Allucquère R. Stone, "Will the Real Body Please Stand up? Boundary Stories about Virtual Cultures", in: *Cyberspace,* (see note 6), pp. 81–118. To quote from p. 81: "I, for one, spend more time interacting with Saint-John Perse, my affectionate name for my Mackintosh computer, than I do with my friends."

23 Cf. Christian W. Thomsen, "Mediarchitecture", Parts I–IV, in: *Architecture and Urbanism (a + u),* nos. 280, 282, 284 and 189, Tokyo 1994, Parts V–XI, *a+u,* nos. 307–312, Tokyo 1996.

24 Cf. especially the catalogue of the "Energieen" exhibition in the Stedelijk Museum Amsterdam from April 8 to July 29, 1990, which gives a detailed introduction to the "Bibliothèque de France" project.

25 Critical Art Ensemble, "Electronic Disturbances, Telecritical Performance", in: *The Last Sex. Feminism and Outlaw Bodies,* Arthur and Marilouise Kroker (eds.) New York 1993, pp. 208–219, quotation p. 211.

26 Cf. the contributions to Gilles de Bure, *Jean Nouvel, Emmanuel Cattani et associés. Vier Projekte in Deutschland,* and Olivier Boissière, *Jean Nouvel, Emmanuel Cattani et associés,* Zurich 1992.

27 Jean Nouvel in: de Bure, (see note 26), p. 12.

28 "Der Bildschirm als Mauer", Paul Virilio in conversation with Andreas Ruby, in: *deutsche bauzeitung,* 6/1994, pp. 52–56, quotation p. 52.

29 Paul Virilio, *Die Eroberung des Körpers: vom Übermenschen zum überreizten Menschen,* Munich/Vienna 1994, p. 109.

30 Virilio, (see note 29), p. 121. For Stelarc's largely ahistorical conception of art, in the old tradition of the machineman, cf. his own contribution "Von Psycho- zu Cyberstrategien: Prothetik, Robotik und Teile-Existenz", in: *Kunstforum,* vol. 132/ Nov. 1995 – Jan. 1996, pp. 73–81.

31 Cf. Donna Haraway, "A Manifesto for Cyborgs: Science, Technology and Socialist Feminism", in: *Feminism/Postmodernism,* Linda J. Nicholson (ed.), New York/London 1990, pp. 190–233, and Donna Haraway, "The Actors are Cyborgs, Nature is Coyote, and the Geography is Elsewhere: Postscript to 'Cyborgs at Large'", in: *Technoculture,* Constance Penley and Andrew Ross (eds.), Minneapolis 1991.

32 In conjunction with the "Telepolis" conference in Luxembourg at the beginning of December 1995, two books writ-

ten and edited by Florian Rötzer (et al.) should be mentioned which are keeping the discussion moving in the '90s: Florian Rötzer, *Die Telepolis-Urbanität im digitalen Zeitalter,* Mannheim 1995, and *Stadt am Netz, Ansichten von Telepolis,* Stefan Iglhaut, Armin Medosch, Florian Rötzer (eds.), Mannheim 1996.

33 Karlheinz Steinmülller, "Versuche über den Cyberspace. Spekulative Bemerkungen zu einer neuen Technik", in: *Wirklichkeitsmaschinen. Cyberspace und die Folgen,* K. H. Steinmüller (ed.), Weinheim/Basle 1993, p. 136.

34 Philip Robinson and Nancy Tamosaitis, *The Joy of Cybersex. The Underground Guide to Electronic Erotica,* New York 1993.

35 Kathy Keeton, "Foreword", in: Robinson and Tamosaitis, (see note 34), p. XIII.

36 Ibid.

37 Robinson and Tamosaitis, (see note 34), p. 15.

38 Keeton, (see note 35). This is in fact a quotation which has been only marginally modified from the chapter "Teledildonics und darüber hinaus", in: *Virtuelle Welten* (see note 46), pp. 329–330.

39 Schmidt, (see note 3), p. 8. Cf. also Siegfried J. Schmidt, "Platons Höhle – ein philosophischer Betriebsunfall?", in: *Platons Höhle. Das Museum und die elektronischen Medien,* Cologne 1995, pp. 36–56, here pp. 49–52, quotation p. 52.

40 Michael Heim, "The Erotic Ontology of Cyberspace", in: *Cyberspace,* (see note 6), pp. 59–80, quotation p. 65.

41 Arthur and Marilouise Kroker, "The Last Sex. Feminism and Outlaw Bodies", in: *The Last Sex,* (see note 25), pp. 1–19, quotation p. 15.

42 Ibid.

43 Cf. Stahl Stenslie, "Cyber SM. A Comment on Tactile Technology", in: *Lab, Das Magazin der Kunsthochschule für Medien,* Cologne, no. 1, 1994, pp. 72–75.

44 Kirk Woolford, "Touch at the End of the Century", in: *Lab No. 1,* (see note 43), pp. 40–43, quotation p. 42.

45 Cf. Ingrid Stoppa-Sehlbach, "Virtual Lifestyle. Ästhetik und Cyberspace", in: *Wirklichkeitsmaschinen,* (see note 33), pp. 85–102.

46 Howard Rheingold, *Virtuelle Welten. Reisen im Cyberspace,* Hamburg 1992, p. 288.

47 Stoppa-Sehlbach, (see note 45), p. 92.

48 Cf. Bernd Flessner, "Archäologie im Cyberspace. Anmerkungen zu Stanislaw Lems Phantomatik", in: *Wirklichkeitsmaschinen,* (see note 33), pp. 25–38, here p. 36.

49 Wolfgang Strauss and Monika Fleischmann, "Cyber-City. Virtuelle Räume der Kommunikation", in: *Multimediale Stadt,* (see note 13), pp. 95–99, quotation p. 97.

50 Rheingold, (see note 46), p. 287.

51 Virilio, "Der Bildschirm als Mauer", (see note 28), p. 56.

52 John Donne, *The Dreame,* c. 1600, first verse, in: *John Donne, The Elegies and the Songs and Sonnets,* Helen Gardner (ed.), Oxford 1965, pp. 79–80.

Sensuous Architecture: The Final Plea

1 Wolfgang Meisenheimer, "Zur Einführung in den Themenkreis", in: *Architektur und menschlicher Körper, ad,* no. 9, Düsseldorf 1982, p. 14.

2 Juhani Pallasmaa, "An Architecture of the Seven Senses", in: *Questions of Perception,* Tokyo 1994, pp. 27–38, quotation p. 29.

3 Barbara Radice, "Editor's Note", in: *Terrazzo,* no. 6, Spring/Summer 1991, p. 27.

4 This theme will be dealt with in more detail in a book by the same author, shortly to be published by Prestel.

5 Quoted in Kaye Geipel, "Strategien architektonischer Verführung", in: *Bauwelt* 22, vol. 87, June 7, 1996, p. 1257.

6 William Gibson, in: *Der Spiegel,* no. 2, January 10, 1994, p. 142.

7 Coop Himmelblau, *Architektur ist jetzt. Projekte, (Un)bauten, Aktionen, Statements, Texte, 1968–1983,* Stuttgart/New York 1983, p. 173.

ad, Annual Journal of the Fachhochschule Düsseldorf, no. 9, 1982, Wolfgang Meisenheimer (ed.): *Architektur und menschlicher Körper*.

ad, Annual Journal of the Fachhochschule Düsseldorf, no. 17, 1989, Wolfgang Meisenheimer (ed.): *Architektur als Darstellung, als Zeichen, als Sprache*.

ad, Annual Journal of the Fachhochschule Düsseldorf, no. 19, 1991, Wolfgang Meisenheimer (ed.): *Architektur für die Sinne*.

Alfredo Arribas. Architecture and Design, 1986–1992. (Arquitectura y diseno, 1986–1992). Introduction: Oscar Tusquets, text: Georg C. Bertsch. Tübingen, Berlin, 1993.

Angerer, Marie-Luise. *Body/Options. Kommunikationstechnologische Rahmenbedingungen für Körper/Repräsentationen/Geschlechts/Identitäten.* Habilitationsschrift, Vienna (in preparation).

Aragon, Louis. *Pariser Landleben. (Le paysan de Paris).* Munich, 1969.

ARCH+, no. 108, Berlin, 1991.

Archigram: a Guide to Archigram 1961–74. London, 1994.

Architectural Design, see *Architecture and Film*, special issue.

Architectural Visions for Europe. Dirk Meyhöfer (ed.). Braunschweig, Wiesbaden, 1994.

Architecture and Film, special issue, profile, no. 112: *Architectural Design*, London 1994.

Architecture and Urbanism (a + u), extra edition, Toshio Nakamura (ed.), Tokyo, December 1988: *Richard Rogers 1978–1988*.

Architecture and Urbanism (a + u), extra edition, Toshio Nakamura (ed.), Tokyo, December 1989: *Peter Cook 1961–1989*.

Architektur als Darstellung, als Zeichen, als Sprache, see *ad*, no. 17.

Architektur des 20. Jahrhunderts. Peter Gössel and Gabriele Leuthäuser (eds.). Cologne, 1990.

Architektur für die Sinne, see *ad*, no. 19.

Architektur und menschlicher Körper, see *ad*, no. 9.

Badewonnen: gestern – heute – morgen. Hansgrohe 'Schiltach' (ed.), with contributions from Karl Michael Armer, Ulrika Kiby, Klaus Kramer and Erich Küthe. Cologne, 1993.

Barthes, Roland. *Fragmente einer Sprache der Liebe*. Frankfurt am Main, 1984.

Bataille, Georges. Die *Tränen des Eros*. Gerd Bergfleth (ed.). Munich, 1981.

Beckford, William. *Vathek*. Frankfurt am Main, 1964.

Besichtigung der Moderne: bildende Kunst, Architektur, Musik, Literatur, Religion; Aspekte und Perspektiven. Hans Holländer and Christian W. Thomsen (eds.). Cologne, 1987.

Betsky, Aaron. *Building Sex: Men, Women, and the Construction of Sexuality*. New York, 1995.

Boissière, Olivier. *Jean Nouvel, Emmanuel Cattani und Partner*. Zurich, 1992.

Boissière, Olivier. *Philippe Starck*. Beatrix Schomberg (ed.). Cologne, 1991.

Boullée, Etienne-Louis. *Architektur, Abhandlung über die Kunst*. Beat Wyss (ed.). Introduction and commentary: Adolf Max Vogt. Zurich, Munich, 1987.

Brennicke, Ilona and Joe Hembus. *Klassiker des deutschen Stummfilms: 1910–1930*. Munich, 1983.

Brooks, Peter. *Body Work. Objects of Desire in Modern Narrative*. Cambridge, Mass., 1993.

Bukow, Wolf-Dietrich. *Ritual und Fetisch in fortgeschrittenen Industriegesellschaften. Formen kultureller Kommunikation*. Frankfurt am Main, 1984.

Calvino, Italo. *The Invisible Cities: a Novel*. London, 1979.

Carter, Angela. *The Infernal Desire Machines of Doktor Hoffman*. Suffolk, 1985.

Carter, Angela. *The Sadeian Woman*. London, 1979.

Christo, der Reichstag und urbane Projekte. Jacob Baal-Teshuva (ed.). Munich, 1993.

Christo. Surrounded Islands. Introduction: Werner Spies, documentation and photographs: Werner Volz. Cologne, 1984.

Clark, Kenneth. *The Nude. A Study in Ideal Form*. Princeton, 1956/1972.

Clemente, Francesco. *The Black Book*. Thomas Kellwein (ed.). Basle, 1991.

Clemente, Francesco. *Evening Raga & Paradiso 1992*. Introduction: Francesco Clemente, Allen Ginsberg and Peter Orlovsky. New York, 1992.

Clemente, Francesco. *Francesco Clemente im Gespräch mit Rainer Crone und Georgia Marsh*. Cologne, 1990.

Coop Himmelblau. Architektur ist jetzt / Architecture is Now. Projects, (Un)Buildings, Actions, Statements, Sketches, Commentaries, 1968–1983. Stuttgart, New York, 1983.

Croce-Spinelli, Michel. *Fetisch und Fortschritt. Berichte aus dem Kongo, Dahome, Gabun und Kamerun*. Munich, 1969.

Coubier, Heinz. *Europäische Stadt-Plätze. Genius und Geschichte*. Cologne, 1985.

Cyberspace. Michael Benedikt (ed.). Cambridge, Mass., 1992.

Dalí, Salvador. *The Secret Life of Salvador Dalí*. London, 1973.

De Kerckhove, Derrick. See Kerckhove, Derrick de.

Deleuze, Gilles und Félix Guattari. *Anti-Ödipus*. Frankfurt am Main, 1977.

Deleuze, Gilles und Félix Guattari. *Tausend Plateaus*. Berlin, 1992.

Das Denken des Marquis de Sade. With contributions from Roland Barthes, Pierre Klossowski, Philippe Sollers and Jacques Lacan. Frankfurt am Main, 1988.

Der Diskurs des Radikalen Konstruktivismus. Siegfried J. Schmidt (ed.). Frankfurt am Main, 1987.

Dislocations. Robert Storr (ed.). New York, 1991.

Döhl, Reinhard. *Hermann Finsterlin. Eine Annäherung*. Stuttgart, 1988.

Donne, John. "The Dreame", from *The Elegies and the Songs and Sonnets*. Helen Gardner. Oxford 1965.

Donner, Wolf and Jürgen Menningen. *Signale der Sinnlichkeit. Filmerotik mit anderen Augen*. Düsseldorf, Vienna, New York, 1987.

DuBois, Page. *Sowing the Body. Psychoanalysis and Ancient Representations of Women*. Chicago, 1988.

Eisenstein, Sergej. *Das dynamische Quadrat*. Translated and edited by Oksana Bulgakova and Dietmar Hochmuth. Cologne, 1988.

Energieen. Luciano Fabro, ..., Robert Wilson. Exhibition at the Stedelijk Museum, Amsterdam, April 8 – July 29, 1990. Wim Beeren (ed.). Amsterdam, 1991.

Erickson, Arthur. *The Architecture of Arthur Erickson*. New York, 1988.

Erikson, Erik Homburger. *Identität und Lebenszyklus. Drei Aufsätze*. Frankfurt am Main, 1966.

Erotik in der Kunst des 20. Jahrhunderts. Angelika Muthesius and Burkhard Riemschneider (eds.), with a text by Gilles Néret. Cologne, 1992.

Europa, Europa. Das Jahrhundert der Avantgarde in Mittel- und Osteuropa, vol. 2. Ryszard Stanislawski and Christoph Brockhaus (eds.). Bonn, 1994.

Felix, Jürgen. *Woody Allen. Komik und Krise*. Marburg, 1992.

Feminism/Postmodernism. Linda J. Nicholson (ed.). New York, London, 1990.

Feuerstein, Günther. *Visionäre Architektur Wien 1958–1988*. Berlin, 1988.

Film, Fernsehen, Video und die Künste. Strategien der Intermedialität. Joachim Paech (ed.). Stuttgart, 1994.

Flaubert, Gustave. *Tagebücher. Deutsche Gesamtausgabe in 3 Bänden*. E. W. Fischer (ed.). Potsdam, 1919.

Francesco Clemente. Early Morning Exercises. A catalogue to the exhibition at the Cabinet d'Art Graphique, Centre Georges Pompidou, Paris, Oct. 26, 1994 to Jan. 16, 1995. Paris, 1994.

Francesco Clemente, Pastelle 1973–1983. Rainer Crone (ed.). Munich, 1984

Frauen in der Kunst, vol. 1. Gislind Nabakowski et al. (eds.). Frankfurt am Main, 1980.

Freud, Sigmund. *Gesammelte Werke*. Anna Freud et al. (eds.). vol. 11: "Vorlesungen zur Einführung in die Psychoanalyse". London, 1940.

Fürstenberg, Diane von. *The Bath*. New York, 1993.

Fusionen. A catalogue to the exhibition on the works of Jean Louis Faure, Alain Fleischer, Bertrand Lavier und George Rousse. Bayer AG, Nov. 9 to Dec. 17, 1988. Leverkusen, 1989.

Geiger, Gabriele. *Frauen – Körper – Bauten. Weibliche Wahrnehmung des Raums am Beispiel Stadt*. Munich, 1986.

Geist, Johann Friedrich. *Passagen: ein Bautyp des 19. Jahrhunderts*. Munich, 1978.

George Grosz: Berlin – New York. Peter-Klaus Schuster (ed.). Berlin, 1994

Gerd Winner. Stadt – Raum – Urban Spaces. Urbane Strukturen Berlin – London – New York 1968–1996. Ernst August Quensen (ed.). On the occasion of the exhibition in the Hildesheim Roemer- and Pelizaeus-Museum, Sept. 21 to Dec. 2, 1996. Lamspringe, 1996.

Gibson, William. *Mona Lisa Overdrive: Science Fiction*. First German edition. Munich, 1989.

Grimm, Jakob. *Märchen der Brüder Grimm*. Berlin, 1937.

Gröning, Karlo. *Geschmückte Haut. Eine Kulturgeschichte der Körperkunst*. Munich, 1997.

Grosz, George. *New York*. Walter Huder and Karl Riha (eds.). Siegen, 1985.

Grosz, George. *Paß auf, hier kommt Grosz. Bilder, Rhythmen, Gesänge; 1915–1918*. Wieland Herzfelde and Hans Marquardt (eds.). Leipzig, 1981.

Hannsjörg Voth, Zeitzeichen – Lebensreisen. Christian W. Thomsen (ed.). Munich, 1994.

Haus-Rucker-Co: Denkräume – Stadträume, 1967–1992. Dieter Bogner (ed.). Klagenfurt, 1992.

Heinle, Erwin and Fritz Leonhardt. *Türme aller Zeiten – aller Kulturen*. Stuttgart, 1988.

Hulten, Pontus. *Niki de Saint Phalle*. Stuttgart, 1992.

Hybridkultur: Bildschirmmedien und Evolutionsformen der Künste. Christian W. Thomsen (ed.). Siegen, 1994

In den Tempeln der Badelust: Architekturen der Sinnlichkeit. Photographs: Gerhard P. Müller, essay: Joseph von Westphalen. Munich, 1986.

Internationales Interior-Design 1990/91. Lucy Bullivant (ed.). Munich, 1991.

Internationales Interior-Design 1991/92. Lucy Bullivant (ed.). Munich, 1992.

Internationales Interior-Design 1993/94. Lucy Bullivant (ed.). Munich, 1994.

Japan-Design. Matthias Dietz and Michael Mönninger (eds.). Cologne, 1992.

Jencks, Charles. *The Prince, the Architects and New Wave Monarchy.* London, 1988.

Jones, Barbara. *Follies and Grottoes.* Rev. ed., London, 1974.

Kasper, Ernst and Klaus Klever. *Das Kaiserbad. Der Neubau und sein historischer Hintergrund.* Aachen, 1995.

Kerckhove, Derrick de. *Brainframes. Technology, Mind and Business.* Utrecht, 1991.

Kern, Hermann. *Labyrinthe: Erscheinungsformen und Deutungen; 5000 Jahre Gegenwart eines Urbilds.* Munich, 1982.

Khajurâho: Tempel der Liebe. Text: Louis Frédéric, photographs: Raghu Rai, preface: Alain Danielou. Cologne, 1993.

Klotz, Heinrich and Andrea Gleiniger. *Der Hang zur Architektur in der Malerei der Gegenwart.* Stuttgart, 1988.

Kodik, Charlotta, Terrie Sultan and Christian Leigh. *Louise Bourgeois: the Locus of Memory; Works 1982–1993.* New York, 1994.

Kramer, Hilton. *Richard Lindner.* Berlin, 1975.

Kratinová, Vlasta, Bohumil Samek and Milos Stehlík. *Telĉ. Eine historische Stadt in Südmähren.* Prague, 1993.

Kulich, Ján. *Teltsch. Das Schloß und die Stadt.* Telĉ, 1994.

Kultur und Technik im 21. Jahrhundert. Gert Kaiser et al. (eds.). Frankfurt am Main, New York, 1993.

Kunstforum International, vols. 132 and 133: *Die Zukunft des Körpers, I und II.* Florian Rötzer (ed.). Ruppichteroth, 1995 and 1996.

Kurt Schwitters: 1887–1948. Joachim Büchner and Norbert Nobis (eds.). Berlin, Frankfurt am Main, 1987.

Lab. Das Magazin der Kunsthochschule für Medien Köln, no. 1, Jürgen Klaus (ed.). Cologne, 1994.

Laqueur, Thomas W. *Auf den Leib geschrieben. Die Inszenierung der Geschlechter von der Antike bis Freud.* Frankfurt am Main, 1992.

The Last Sex. Feminism and Outlaw Bodies. Arthur and Marilouise Kroker. New York et al., 1993.

Lautréamont, Comte de. *Les chants de Maldoror.* With original illustrations by Salvador Dalí. Paris, 1934.

Lebbeus Woods, Centricity: architekturphilosophische Visionen. Kristin Feireiss (ed.). Berlin, 1987.

Lehndorff, Vera and Holger Trülzsch. *Oxydationen.* Altenham-Emertsham bei Hamburg, 1979.

Louise Bourgeois: Skulpturen und Installationen. Carl Haenlein (ed.). Hanover, 1994.

Lund, Nils-Ole. *Collage Architecture.* Introduction: Christian W. Thomsen. Berlin, 1990.

Massimo Iosa Ghini. Düsseldorf, 1993.

Meyer-Thoss, Christiane. *Louise Bourgeois: Konstruktionen für den freien Fall.* Zurich, 1992.

Mitchell, William J. *City of Bits.* Cambridge, Mass., 1995.

Miyake, Issey. *Bodyworks.* Tokyo, 1983.

Miyake, Issey. *Issey Miyake.* Photographs by Irving Penn. Boston, New York, 1988.

Mott, George and Sally Sample Aall. *Follies and Pleasure Pavilions.* Introduction: Gervase Jackson-Stops. London, 1989.

Multimediale Stadt: Entwicklungen, Trends, Visionen auf dem Weg ins nächste Jahrhundert. Ingrid Stoppa-Sehlbach (ed.). Gelsenkirchen, 1993.

Niedermeier, Michael. *Erotik in der Gartenkunst. Eine Kulturgeschichte der Liebesgärten.* Leipzig, 1995.

Niki de Saint Phalle. Bilder – Figuren – phantastische Gärten. Carla Schulz-Hoffmann (ed.). Munich, 1987.

Nouvel: Jean Nouvel, Emmanuel Cattani et Associés. Iwona Bladzwick (ed.). Zurich, 1992.

Oldershaw, Barbara. *Constructive Criticism of the Man-made Environment. Feminist Approaches to Buildings and Cities, 1970–1986.* Master's Thesis, University of California at Los Angeles, 1987.

Oskar Schlemmer: der Maler, der Wandgestalter. Karin von Maur (ed.). Stuttgart, 1977.

Partsch, Susanna. *Loire. Städte, Schlösser und Gärten von Giens bis Angers.* Photographs: Hermann Josef Wöstmann. Munich, 1993.

Percy, Ann. *Francesco Clemente: Three Worlds.* With essays by Stella Kramrisch and Ettore Sottsass. Philadelphia, 1990.

Platons Höhle. Das Museum und die elektronischen Medien. Michael Fehr, Clemens Krümmel, Markus Müller (eds.), Cologne, 1995.

Poe, Edgar Allan. *Tales of Mystery and Imagination.* London, 1965.

Postmoderne: Zeichen eines kulturellen Wandels. Andreas Huyssen and Klaus Scherpe (eds.). Reinbek bei Hamburg, 1986.

Questions of Perception: Phenomenology of Architecture. Steven Holl, Juhani Pallasmaa and Alberto Pérez-Gómez. *Architecture and Urbanism (a + u),* special issue, Tokyo, July 1994.

Radice, Barbara. *Ettore Sottsass. Leben und Werk.* Munich, 1993.

Radin, Paul, Karl Kerény and C. G. Jung. *Der göttliche Schelm. Ein indianischer Mythenzyklus.* Hildesheim, 1979.

Rheingold, Howard. *Virtuelle Welten. Reisen im Cyberspace.* Hamburg, 1992.

Roben wie Rüstungen: Mode in Stahl und Seide einst und heute. Illustrations: Roberto Capucci. Vienna, 1991.

Robinson, Philip and Nancy Tamosaitis. *The Joy of Cybersex. The Underground Guide to Electronic Erotica.* New York, 1993.

Rötzer, Florian. *Die Telepolis. Urbanität im digitalen Zeitalter.* Mannheim, 1995.

Rot & [und] Weiß. Drawings: Hannsjörg Voth, photographs: Ingrid Amslinger. Zirndorf, 1981.

Rudofsky, Bernard. *Streets for People: a Primer for Americans.* Garden City, N.Y., 1969.

Ruggiero, Guido. *The Boundaries of Eros. Sex Crime and Sexuality in Renaissance Venice.* New York, 1985.

Sade, Donatien Alphonse Marquis de. *The 120 Days of Sodom and Other Writings.* Compiled and translated by Austin Wainhouse and Richard Seaver. New York,1966.

Sade, Donatien Alphonse Marquis de. *Philosophie im Boudoir.* Munich, 1977.

Santiago Calatrava: Ingenieur-Architektur. Werner Blaser (ed.). With contributions by Kenneth Frampton and Pierluigi Nicolin. Basle, Boston and Berlin, 1989.

Santiago Calatrava 1983/1993. Richard C. Levene et al (eds.). *El Croquis,* vol. 38+57 (special issue), Madrid, 1994.

Die Schlösser der Loire. Photographs: Axel M. Mosler, text: Thorsten Droste. Munich, 1994.

Schmidt, Siegfried J. *Cyber als Oikos? Oder: Ernste Spiele.* Unpublished manuscript. Siegen, 1995.

Sennett, Richard. *Flesh and Stone.* New York, London, 1994. German edition: *Fleisch und Stein. Der Körper und die Stadt in der westlichen Zivilisation.* Berlin, 1995.

Sexuality and Space. Beatriz Colomina (ed.). New York, 1992.

Singer, Herbert. *Der galante Roman.* Stuttgart, 1961.

Spies, Werner. *Lindner.* Paris, 1980.

Sprung im Spiegel: filmisches Wahrnehmen zwischen Fiktion und Wirklichkeit. Christa Blümlinger (ed.). Vienna, 1990.

Die Stadt als Gabentisch: Beobachtungen der aktuellen Städtebauentwicklung. Hans G. Helms (ed.). Leipzig, 1992.

Stadt am Netz. Ansichten von Telepolis. Stefan Iglhaut, Armin Medosch, Florian Rötzer (eds.). Mannheim, 1996.

Stadt und Utopie: Modelle idealer Gemeinschaften. Idea and conception: Lucie Schauer. Berlin, 1982.

Stanley Tigerman. Buildings and Projects, 1966–1989. Sarah Mollman Underhill (ed.). New York, 1989.

Strategies in Architectural Thinking. John Whiteman, Jeffrey Kipnis and Richard Burdett (eds.). Cambridge, Mass. et al, 1992.

Strauss, Botho. *The Young Man.* Evanston, Illinois, 1995.

Sudjic, Deyan. *Norman Foster, Richard Rogers, James Stirling: New Directions in British Architecture.* London, 1986.

Technoculture. Constance Penley and Andrew Ross (eds.). Minneapolis, 1991.

Terrazzo. A Biannual Publication on Architecture and Design. Nos. 2, 3, 5, 6. Milan, Spring 1989, Fall 1989, Fall 1990, Spring/Summer 1991.

Thomsen, Christian W. *Visionary Architecture: From Babylon to Virtual Reality.* Munich, New York, 1994.

Thomsen, Christian W. *Dieter Sieger: Architect, Shipbuilder, Designer.* Tübingen, 1994.

Thomsen, Christian W. *Eberhard Zeidler. In Search of Human Space.* Berlin, 1992.

Thomsen, Christian W. *Experimentelle Architekten der Gegenwart.* Cologne, 1991.

Thomsen, Christian W. *LiterArchitektur. Wechselwirkungen zwischen Architektur, Literatur und Kunst im 20. Jahrhundert.* Cologne, 1989.

Tschumi, Bernard. *Architecture and Disjunction.* Cambridge, Mass., 1994.

The Unsheltered Woman: Women and Housing in the '80s. Eugenie Ladner Birch (ed.). Piscataway, N.J., 1985.

Verny, Thomas and John Kelly. *Das Seelenleben des Ungeborenen.* Munich, 1981.

Vicino Orsini und der Heilige Wald von Bomarzo. Ein Fürst als Künstler und Anarchist. Text by Horst Bredekamp, photographs by Wolfram Janzer. Worms, 1985.

Virilio, Paul. *Die Eroberung des Körpers: vom Übermenschen zum überreizten Menschen.* Munich, Vienna, 1994.

Von Fürstenberg, Diane, see Fürstenberg, Diane von.

Wappenschmidt, Friederike. *Der Traum von Arkadien: Leben, Liebe, Licht und Farbe in Europas Lustschlössern.* Munich, 1990.

Weigel, Sigrid. *Topographien der Geschlechter. kulturgeschichtliche Studien zur Literatur.* Reinbek bei Hamburg, 1990.

Weiß, Klaus-Dieter. *Urbane Handelswelten. Zeilgalerie Les Facettes.* Photographs: Dieter Leistner. Berlin, 1994.

Weiss, Peter. *Rapporte, 1.* Frankfurt am Main, 1968.

Williams, Stephanie. *Docklands.* London, 1993.

Winner: Bilder und Graphik, 1970–1980. Dieter Blume (ed.). Braunschweig, 1980.

Wirklichkeitsmaschinen. Cyberspace und die Folgen. Karlheinz Steinmüller (ed.). Weinheim, Basle, 1993.

Wollschläger, Martin. *Fetischismus, Transvestitismus, Transsexualität, Homosexualität.* Cologne, 1983.

Women and the American City. Catharine R. Stimpson et al (eds.). Chicago, 1981.

Woods, Lebbeus. *Anarchitecture. Architecture is a Political Act.* London, 1992.

Zilcer, Judith. *Richard Lindner. Gemälde und Aquarelle 1948–1977.* On the occasion of the exhibition in the Munich Haus der Kunst, Feb. 7 to April 27, 1997. Munich, 1997.

Die Zukunft des Körpers, I and II. See *Kunstforum International,* vols. 132 and 133.

Index

Page numbers in bold indicate locations of illustrations

Photo Credits

Architecture and Urbanism (a+u), Peter Cook 1961-1989, Extra Edition, ed. by Toshio Nakamura, Tokyo, December 1989: p. 62 left and right

Architekton, Dieter Leistner: pp. 124, 145, 163

Arch. Photo / Eduard Hueber: pp. 53 top, 162

Architektur und Wohnen 3/78: p. 89

Das Bad. Eine Geschichte der Badekultur im 19. and 20. Jahrhundert, by Herbert Lachmayer, Sylvia Mattl-Wurm, Christian Gargerle, Salzburg / Vienna 1991 (François Hers): p. 51 bottom

Richard Barnes, San Francisco: pp. 13 top, 164 top and bottom left

Gert von Bassewitz: pp. 52 top, 160 top, 167

Bayerische Verwaltung der Schlösser, Gärten und Seen, Museumsabteilung, Munich: p. 50

Gaston Bergeret: p. 144 bottom right

Leonardo Bezzola, Bätterkinden: p. 84 left

Antonio Bignami, IMG.: p. 46 top left

Luc Boegly, Archipress: pp. 24, 25

Peter Böttcher: p. 140 top right

Robert Bosch GmbH, Stuttgart: p. 60 top left

British Film Institute, London: pp. 131, 132, 133

Donatella Brun, New York: pp. 142 bottom right, 143 top left

Richard Bryant, Arcaid: pp. 41, 155 left and right

Busam/Richter, Dortmund: p. 94

Santiago Calatrava, Zurich: pp. 18 bottom right, 19, 20 top and bottom, 21

Robert César, Archipress: p. 97

Charles Gwathmey and Robert Siegel, Buildings and Projects 1964-84, by Peter Arnell and Ted Bickford, New York 1984: p. 157 right

Peter Cook, London: pp. 9, 92 bottom, 93 top, 95

Coop Himmelblau, *Architektur ist jetzt. Projekte, (Un)bauten, Aktionen, Statements, Zeichnungen, Texte, 1968-1983,* Stuttgart / New York 1983: pp. 22, 139 top left and bottom

Stéphane Couturier, Archipress: p. 165, 172

Michael S. Cullen, Berlin: p. 78 bottom

Lynn Davis Architects, Sandwich, Kent: p. 86

Thomas Delbeck: p. 158 top right

Peter Dunas, Luigi Colani und die organisch-dynamische Form seit dem Jugendstil, Munich 1993: p. 53 bottom left

Hagen Ernstbrunner, Vienna: p. 140 top left

Filmarchitektur. Von Metropolis bis Blade Runner, by Dietrich Neumann, München – New York 1996: p. 128 top right

Arwet Foß, Hamburg: p. 123

Klaus Frahm/Contur: pp. 87, 152

Johann Friedrich Geist, *Passagen, ein Bautyp des 19. Jahrhunderts,* Munich 1982: pp. 105 top left, top middle, top right, bottom left, 106 top and bottom

Manfred Gerner, Fulda: p. 59 top

Jeff Goldberg/Esto Photographics: p. 153, 154

Hans Hammarskiöld: p. 85 right

Naoya Hatakeyama: p. 151

Haus-Rucker-Co: Denkräume-Stadträume, 1967-1992, by

Dieter Bogner, Klagenfurt 1992: p. 138 bottom

Thomas Heinle, Stuttgart: p. 58 right

Volkmar Herre, Stralsund: p. 31 bottom

Archiv Hans Hollein, Vienna: pp. 15 top left, 18 bottom left

Atelier Hollein/Sina Baniahmad, Vienna: p. 18 top left

Franz Hubmann: p. 15 bottom left and right

Almut Imlau: p. 138 top right

Internationales Interior Design 1990/91, by Lucy Bullivant, Munich 1991: pp. 68 left, 91, 92 top, 96 left

Massimo Iosa Ghini, Milan: p. 8 top

Christopher Irion: p. 161

Yasuhiro Ishimoto: p. 12 top

Magyar Képek, Budapest: p. 45 top

Luftbild Klammet und Aberl, Ohlstadt: p. 100

Barbara Klemm, *Frankfurter Allgemeine Zeitung:* pp. 78 top right, 79

Angela Krewani: pp. 80 top and bottom, 114 top left

Erich Krewani: p. 40 top and bottom right

Kunstbibliothek, SMPK, Berlin: p. 128 top right

Kunstforum International, vol. 132, *Die Zukunft des Körpers I* by Florian Rötzer, Ruppichteroth 1995: p. 146 top left

Landesbildstelle Baden, Karlsruhe: p. 11

Bernard Larsson für *Madame:* p. 10 top left

Wolfgang Lauter, Munich: pp. 26, 44, 105 bottom right, 107

Lebbeus Woods, Centricity: Architekturphilosophische Visionen, by Kristin Feireiss, Berlin 1987: p. 57

Rolf Legler, Munich: p. 10 top middle

Vera Lehndorff and Holger Trülzsch, *Oxydationen,* Altenham/Emertsham bei Hamburg 1973: p. 12 bottom

Wulf Ligges, Flaurling: p. 10 top right

Nils-Ole Lund, *Collage Architecture,* Berlin 1990: pp. 60 bottom right, 88 top

Max, Sixth Edition, Hamburg, April 1996: p. 147

Franziska Megert: p. 141 top left

Courtesy Robert Miller Gallery, New York: pp. 81 top right, bottom left and right, 82 top and bottom, 83 top

Moderna Museet, Stockholm: p. 85 left

Jochen Mönch, Bremen: p. 101

George Mott, New York: pp. 32 top, 33 left and right, 34 top and bottom

Gerhard P. Müller: p. 55

Nacasa & Partners Inc.: p. 90 top

Jean Nouvel: p. 144 bottom left

Olympia & York Canary Wharf Ltd., London: p. 116 top and middle

Stewart O'Shields, New York: p. 46 bottom

Keith Palmer and James Steinkamp: p. 157 left

Pan Foto e.V./Günter Zint, Hamburg: p. 8 bottom

Panda Photography Ltd.: p. 103 bottom

Dr. Parisini, Vienna: p. 58 bottom and top left

Markus Pillhofer: p. 144 top

Pierluigi Praturlon, Rome: p. 134

Raghw Rai: pp. 56, 59 bottom

Erwin Reichmann, Vienna: p. 138 top left

Ralph Richter/Architekturphoto: p. 118, 119 left and right, 120, 121 top and bottom, 122

Georges Rousse, Paris: pp. 4-5, 6

Russian State Library, Moscow: p. 126

Rudolf Schäfer, Berlin: p. 102 top

R. Schenkirz: p. 169 left and right

Atelier Ingrid Schütz and Heyne Verlag, Munich: p. 141 bottom right

T. Shinoda: p. 146 bottom

Dieter Sieger: p. 52 bottom

Stadt und Utopie: Modelle idealer Gemeinschaften, catalogue to the Neuer Berliner Kunstverein's exhibition of the same name, Berlin 1982: p. 66 left

Philippe Starck, Paris: pp. 7, 54, 90 bottom

Stelarc: p. 136

Stahl Stenslie, Cologne: pp. 148, 149 top left and right, 149 bottom

Peter Stepan, Munich: pp. 83 bottom, 84 right

Stiftung Deutsche Kinemathek, Berlin: pp. 127, 128 top left and bottom, 129 top left, right and bottom

Wim Swaan: pp. 37 top and bottom, 38 top and bottom, 39

Keiicki Tahara: p. 93 bottom

Terrazzo, A Biannual Publication on Architecture and Design, no. 1, Milan, Autumn 1988: p. 64, 68 right

Terrazzo, A Biannual Publication on Architecture and Design, no. 2, Milan, Spring 1989: p. 75

Terrazzo, A Biannual Publication on Architecture and Design, no. 3, Milan, Autumn 1989: p. 67

Terrazzo, A Biannual Publication on Architecture and Design, no. 5, Milan, Autumn 1990: pp. 65 top right, 66 bottom right

Sabine Thiel-Siling, Munich: pp. 10 bottom, 78 top left, 113 top, 114 bottom left and top right, 116 bottom, 117

Christian W. Thomsen, Siegen: pp. 2, 13 bottom, 16, 17, 23, 31 top right, 36, 40 left, 99, 104, 108 top, 109 top and bottom, 110 top and bottom, 111 left and right, 112, 113 bottom, 114 bottom right, 140 bottom, 158 top left and bottom, 159, 160 bottom, 164 bottom right, 168, 171

Inge Thomsen, Siegen: pp. 63, 170

Ivan Ulrych, Luboš Stiburek, Karel Křížek: pp. 102 bottom, 103 top, middle

Rafael Vargas, Barcelona: pp. 42, 43

Woody Vasulka: p. 150

Paul Warchol, New York: pp. 96 right, 98

Wolfgang Wesener: p. 35

James F. Wilson: p. 166

Gert Winkler: p. 139 top right

Winner: Bilder und Graphik, 1970-1980, by Dieter Blume, Braunschweig 1980: p. 115 top and bottom

Herrmann Josef Wöstmann, Kerpen-Buir: pp. 27 top, 28, 29 top

Manfred Wolff-Plottegg, Graz: p. 53 bottom right

Gerald Zugmann, Vienna: pp. 14, 137 bottom

Front cover and spine: Frank O. Gehry, The Guggenheim Museum, Bilbao, 1997
(Photo: Christian Richters)
Back cover: Georges Rousse, Embrasure IV, 1987
Frontispiece: Brian Murphy, House in a canyon in
Santa Monica, California (Photo: Christian W. Thomsen)

Illustrations on pp. 4–5: Georges Rousse, Bercy, 1985
Sources of illustrations and photographs: see page 183

Library of Congress Cataloging-in-Publication Data is available

Translated from the German by Alex Atkins
Copy-edited by Claudine Weber-Hof

© Prestel-Verlag Munich · New York
© of works illustrated by the artists and architects, their heirs or assigns except
in the following cases: Louise Bourgeois, George Grosz, Alfred Kubin, Richard
Lindner, Niki de Saint Phalle, Kurt Schwitters, Maurice de Vlamnick
by VG Bild-Kunst, Bonn, 1998

Prestel-Verlag · Mandlstraße 26 · D-80802 Munich
Tel.: (+49-89) 38 17 09-0, Fax: (+49-89) 38 17 09-35
and 16 West 22nd Street, New York, NY 10010 USA
Tel.: (212) 671 8199, Fax: (212) 627 9866

Prestel books are available worldwide. Please contact your nearest bookseller
or write to either of the above addresses for information concerning your
local distributor.

Design: Maja Thorn, Berlin
Reproduction and typesetting: Mega-Satz-Service, Berlin
Printing and binding: Gorenjski Tisk, Slovenia

Printed on acid-free paper

ISBN 3-7913-1807-1